Secret Beaches
of Central Vancouver Island

CAMPBELL RIVER *TO* **QUALICUM**

THEO DOMBROWSKI

HERITAGE

VANCOUVER · VICTORIA · CALGARY

Heritage House Publishing Company Ltd.
www.heritagehouse.ca

LIBRARY AND ARCHIVES CANADA CATALOGUING IN PUBLICATION

Dombrowski, Theo, 1947–
    Secret beaches of Central Vancouver Island: Campbell River to Qualicum /
Theo Dombrowski.

Includes index.
Also issued in electronic format.
ISBN 978-1-926936-03-1

    1. Beaches—British Columbia—Vancouver Island—Guidebooks.
2. Recreation areas—British Columbia—Vancouver Island—Guidebooks.
3. Campbell River Region (B.C.)—Guidebooks. 4. Qualicum Beach
Region (B.C.)—Guidebooks. 5. Vancouver Island (B.C.)—Guidebooks. I. Title.

FC3844.D647 2011   796.5′3097112   C2011-900370-8

editor: Lenore Hietkamp
proofreader: Karla Decker
designer: Jacqui Thomas
maps, artwork and photographs: Theo Dombrowski

 This book was printed on FSC®-certified, acid-free paper, processed
chlorine free and printed with vegetable-based inks.

Heritage House acknowledges the financial support for its publishing program from the
Government of Canada through the Canada Book Fund (CBF), Canada Council for the
Arts and the province of British Columbia through the British Columbia Arts Council
and the Book Publishing Tax Credit.

Printed in Canada

CONTENTS

INTRODUCTION

View from Heard Road

Imagine yourself spending a glorious afternoon on Saratoga Beach, one of several such beaches on Vancouver Island's north-central coast (and described in this book). You wade through warm, turquoise waters over silky-soft sand while gazing at wheeling gulls against a backdrop of snow-decked crags. Imagine yourself struggling to find words to do justice to your experience. If you're a normal mortal, you will probably come up with something like, "Mmmm."

Imagine yourself, a day later, at a shoreline with similar elements, such as Island View Beach on the Saanich Peninsula (described in volume two of the *Secret Beaches* series, *Greater Victoria: View Royal to Sidney*). Obligingly arranging themselves around you are sun, sand, mountains and even wheeling gulls. If you are a connoisseur of beaches, even though you might again transcribe your experience as "Mmmm," you will also immediately want to make a comparison between the two beaches.

But stop. Should we make such comparisons? We are told that we should never compare our nearest and dearest—our children. We are told we should never look from one child to another and say, "Savannah is prettier than Sierra, but Sierra is brighter." Some would argue that we should likewise avoid comparisons among the wonderfully profuse and diverse beaches of Vancouver Island. Comparisons do a disservice to the distinctive qualities of beaches as much as to those of children.

Just as the parents who dote on their children can't help but note differences between their Savannahs and their Sierras, though, so beach-goers who love the beaches of Vancouver Island can't help but compare them. In some cases, the differences might be subtle, as between the up-island beach and the Saanich Peninsula one. In other cases, the differences are striking. While at many beaches, as at our first two, hectares of firm, silver sand stretch out to distant low-tide waters, at others, cliffs of sheer rock plunge hundreds of metres into the waves. Similarly, the beachgoer might find a tiny cove alight with pebbles and tidal pools at one spot, at another, an estuary rich with intertidal vegetation and busily bobbing shorebirds, or, at yet another, a headland lunar with strangely sculpted sandstone and gnarled Garry oaks.

Having gloried in the beaches in the first two volumes of this Secret Beaches series—the shore from Qualicum to the Malahat and that of the Saanich Peninsula—you will notice that some types of shoreline are completely absent between Campbell River and Qualicum, the region covered by this third volume. Are you looking for steep shores of solid rock from which to fish? Don't expect this kind of shore here. Are you looking for weathered headlands inset with pebbly coves? You won't find any. As for stretches of smooth rock shelf for easy strolling, those, too, you won't find. What you will find, however, just might thrill you.

And those most likely to be thrilled are children. Children who love lots of silvery, warm sand and seashells high on the shore among tangles of sea logs will be thrilled by many, many beaches along this part of the coast. Children who love splashing or castle building on bars of low-tide sand interspersed with giant sandy tidal pools will likewise be thrilled with many of the beaches mentioned here.

Adults who enjoy driving virtually onto the shore will be excited to make discoveries on this section of coast. Those with walking difficulties and those who love to picnic in the car while a storm howls can find scores of perfect spots. Kayakers who would prefer to put their energy into paddling rather than lugging their craft down steep banks or along endless trails will also be happy with the dozens of easy entry points.

Another group of beachgoers who will be pleased with what they find here are those who like to walk long distances along level beaches beneath wooded banks or by huge tidal pools and curious gravel spits. The lovers of shoreside solitude will likewise discover myriad spots to savour their isolation—or share it. While this coast has densely built pockets of shorefront houses, it also still has many heavily wooded sections of shore where the intrepid visitor can be utterly alone—or, at least, feel that way.

To this considerable list of happy beachgoers let us add the lovers of mountains. Now, it is true that at many spots between Qualicum and Victoria, crags and glaciers arrange themselves in spectacular abandon. Still, for sheer numbers of beaches with stunning views of these features, this more northerly section of coast is unrivalled.

THE VANCOUVER ISLAND BEACH

The word "beach" is used here in the way that most people who live on Vancouver Island would use the word—loosely. For us, a "beach" is simply a shorefront. It can be covered with sand, pebbles, boulders or even slabs of rock. Now, we all know that some people, usually from southern climes, become (politely) superior when they consider our use of the word "beach." To them, unless it is an unbroken expanse of golden sand bashed by surf, it is not a beach at all. Let such people take themselves elsewhere. The rest of us know what a beach is, and we love our beaches!

Finding these beaches is not always easy, but that is part of their charm. Maps can be a real problem, and in this section of coast more so than farther south. Those planning to use a GPS or Google Maps with its "Get Directions" will often come a cropper, either because those associated databases contain many mistakes or because they simply haven't entered the information for many of the tiny roads in this area. Try finding your way to "Davey Janes Road," for example. You can't. Official maps issued by the regional districts pose the opposite kind of problem. They show literally dozens of little roads leading to the coast where, as yet, no such roads exist. At some such places you will find a track or a path through woods. At most, however, you will encounter nothing but a wall of dense vegetation—that is, if you can even find where the turnoff is supposed to be when in front of you stretches a long, straight road lined with no landmarks. Sometimes locals are less than helpful. Law-abiding visitors are understandably taken aback when they arrive at a grassy track leading to the shore and see a sign saying PRIVATE, cocked at such an angle as to leave unclear exactly what is private. Conditions always change, of course, especially in this fast-growing area, where a lot empty yesterday can have houses springing up on it tomorrow. Still, using the maps and directions in this book should be helpful in getting you to hidden places that you had no idea existed or would have great difficulty finding unaided.

PUBLIC ACCESS—AND PUBLIC RESPONSIBILITY
Two key principles underlie the writing of the guidebooks in this series:

- The kind of person who will make a point of seeking out a little-known beach will be the kind of person who values quiet beauty and undamaged natural settings.

- In keeping with the ideals of the community of which we are all a part, everyone who lives on Vancouver Island (and, indeed, visitors to our paradise) should be able to enjoy waterfront that is, after all, public property.

Even though public property is available for everyone to find, it is important to keep in mind the status of this public property. Most of the "public access" routes leading to beaches are on government-owned land lying between private waterfront lots. These routes lead to publicly owned "foreshore," the area between high and low tides. Even when the land above the foreshore is private, the public generally has the privilege of using the foreshore and the water below it, though not the right to do so. When this area has been granted special status, such as a lease or "tenure" for farming oysters, the public is not permitted there. Usually signs are posted if visitors are restricted from using the foreshore.

BEACH ACCESS WARNING
Quite understandably, many waterfront property owners and other locals want to keep their secret beaches secret. Who, after all, doesn't enjoy seclusion by the waterfront (other than, perhaps, those who have been working hard at the gym to build the perfect Beach Body)? More important, what property owners welcome cars blocking driveways and high-decibel midnight parties, not to mention rotting litter, aromatic dog

excrement, gutted berry patches, depleted clam and oyster beds or ugly firepits? No one finds abuse acceptable, neither waterfront owner nor visitor. On the other hand, we need not despair that with increased use will come increased abuse. We can all hope that the more people who visit the shorefront, the more beachgoers there will be to encourage its preservation. Everyone who loves our shores finds in the pleasures and peace of the "secret beach" the inspiration to act on behalf of it and all other areas of natural beauty.

BEACHES IN THIS BOOK

Fewer than half of the public access spots between Campbell River and Qualicum appear in this book. Why? Many access routes, as already mentioned, don't live up to their name: they are not accessible! Many, many are overgrown tangles of bush, even when they are not located down plunging banks. Other spots, though, are omitted because they are not quite "secret" enough or are too much part of a cityscape. Thus, for example, you will find none of the waterfront spots within the Campbell River city limits here. Likewise, you won't find any of the interesting parks and walks around Courtenay and Comox, not only because they are surrounded by city, but also because they belong more to the waterfront of a river estuary than sea. Two big public beaches are excluded for the simple reason that they are very well signposted and very popular— Miracle Beach and Qualicum Beach. Also excluded are many roadside stops in an area rich in seaside roads. Last to be excluded are those beaches that are simply too unappealing, or are near similar but more appealing spots. The preferable spots may offer better parking, for example, or an easier path.

In contrast, a few places have been included whose choice may seem surprising. Prominent among these are those roadside spots included simply because it would be criminal not to draw attention to their features. Others appear here, even though they are parks, because they are so far off the beaten path that few visitors use them or even seem to know of their existence. Last to raise eyebrows for their inclusion are those that, by many people's standards, are not very attractive or, at least, not "proper" beaches. One such spot might be a stream estuary with meadows of salt-tolerant vegetation and rich birdlife. Another might be a convenient place to launch a kayak and enjoy a car picnic but not do much else. Others have an idiosyncratic character. They are the kinds of places you might like to visit once every few years, more out of interest than anything else.

There is no reason you should trust the value judgements that lard this book. They arise from irrepressible enthusiasm or from mild distaste, not from a strong desire to warp visitors' reactions to their beach experience!

CHOOSE THE RIGHT BEACH

Let us imagine you suddenly decide that what you need most in the world is an afternoon at the beach. Let us also imagine that what you want most out of your afternoon is complete solitude as you bask in soft sand behind beach logs finishing off your novel. Or launch your kayak. Or photograph a sunset. Where should you go?

A quick look at the last section of this book, called "Best Bets," will help you on your way to exactly the best bit of the water's edge for what you want. The categories in this section cover many interests—playing in the sand, walking along the shore, photographing a sunset or picnicking in a shorefront parking spot. You might be looking for a convenient picnic spot for a visiting aunt with walking difficulties. You might want a place where you and your extended family can find lots of parking and sunbathing space. You might want to go where you can practise your skimboarding or fly a kite. Find the category and narrow in on just the right beach for you.

THE GREAT BEACH EXPERIENCE

Armed with this book, then, and sensitive to the possible impact of their beach-going on local residents and the beaches themselves, the adventurous can head out with camera, sunscreen and picnic basket—or kayak, easel and Frisbee. To be sure that you have a wonderful beach experience, however, consider the following.

Weather The first question that anyone with an iota of West Coast experience will ask before going to the beach is, "What will the weather be like?" Even a sunny day does not guarantee a pleasant experience. As any *real* West Coaster will tell you, your beach experience is affected by not just the cloud cover and precipitation, which you can find out from basic weather forecasts, but also the *wind*. First, use this book to identify which beaches are partially or fully exposed to which winds. Then turn to the forecast. Unfortunately, most radio or newspaper weather forecasters will tell you little or nothing about the wind, except for tossing in the occasional phrase "windy near the water."

Enter the *marine forecast*. This kind of forecast is readily available by telephone as a recording (250-339-0748) or on the web as printed script at http://www.weatheroffice.gc.ca/. To find the online forecast simply type "marine forecast Comox" in your search window and follow links to "marine info," then "Georgia basin," then "north of Nanaimo." Soon you will be looking at a prediction something like "winds light this morning, rising to northwest 15 to 20 knots late morning and dropping to 5 knots, variable this evening." In fact, a version of this particular forecast is the one you are most likely to find during the summer (when, let's face it, most of us head to the beach). Almost every warm, sunny day with settled conditions begins with barely a breeze. Before long, however, the first ripples spread across the mirror-like surface, and soon the first whitecaps appear. For the next several hours the strait is alive with the brisk, deep-blue charge of waves.

These conditions, however, can make for some chilly sunbathing or sandcastle building. This is where your handy book is so important. Except on the warmest days, and unless you enjoy the exhilaration of beachcombing with wind in your hair, you will have to make some decisions: wait until late morning, when northwest winds may have subsided; bring a sweater; or *look for beaches that are not exposed to northwest winds.*

But don't get cocky. This particular daily pattern is common, but in some conditions, and especially during very warm weather, not inevitable. The northwest wind can blow all day long and all night. If, for example, you head off late afternoon to Singing Sands Road expecting a sun-flooded dinner picnic and a sunset paddle over silken seas, you might take one look at the foaming whitecaps and redirect yourself to Lazo Road. Check the forecast, or be prepared to be flexible with your plans.

Although northwest winds are typical of sunny weather in the summer, they aren't inevitable. Look to the southeast! The kind of southeast wind that comes with a sunny day seems most often to arise in the afternoon and fade in the evening. Even when this wind is more refreshing than you want, if you use this book properly, you can find delightful beaches either fully or partially protected where you can enjoy a blissful bask. Take note, too, that during bad weather, any winds will be most likely from the southeast. Before trusting too fully in a wind forecast, though, remember that winds can be fluky, curving around headlands just where they aren't wanted. Furthermore, in the southern part of this particular region, beware the "Qualicum wind." This wind, though rare, can be a little dangerous, particularly for beachgoers planning an evening paddle and, as the name suggests, particularly in the Qualicum area but extending to Nanoose Bay in the south and Bowser in the north. A Qualicum wind can arise suddenly and can be intensely gusty, rising to 25 knots, and in most places it is "offshore"; that is, it will tend to blow the weak paddler away from the shore. For a fascinating account of this and all the other winds in this area, you can easily find an analysis by Owen Lange of Environment Canada through a web search.

But don't avoid all blustery days. You might, in fact, particularly enjoy a strong wind. In a storm from the southeast, for example, it can be thrilling to drive to Lazo Road and watch the giant waves crash around you. Likewise, kite flying can be a great diversion on a windy day—if you choose a long flat beach such as Williams Beach and arrive at low tide, when that lovely long stretch is not underwater! Then, too, there are those (few) stiflingly hot days we have each summer when a windy section of shore feels delightful while sheltered beaches feel the opposite. Deep Bay Spit, for example, can get blisteringly hot.

And don't avoid foul, rainy weather. In even the worst weather, you can, by consulting this book, find many spots to drive your car in full view of the shore and enjoy a cozy car picnic while simultaneously feeding your soul on the splendours of the waves. In fact, winter, when we are treated to most of the foul weather, is also the best time for spotting sea lions and many species of waterfowl that spend their summers in the far north. Be careful, though, if you venture onto the shore, since both logs and rocks are often more slippery in winter than in summer.

Sun direction Do you want to sunbathe on a baking bit of shore or picnic in a patch of cool shade? Use this book to select just the right beach. We tend to think of beaches as being permanently in sun on a sunny day. Because the coast of Vancouver Island has many large trees and many steep shores, however, a particular piece of shore can be deeply in shadow for part of the day. Use this book to consider the right time of day for finding sun or shade on your beach.

You will find that, on this part of Vancouver Island, the morning is most often the sunniest time of day, at least for the upper shore. This pattern arises—think about it—because the coastline in most places faces northeast. There are many exceptions to this pattern, however. You will find in this book many spots that get sun throughout the day, and a few (a very few) that allow you to picnic while basking in the direct rays of the evening sun. Don't forget the seasons, though. Both the length of shadows and their timing will vary significantly between even June and September, let alone in December.

Tides Beaches can, of course, change character completely between high and low tide. This is particularly the case where tides go out a long way. The same beach that is a tempting swimming spot with turquoise waters over sun-dappled pebbles can, at low tide, be a broad swath of oysters, barnacle-covered boulders and tidal pools. Likewise, panting for a swim, you might arrive at a beach to find a pleasantly sandy shore, yes—but *far too much* of this pleasantly sandy shore between you and the water. Conversely, and especially in winter, you might arrive shod and snack-laden for a favourite shore tromp—only to find that the shore is under water. You cannot use this book to predict tides, except in a very general

View from Shell Road

way. You can, however, use it in combination with your tide tables to decide when to go to your chosen spot.

Learn about tidal patterns. As most Islanders know, we have two high tides each day and, it follows, two low tides. Most Islanders also know that the sequence moves forward about an hour each day, so that if, for example, the tide is high at 4:30 p.m. on Tuesday, it will be high at approximately 5:30 on Wednesday. Not all Islanders, however, are familiar with other patterns. In the summer the tides tend to follow one pattern, and in the winter the reverse.

Knowledge of this seasonal shift should help you in your planning: tides are generally *in* during the day in winter and generally *out* during the day in summer. That general effect is created because in mid summer, any high tide during the middle of the day will not be very high; in fact, it will often seem like a half tide. Similarly, any low tide in late afternoon or evening will not be very low; it, too, will seem like a half tide. Needless to say, kayakers, who prefer to put their energy into paddling rather than lugging their craft, love these tides. In contrast, if the low tide occurs mid morning, it is likely to be very low, and its companion high tide in mid to late afternoon is likely to be very high. On wide expanses of beach, this water comes rushing in over the warmed pebbles or sand. These tides often produce the warmest swimming, though the warmth can be a little patchy as the newly warmed surface water is still "floating" over the comparatively colder water.

This, then, is the pattern of midsummer. In early and late summer, the pattern is a little different. If you're looking for days with extreme tides in early summer, expect an afternoon low tide to be extremely low; in late summer, expect a morning low tide to be equally low. Confused? Simply search out one of the dozens of websites that provide tide tables. The most official one is that of Fisheries and Oceans Canada: http://www.waterlevels.gc.ca/.

Children We all associate the seaside with children and sandcastles. Public access routes can certainly lead you to many wonderful spots with sand and warm tidal pools. Nevertheless, one strategy for finding beaches for children away from the big beaches is to recognize that even a small area of sand can provide scads of fun. Almost half of the spots in this book have at least one sandy patch. Another strategy is to recognize that even beaches with no subtidal sand often have a huge natural sandbox of loose, dry sand among beach logs. Remember how much fun it was, as a child, burying your father's legs, or plowing trucks through collapsing landscapes?

Another strategy is to break the stereotypes. Children can play for hours in rocky tidal pools attempting—fruitlessly—to catch "bullheads" (actually sculpins), or building little kingdoms of seaweed, rocks and seashells for their shore-crab citizens. Likewise, and particularly with adults leading the way, children can discover wonderful creatures under boulders at low tide that most beachgoers don't even know exist—the frantically wiggling eel-like "blennies," for example, or the bulbous-headed cling fish, or the deliciously slimy leather star.

Some beaches, too, are magical with polished pebbles. Even adults can spend hours sifting through the multicoloured little gems. Other beaches have great skipping stones, or stones perfect for making not sand-castles but rock castles. And don't forget the hours of play that can be had on the tangles of beach logs just begging to be climbed over, conquered or converted into rocket ships. (Do be wary, though: rolling beach logs can be lethal.)

Because there is nothing much on our beaches that will hurt children, life is made comparatively easy for protective parents. Perhaps the greatest threat is the oyster or barnacle, lurking to inflict the wounds that constitute the rite of passage for all Vancouver Island children. Despite the relative safety of our beaches, remember to toss antibiotic cream and some colourful Band-Aids into the beach bag along with the sunscreen.

Not all of the beaches in this book are suitable for children, though. Adults will enjoy a steep path down a wooded bank to a secluded nest on a rocky shore with a dreamlike view of the Coast Mountains. They will not, however, enjoy watching their children wail as they attempt to struggle through a maze of weed-covered giant boulders, crashing and slithering to a bloody-handed halt.

So read the descriptions and advice in this book carefully. If you have a high panic threshold and nimble, adventurous children, you can have a wonderful time at some of the lumpier beaches. Do, however, consider what you will be facing and what decisions you will have to make once you get there. And, of course, be prepared to move on if a beach isn't suitable for your children. One of the delights of this area is that beaches even a hundred metres apart can be wildly different in character.

Signs Glorious confusion and amazing inconsistency reign in the world of beach signs. Some beach access spots are heavily burdened with signs. Many have none. Some have one kind, some another. In some places you will find two access spots 100 m apart, one of them carefully signposted, the other with only a half-hidden path to guide your way. You will see some signs referring to the Strathcona-Comox Regional District, though that region was subdivided in 2008 and no longer exists. Now the shore between Campbell River and Oyster River is administered by the newly created Strathcona Regional District. That between Oyster River and Deep Bay is overseen by the Comox Valley Regional District (CVRD), although in the middle of this stretch, the City of Courtenay and Town of Comox administer the shore within their borders. From Deep Bay to Qualicum, the land is overseen by the Regional District of Nanaimo (RDN). Of all of these, only the RDN is even remotely interested in posting PUBLIC ACCESS or BEACH ACCESS signs—or any signs very much, other than the occasional ones prohibiting overnight parking, collecting shellfish or lighting fires.

Still, knowing what signs to expect can be crucial. Signs will help you know you're not lost. At several locations, in fact, the only indication that you have come to a public access trail is a single sign warning against collecting shellfish. More important, signs will help you plan. If you know that you must leave a shore at 10 p.m., there's no point selecting the spot for viewing the annual mid-August meteor shower. Likewise, if you're planning a wiener roast, you will want to know where fires are not allowed or where you must get a fire permit first. Dog walkers will want to know where Arnold must stay on a leash or is not allowed at all. Similarly, if you're hunting for ingredients for your paella, don't come to a beach where the shellfish are contaminated. Signs can change quickly, though, so don't treat everything you read in this book as gospel. Below are the signs you are most likely to encounter.

Public access, beach access or public beach access These are the friendly, welcoming assurances that you are at the right spot and belong here. Many public access routes do not have them, however— and there are almost none in the CVRD. At a few places, original signs have been carefully crafted, carved or painted out of a whole range of materials. They make you feel welcome, but their source is tantalizingly mysterious.

Park Some parks are merely designated areas, completely undeveloped; others are beautifully managed parklands with benches, picnic tables and washrooms. The largest and, generally, most beautiful parts of shorefront you will find in this book are community parks, "nature" parks, regional parks, municipal parks or even provincial parks. Don't limit yourself to parks, though, or you will miss some real gems.

Danger/Shellfish area closed Some of these signs have been in place for decades and are so faded that one wonders about them. One particularly wonders about those that are posted where beaches are also oyster leases. One version of these signs has a prominent skull and crossbones to give a ghoulish panache to the message. These latter signs are actually less absolute than those declaring the area closed, mostly alerting you to the dangers of paralytic poisoning via "red tide." Unless you make some rigorous inquiries, it is best to heed the warning of these signs. Death by paralysis? Not a good way to go.

Dead-end road/No turnaround These are the yellow and black road signs at the beginning of a cul-de-sac that make you feel really, really unwelcome. It is tempting to speculate how these signs found their way to the beginning of some dead-end roads and not others. Occasionally, just occasionally, one wonders about the enthusiasm locals feel for having outsiders in their neighbourhood. Not surprisingly, the NO TURNAROUND signs are misleading. Unless you are driving a semi-trailer, you will find yourself perfectly capable of turning around at the end of these roads— you are not condemned to remain, as they suggest, forever marooned.

No camping or overnight parking Again, this is sometimes the only indication that you have found a public access spot. Presumably there have been bad experiences with Winnebago juggernauts. One wonders, though, where the harm lies in a camper dozing away for a few hours on a secluded spot on a secluded road. Still, the sign should be heeded, even if you are hoping to use this book to find a spot to spend a night by the sea. Often the hours are posted, again with intriguing diversity. Usually they are 10 or 11 p.m. to 5, 6 or 7 a.m.

Tsunami warning A few beaches are posted with signs that show a dramatic wave washing ashore. These signs warn beachgoers to move to higher ground in case of earthquake. This is a good warning, but one wonders why they dot the shores between Nanaimo and Victoria but are almost completely absent in this region.

No fires, fire ban or no open fires ometimes conveyed through words, sometimes through symbols, these are, perhaps of all the signs, the most important to heed.

Dog or pet signs ne assumes the pets in question are dogs. It is hard to imagine what else these might mean. Sometimes the signs tell you to keep your pet on a leash, sometimes just at certain times of year. Just as often they are concerned with your pet's excrement. At a few access points, plastic bags are provided; at some you are asked to top up the supply with shopping bags. If you visit a lot of beaches, you will notice that there is no other issue about which locals seem quite so enthusiastic in creating homemade signs.

Wildlife management area At many access points in the Qualicum area, attractive blue diamond-shaped signs will tell you YOU ARE ENTERING PARKSVILLE–QUALICUM BEACH WILDLIFE MANAGEMENT AREA. Lest you feel that you mustn't enter, they pleasantly add WELCOME in large letters.

Brants In the Qualicum area, wherever you find access to a flat beach, you may see an additional large sign with two pictures, one of a beach covered with the migrating brant geese, another with a dog running along the beach. DO NOT DISTURB! and WHOA! make their points loudly and clearly—and all the more so when you are told that a hefty fine awaits you if you let your dog loose among the geese.

Parking Whether or not your access spot is along a through road or at the end of a cul-de-sac, you might find parking is not great. Almost invariably, though, you will find parking for two or three cars, usually on the shoulder of the road. While in general the smaller public access spots in this book are not suitable for groups, you can find some spots where more than half a dozen cars can park comfortably. You should, of course, be sensitive about blocking driveways.

Facilities Few of these spots have public toilets. The last thing locals or other beachgoers want to face is the unpleasant sight of toilet paper festooned from wild rose bushes. One word of advice: plan! Remember that the same applies to your toy poodle or your Irish wolfhound—even if there is no "pet" sign. Even worse than festoons of toilet paper is a mound of dog excrement. If you are going to take Vlad or Esmerelda to the beach, bring a pooper scooper and plastic bag.

Boat launching Only a few of the spots in this book are suitable for launching boats of any weight—say a dinghy with a small outboard. Many more spots are suitable for launching kayaks and canoes, especially since this area is rich in places where you can drive virtually onto the shore. Do check your tide tables, though, and read this book to learn how much shore is exposed at low tide as well as how easy it is to walk on. The best spots for launching kayaks are listed in the final chapter, but other spots can be used, depending on tides and your determination.

Beach fires Don't even think about having a beach fire during fire season, even when you crave s'mores. Enjoy the tranquility and freedom from lungfuls of smoke. Even when beach fires are permitted, be considerate to others and build your fire well below the high-tide line or in established firepits. Nothing ruins the pristine pleasures of a shiny pebble beach more than an ugly firepit or logs scarred with ashes. In addition, remember that rocks close to a fire turn an ugly orange-brown, permanently blemishing the beach.

Beachcombing Do you most like to use a public access spot as the beginning of an exploration of a piece of shoreline? Whether you enjoy poking through tidal pools or striding along with the wind in your hair, many of these access points will allow you considerable opportunity for uplifting waterfront walks. There are a few things to remember, though, before you set off along the beach. First, note that land below the high-water mark cannot be privately owned. Unless you are approaching a commercial tenure, therefore, don't be intimidated if your walk takes you embarrassingly close to someone's front yard. Do, however, respect private property and, as much as possible, keep your distance.

And don't forget to consider tides. Some carefree rambles can turn at high tide into awkward scrambles beneath overhanging tree branches. At the same time, you needn't worry much about tides. It is true that at many points on the island's west coast, being trapped at high tide can lead you into dangerous situations. On this coast, you will suffer only inconvenience. Finally, consider the season. Many rocky beaches, easy to stroll along in summer, can be dangerously slimy in winter.

Seclusion You may feel motivated to hunt down a small, remote beach to get away from the madding crowds that throng the big public beaches. If so, you might be unhappy that about a third of the beaches in this book lie between private houses. Take heart! At many of these places you can expect to sit for hours at a time, virtually alone, contemplating, undisturbed, the play of light on the waves and the cry of the gulls, or how you are going to tell your partner that she snores.

Beaches can be secluded in four different ways, as you will find in the seclusion sections of this book. First, a few spots border on undeveloped or otherwise "wild" land. Second, at some spots you can walk hundreds of metres out to the low-tide line, far away from everyone. Third, some access points are rarely if ever used, even by local residents. Last, neighbouring houses are sometimes built well back from the bank or behind a screen of trees.

Compass directions Compasses? Don't be alarmed; you don't need a compass for any of these spots. The point is simply this: all real Islanders use the terms "north" and "south" with the very misled, and misleading, implication that Victoria is at the south end of the island and the rest of the island is to the north of it. In fact, as Islanders point out to each other at regular intervals, the "northern" tip of the island is actually northwest of its "southern" tip. Thus, for example, visitors can observe the interesting phenomenon that, as they drive "north" from Victoria, they pass the clearly marked 49th parallel in Ladysmith. Continuing "north" to Parksville, they then turn "west" to head out toward Pacific Rim Park—only to find themselves crossing the 49th parallel again as they approach the park! They have really been driving more west than north in going to Parksville and driving more south than west in driving toward Pacific Rim Park. Still, because we all participate in the tradition, let's continue to do so. When you read that there is, say, a sandy patch at the north end of a beach, understand this simply to mean "away from Victoria"!

Mountain views Something that Islanders take for granted, or don't really think about, is that the east coast of Vancouver Island offers a kind of view that is extremely rare on a world scale. For most people on planet Earth, a "sea view" means a view with perhaps an odd promontory or two, maybe some islands, but beyond that, the horizon—the blank, unadorned horizon. To get such views on Vancouver Island, of course, you need to go the west coast. For Islanders on the east coast, especially between Bowser and Courtenay, a view means promontories and islands, yes—but it also means mountains, and, in most cases, the Coast Mountains. North of Comox and the closer you get to Campbell River, the mountains become little short of spectacular, one crag vying with another for cragginess.

From certain perspectives—from, say, Cape Lazo looking south—a small section of horizon appears completely open. Of course, that is an illusion. After all, just below the lip of the horizon lie islands, hills and—mountains. And, since most views in this central bit of the Island are thick with mountains, those who would most enjoy the view will look at the mountains, *really* look at the mountains, and grow to appreciate them. Such connoisseurship is made all the more piquant because all the best mountains are not visible from any one spot. Each area along this part of the coast offers different lofty pleasures.

Don't assume that the familiar misty blue silhouettes of the Coast Mountains are the best views of the mountains you can get. If you like the mountains, make a point of coming to a favourite viewing spot in the evening, near sunset and on a clear day, and you will see the mountains jump out of their background, thrown into relief by the low shadows. And don't forget the rather obvious point that it is in the winter and spring, when they are covered with snow, that they are at their (photogenic) best.

If you were to set out on your exploration of beaches at Campbell River, you would start with some of the most spectacular mountain scenery anywhere. In fact, this book, like volume one, covering Qualicum to the Malahat, is arranged in a north-to-south sequence. If you are driving from the south, you may well wish to take the fast "inland highway," or highway 19, partway and then one of the connecting roads out to the old highway, 19A. The assumption lying behind all the driving directions in this book is that you are beginning your exploration on 19A, driving either northward or southward. For the sake of simplicity, highway 19A is referred to as "the highway."

Checklist With this book, you can set out from anywhere on the Island for a perfect day of beach exploration. You may be alone or with a car full of excited family members. You may be unencumbered or packed with gidgets and supplies. Before you set out, you might want to scan the following handy checklist of things you may need to find out or bring with you.

For your pre-trip planning, check:
- ✓ tide tables (http://www.pac.dfo-mpo.gc.ca/)
- ✓ marine weather forecast (http://text.www.weatheroffice.gc.ca/)
- ✓ Fisheries notices about gathering shellfish
    (http://www.pac.dfo-mpo.gc.ca/)
- ✓ need for fire permits

And for your trunk:
- ✓ sunscreen, sunglasses, sun hat, other protective sunwear
- ✓ bathing suit and towel, extra (dry!) clothing and water shoes/ crocs for children—even in cold weather
- ✓ beach umbrella, folding chairs, beach mats
- ✓ water bottles, picnic supplies
- ✓ extra garbage bags to carry away your trash
- ✓ binoculars, camera, tripod, easel, painting and sketching supplies, reading material
- ✓ Frisbees, kites, skimboards, buckets and spades, inflatable toys

For your dog:
- ✓ leash, treats, water dish, plastic bags for cleanup

For your children's safety:
- ✓ first-aid supplies and PFDs

If you start driving south from Campbell River along coastal highway 19A, within minutes you will have dozens of roadside beach spots beckoning you. Before leaving downtown Campbell River, though, spot the well-signposted terminal for the ferry to Quadra Island. This ferry can be your stepping stone to some amazing beaches both on Quadra Island and on the next island across from Quadra, Cortes Island. Not only do tiny coves await exploration, but also striking geographical formations and other places of interest—Rebecca Spit, Cape Mudge Lighthouse, Kay Dubois Trail, Manson's Landing, Smelt Bay, Squirrel Cove, Van Donop Inlet and more. Full guides to the best of these hidden beaches and parks appear in volume four in this series, *Secret Beaches of the Salish Sea*.

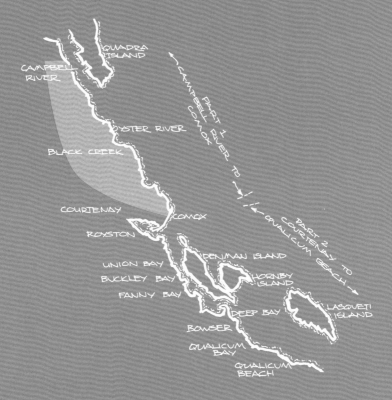

QUADRA
ISLAND

CAMPBELL
RIVER

PART 1
CAMPBELL RIVER TO
COMOX

OYSTER RIVER

BLACK CREEK

COURTENAY

COMOX

ROYSTON

PART 2
COURTENAY TO
QUALICUM BEACH

UNION BAY

DENMAN ISLAND

BUCKLEY BAY

HORNBY
ISLAND

FANNY BAY

LASQUETI
ISLAND

DEEP BAY

BOWSER

QUALICUM
BAY

QUALICUM
BEACH

PART 1 Campbell River to Comox

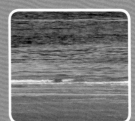

THE SECTION OF COAST FROM CAMPBELL RIVER to Comox is like no other on Vancouver Island. Nowhere else can you experience so fully the scope of the inland "sea," including the Strait of Georgia, that is coming to be called the Salish Sea. Nowhere else, either, can you see such an uninterrupted chain of spectacular peaks towering behind the low undulations of the islands on the far side of the strait. Even these islands are unlike any you will see elsewhere—among them tiny Mitlenatch Island, the "Galapagos of British Columbia"; Savary, the "island of sand"; and East Redonda, remarkable for having the highest mountain not on the mainland of North America or Vancouver Island.

Of even more interest to most beach explorers is the fact that no other section of Vancouver Island has so many beaches that conform so closely to a child's notion of a beach. Whether entirely composed of long tidal stretches of sand and tidal pools, or mixed with areas of pebbles and small rocks, kilometres at a time of exposed, sun-baked low shoreline face the strait. Some of these are so close to the coastal highway, you need only pull over onto the shoulder of the road. Others are hidden off complex networks of back roads. As a general pattern, the closer you get to Comox, the more you have to search—and, some would say, the more you are rewarded.

Our exploration begins immediately outside Campbell River's city limits—but with a quick mention of those spots within the city limits that are not included in this book. Simply by driving south along the coastal highway 19A through Campbell River, you will find yourself passing many intriguing rest stops, picnic sites, launching areas, seaside walkways and esplanades. Don't discount the possibility of visiting any or all of these just because they are such integrated parts of the cityscape or because they aren't listed in this book. Among the well-signposted spots worth visiting are the Rotary Beach Park and Seawalk, Frank James Park and Ken Forde Park. The 50th parallel marker is particularly interesting if you noticed the 49th parallel marker at Ladysmith and contemplate the fact that since passing that marker, you have covered one-ninetieth of the distance from equator to North Pole!

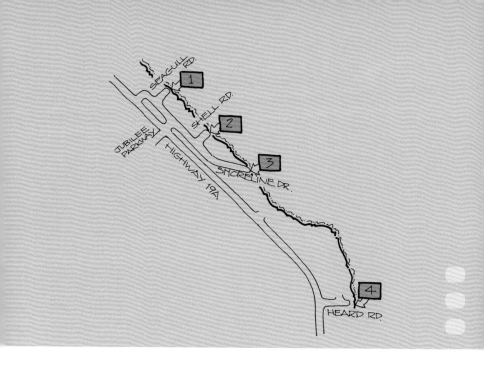

1 SEAGULL ROAD

Easy access to an upper shore of pebbles and logs and a lower shore of rocky tidal flats with boulders, pools and areas of flat rock

Location, signs and parking About 10 km south of downtown Campbell River, you will see traffic lights at a major intersection leading to the Jubilee Parkway. Turn onto the few metres of road opposite Jubilee and immediately left onto Shoreline Drive and carry on for just over 100 m. From the northern end of Shoreline Drive, turn onto Seagull Road, politely ignoring its No Turnaround sign. Drop steeply and directly a short distance to the end of the road, where you will find yourself staring straight out to sea. If you have felt a little frustrated elsewhere with the subtle hostility some locals seem to demonstrate toward visitors, your heart should be gladdened by what you see at this spot. Some kind and creative soul has planted a bit of garden here and, to boot, has provided not only a bench but also stonework decorations including pebbles in a log, bearing the word you most want to see: Welcome. Do be aware, however, that you will have to park carefully at the end of the road if you are not going to block the driveways close by on either side—and thereby make yourself considerably less than welcome. Don't expect to see any other signs.

Path Although you might have to be a little careful with your footing over the logs, you need take only a few steps to reach the shore.

Beach Come at high tide if you want to experience this bit of shore at its prettiest. You will find plenty of beach logs and one weathered stump to provide you with all of the backrests and improvised tables you will need as you settle down among the coarse sand and occasional rocks. Low tide presents you with a less conventionally pretty shore, but a fascinating one nevertheless, comprising an expanse of mixed rock, boulders, tidal pools and, in a few spots, flat patches of solid rock.

Suitability for children Not the most likely choice for those on unsteady little legs, this beach can still provide plenty of entertainment for sure-footed children eager to poke around rocks and explore tidal pools. Neglect to bring water shoes at your peril.

Suitability for groups Two or three cars' worth of family or friends could park along the cropped grass shoulder before the end of the road, but this is a thoroughly inhabited residential area so don't plan for a large group.

View The view is wonderfully varied. To the north you will see the shoreline curving toward a distant point and, behind it, downtown Campbell River. The sandy cliffs at the southern end of Quadra Island partially block distant Cortes, Hernando and Savary islands. The mainland mountains are especially striking here as they taper off toward the horizon of the southern strait and the distant bumps of Texada Island.

Winds, sun and shade Expect to garner all that the sun's rays have on offer when you come—you won't find much in the way of shade for most of the day. A middling fir tree at the right side of the foreshore does, however, cast enough shade during the afternoon that you can nurse a sunburn if you are willing to stay among the logs and pebbles. For good or ill, both a northwest wind and southeast wind blow along the shore.

Beachcombing Don't bring your iPod to this spot if you expect to jog or even walk easily. You will be far too distracted by the need to find secure footing along the loose rocks of the upper beach to pay much attention to the tunes. Along the lower shore you should be equally distracted by the biological and geological curiosities of the rocky shore. If you feel the need to explore more and are up for a bit of stumbling, you will find nothing to stop you from wandering a considerable distance in either direction.

Seclusion Although the houses on either side are set well back and surrounded by gardens, this spot is very much in full view not just of these houses but also of some others on the bank above. Even so, on this very quiet piece of shore you should feel pleasantly alone, especially if you stroll out along the tidal flats or explore in either direction.

2 SHELL ROAD

A short, steep paved road ending at a concrete barrier and an extensive shore of mixed gravel, sand, boulders and rocky outcroppings

Location, signs and parking About 10 km south of downtown Campbell River you will see traffic lights at a major intersection leading to the Jubilee Parkway. Turn onto the few metres of road opposite Jubilee and immediately right onto Shoreline Drive and carry on for just over 100 m. Turn left onto Shell Road and swoop down the ski-jump-like paved bit of road to the concrete barriers. You won't see signs telling you that mustn't engage in specific irresponsible activities, but the fact that this is, indeed, a public access could hardly be more obvious. Three or four cars can park here easily without blocking driveways.

Path While only a few steps separate your parked car from the shore, those steps are awkward, to say the least. Once hoisting yourself over the concrete barrier, you will have to do a little fancy footwork down the jagged chunks of stone retaining wall. A wooden walkway to the left of the access appears to be the neighbour's, so you will want to respect that fact. Put this spot firmly on your list of favourites to bring your crab salad sandwiches and Thermos of coffee: on a blustery day you can enjoy the full view without budging from your car.

Beach The beach could hardly be more varied—or more vast. When the tide decides to go out, it goes out a long way—almost 300 m. Once there, it reveals a large, nearly level area with patches of (slightly squelchy) sand, flat sedimentary rock, tidal pools and boulders. A lump of sandstone formations slightly to the south is especially intriguing. This low-tide version of the beach is probably the most attractive one. The high-tide version is considerably less welcome. Unlike most upper beaches along this coast, this one does not offer posterior-friendly sand or pebbles, but only fist-sized rocks amid a few logs and, on occasion, piles of drying seaweed.

Suitability for children You will have to be prepared to manoeuvre a wobbly child over the concrete barrier and down the jagged lumps of rock. Once on the tidal flats, however, you can relax a little. As long as tender feet are protected from barnacles and broken shell, the child attached to the feet can have a great time with hermit crabs, shore crabs, starfish, limpets and other creatures eager to entertain visitors. The shore is sufficiently flat that a kite could be flown here, but only if it doesn't require very much frantic running to get it airborne.

Suitability for groups Don't bring more than a few friends or family here, and then only if your group plans to wander rather than picnic.

View While the mainland mountains and Cape Mudge at the southern tip of Quadra Island are the highlights of the view, the low profiles of distant islands and the distinct, yellowish bump of Mitlenatch Island are also visible.

Winds, sun and shade Expect the full whammy. Wind and sun, sun and wind: as long as there is any sun, from any direction, and as long as there is wind, from any direction, you will feel it.

Beachcombing Beach exploring is easiest, and most varied, on the tidal flats directly in front of the access road. Beach explorers will almost certainly get wet feet, though, unless they are prepared to do a lot of leaping and balancing. Plan your footwear accordingly. There is nothing to stop you from walking a great distance in either direction, but you will have to be prepared to manage loose rocks along the upper beach and large rocks on the lower beach.

Seclusion Large but open lawns are all that stand between you and the shorefront houses, so don't expect a tryst to remain very secret. As you wander the shore, however, either alone or with kindred spirits, you are unlikely to encounter many, or possibly any, others.

3 SHORELINE DRIVE (CAMPBELL RIVER)
A shorefront parking spot with a slight drop onto a broad sweep of level rocky outcroppings, tidal pools and boulders

Location, signs and parking If you are using a GPS or Google Maps, be aware that there is a different Shoreline Drive also in the area covered by this book—the Regional District of Nanaimo (RDN)—but farther south, near Bowser. For this access, turn off the highway a short distance south of the Campbell River city limits onto Shoreline Drive, where traffic lights indicate an intersection with the Jubilee Parkway. Follow Shoreline Drive 300 m or so to its southern end. You won't see any telltale—or admonishing—signs, but you will see an unambiguous grass-and-gravel patch leading directly to the shore and separated from the private property on either side by carefully arranged logs. This level and open grassy area can accommodate several cars.

Path The lack of path is the chief drawback to this otherwise intriguing spot. While you can drive virtually onto the shore, once there, you are faced with an awkward drop of about a metre to the shore itself. The fact that some locals evidently use this as a spot to dump garden clippings doesn't make life easier for the shore-bound visitor. Still, if you are willing to invest in a clumsy minute or two, you are likely to have an interesting seaside experience. On the other hand, if a car picnic is on your menu of activities, load up your muffins and mangos secure in the knowledge that you needn't budge an inch from behind the windshield wipers to enjoy a fine sea view.

Beach This is one of the only pieces of shore in the entire stretch of land between Qualicum and Campbell River where the beach is primarily solid rock outcropping. Composed largely of nearly level, layered slabs of sedimentary rock, the shore, at low tide, creates a 200 m wide tableau of tidal pools mixed with patches of smooth pebbles and broken rock. The upper beach has a pretty area of logs, coarse sand and rounded rocks, good for picnicking or basking. Nevertheless, the proximity of broken concrete projects and the tendency of the area to collect seaweed might mitigate your pleasure a titch.

Suitability for children Any child arriving here will have to be light enough to be hoisted up and down the short drop to the shore—or large enough to scramble the distance under his or her own steam. Come at high tide if you want a little harmless splashing and the security of knowing that the water remains shallow for a considerable distance from shore. If you want to introduce a wobbly child to the pleasures of exploring tidal pools, choose this beach at low tide. You won't find many shores that offer such a palette of scuttling creatures so easily approached across level rock. Water shoes are a must.

Suitability for groups Don't plan an outing that requires more than two or three cars. And don't bring anyone who can't cope with an awkward bit of initial footing.

View You are considerably south of Quadra Island here, but the sandy cliffs of Cape Mudge are clearly visible. The spectacularly jagged mountains of the mainland provide a backdrop for the low profiles of Cortes, Hernando, Savary and Harwood islands. From here, Mitlenatch Island, isolated in the centre of the strait, is only a tiny knob. If you see a smoke plume slightly to the south, attribute it to Powell River's pulp mill.

Winds, sun and shade The generally cool and sometimes blustery southeast wind packs a fair wallop here, but at an angle to the shore. Summer breezes from the northwest likewise are not even slightly buffered. The sun's rays follow suit: not a morsel of shade is to be found anywhere, anytime.

Beachcombing This is a great spot to choose for wandering a considerable distance over interestingly varied shore. While the low-tide area can make for uncomfortable stumbling among seaweed-covered boulders, the mid-shore allows lots of easy strolling and peering. Do expect to get wet feet, though, so plan either to let the water in and out of your foot gear or keep it out altogether. Think water shoes or gumboots.

Seclusion Only large lawns separate the shore from the houses on either side, so don't expect to creep onto the shore unseen. This is a quiet neighbourhood, however, so once onto the shore you will see few, if any, other starfish hunters.

4
HEARD ROAD
A level approach to the largest expanse of low-tide mixed shore, stretching for many kilometres

Location, signs and parking About 10 km south of downtown Campbell River and 8 km north of the Shelter Bay rest stop, look for Heard Road and follow it a short distance to its end. A venerable log has been placed at the end of the road with a Fisheries notice warning you of dire consequences should you munch on a contaminated shellfish. Don't. The only other signs here are two small No Parking signs, both of them placed ambiguously along the sides of the road, but, it seems, excluding the end of the road itself.

Path A decorative rope-and-stanchion fence indicates the property line to your left, while to your right, a dense leafy hedge performs the same function. Forge ahead through a narrow but usually well-beaten path curving through a thicket of weeds for about 10 m. You will arrive at one of the densest clutters of logs you are likely to find anywhere. While the approach is thus generally welcoming to those with difficulty walking, keep in mind that the logs can be something of a hurdle. Not, fortunately, literally.

Beach A true connoisseur of varied shorelines will want to put this spot into a special category. This is not the place to come if you want to get wet quickly—at least at low tide. When the tide has withdrawn as far as it's going to, it reveals a vast area of flat rock, tidal pools, sandbars, boulders and gravel stretching 400 m toward the southern horizon. The upper beach is welcoming but more ordinary. Here you can find a pleasant place to picnic, especially given the choice of logs with which to improvise backrests and the band of pebbles in which to arrange your towel padding.

Suitability for children Most children can be managed onto the beach with only a little log scrambling, and while there, they can be treated to an array of watery entertainments. Whether you choose low tide, however, to take a romping child far, far out across the varied shore, or high tide to set a splashing child loose in water that is guaranteed not to drop off quickly, do make sure you bring footwear to protect little feet.

Suitability for groups This could be a spot of real interest to a shore-exploring group, but is not otherwise a likely choice for bringing even a small crowd. The parking is limited, the shore is unconventional and the facilities are non-existent.

View While the view from everywhere on this coast is more or less gorgeous, it has to be said that the one from the Heard Road access is not nearly as varied or rich as that from most nearby spots. This is especially the case if you keep your view-gazing eyes at the top of the access strip. From here the distant horizon and the mainland mountains far south are pleasant, but hardly spectacular. If you wander out onto the low tide flats, however, you can treat yourself to a full whammy of the closer mainland mountains and islands—including the strange Mitlenatch environmental reserve.

Winds, sun and shade

The upper beach is a little more sheltered from a northwest blow than most other spots along this section of coast, but not so the tidal flats, where you could lose your hat in a gale.

A southeast wind hits the spot dead on. Don't expect shelter from the sun, either, although a cluster of willows on the neighbouring property does throw a little shade on the upper beach in late afternoon.

Beachcombing If your notion of beachcombing includes exploring a hugely varied and vast area, then you could do no better than come to this spot at low tide. The going is mostly easy out to the low-tide spit directly in front of the access spot, but bring footwear appropriate to negotiating large tidal pools and slippery rocks.

Seclusion The houses on either side and along the beach are well positioned not to miss a single morsel of action. Still, no one much comes to this spot. Wander out or along the shore and expect to meet only the very occasional kindred spirit.

While you're here, note that at the north end of Shelter Bay you can pull off onto a rest area with a park bench and easy access to a magnificently sandy beach.

Also while you're here, consider visiting the access off the end of Crane Road in Stories Beach. You will find a rocky shore with shelving outcroppings and, a short distance north, a large expanse of sand also accessible from the shoulder of the highway.

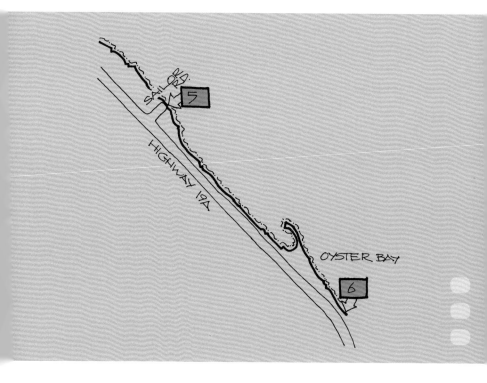

5

SAILOR ROAD

Quiet and shady level access to a mixed shore of boulders and patches of soft sand, a good spot for launching a kayak

Location, signs and parking On a treed section of highway, about 2 km north of the Oyster Bay Rest Area, look for the Sailor Road signpost. Drive the short distance to the end of Sailor Road and pull ahead as much as you dare through the increasingly sandy strip of road toward a barricade of bleached logs, evidently put in place to prevent cars from driving even farther onto the shore. The driveways from the houses on either side leave Sailor Road well back from the end of the road, so several cars can be parked here. You will see no signs welcoming you, forbidding you or cautioning you, but you can guess what they might say if they were there.

Path Those with walking difficulties or managing short-legged creatures with a reluctance to walk will be pleased they've arrived here. A dozen curious steps will bring you from the end of the road onto a pebbly area amid a few logs.

Beach The beach will probably be of most interest to kayakers eager to get their craft afloat with a minimum of lugging or twisted ankles. Even at low tide, the water does not retreat more than a few dozen metres from your vehicle. In addition, although much of the shore is a fairly rough-and-tumble mixture of barnacle-covered rocks and occasional boulders, almost directly in front of the access spot is a wide strip of sand leading to the low-water line. The same sand, though a little sticky, could be of interest to the other sort of paddler as well, or even a shore-goer wishing to break into a full dog-paddle. Picnickers will find a small strip of pebbles on which to spread out their wares, but few logs with which to improvise tables or backrests.

Suitability for children Considering that a few minutes in either direction can take you to large sandy beaches, you will probably not want to choose this beach for the express purpose of delighting your child. On the other hand, if you come here for your own pleasure, you can expect to find enough diversions to keep most children happy.

Suitability for groups While you could bring a few cars' worth of fellow kayakers here, the spot is not otherwise an obvious choice for a group.

View The view offers most of the beauties of this whole stretch of remarkably scenic coast, replete as it is with wonderfully spiky mountains and overlapping islands. The fact that you are virtually in the middle of a very large bay, with Salmon Point to the south and Shelter Point to the north, gives a grand frame to your view.

Winds, sun and shade Even though you are in the middle of a bay, this bay is so wide and so shallow that both northwest and southeast winds can be felt with all the freshness or bluster they are inclined to dole out. On the other hand, if you are looking for a spot with plenty of protective shade, both for your car and for your picnic, you can't do much better than choose this spot. From late morning to evening, fine clusters of firs on both sides give you as much protection from the sun as you're likely to find anywhere.

Beachcombing Although the tide doesn't reveal a huge width of shore, you can find plenty of beach along which to stretch your eager legs. Indeed, except for the fact that you are likely to grow weary from walking through loose rock on the upper beach or barnacle-covered rock on the lower beach, you can go as far in either direction as your irrepressible dachshund is eager to drag you.

Seclusion You won't find much more seclusion at any spot within many kilometres in either direction than you will find here. Although houses lie on either side, both are well screened from the upper beach by a lot of enthusiastic foliage. If your hair is up, you can feel very, very comfortable letting it down.

6

OYSTER BAY REST AREA

Although technically just a "rest area," one of the most gorgeous sandy beach parks you will find ... anywhere

Location, signs and parking Although it is tempting to insist, "You can't miss it," in fact you can. Because this spot is not identified with a large park sign, many explorers drive cheerfully by without fully realizing what watery and sandy pleasures they are missing. Your destination is just off the highway 100 m south of the Driftwood Restaurant. Keep your eyes peeled for a sign saying Oyster Bay Shoreline Park and south of it, the comparatively discreet sign saying Rest Area. If you want to drive virtually onto the beach to hunker down in your car and picnic on roast beef, mustard and onion sandwiches while the winds do their worst (or best), turn toward the shore at the unpaved southern end of the rest area. Otherwise, join the few other cars you are likely to find on the paved area close to information signs, toilets and picnicking facilities.

Path If you have to manage skimboards, kites, umbrellas, Frisbees, ungainly kin and the like onto the beach, you might want to choose the unpaved area, where you need stagger just a few metres across loose sand and logs onto the beach. From the paved area you have a choice of broad, level, crushed gravel paths. While all lead to the shore, most visitors will want to choose a path leading most directly there—not just because most are eager to get sand between their toes, but also because the long trail heads north through Oyster Bay Shoreline Park. This trail, through beach grass and small firs, leads to a raised gravel spit/breakwater interesting to visit but dropping to a muddy shore.

Beach It is difficult to moderate one's enthusiasm for this beach. Dig out your superlatives and exhaust every last one. Even connoisseurs of large sandy beaches will be hard pressed to find much fault with it. The beauties start with the large dune-like area of beach grasses and weathered logs and extend all the way to the distant low-tide line across virtually unblemished sand and tidal pools. While the tide doesn't go out nearly as far here as at some of the other large Island beaches—not the 200 m stretch of Rathtrevor or Parksville—it still uncovers more than enough space for every kite you want to fly or Frisbee you want to throw. In addition, even on a hot summer's afternoon the spot is largely ignored, perhaps because it is so close to the highway and part of a long strip of roadside sand.

Suitability for children If we start with the premise that children love sandy beaches, then all the rest follows. While there are many sandy beaches along this stretch of coast, many of them require running the gauntlet of rocky zones or skirting large patches of eelgrass. Not so this one. In addition, the tide doesn't drop so far that you have to run a marathon to reach the water's edge. Your barefoot, scampering children will always find lots of water with which to wreak havoc.

Suitability for groups As with children, so with groups. This is by far the best group site for many kilometres in either direction. You will want to stop well short of bringing a high school reunion here, since neither the parking nor the facilities can stretch to more than a few dozen people. Still, plan several cars' worth of hyperactive children or curmudgeonly uncles and garrulous aunts, secure in the knowledge that they will have lots of space to park, picnic or frolic.

View Choose a clear day, and you will be stunned with the beauty of the view. Although you might prefer the view slightly north, where Quadra and Cortes loom larger, you will still find the array of mountain peaks and undulating islands inviting. Because the shoreline is slightly convex here, too, you will find the view extending far, far toward the southern horizon and, to the north, to the outlying districts of Campbell River.

Winds, sun and shade If there is wind you will feel it and be either refreshed or chilled. Remember, though, that on the lower beach the wind is always strongest. If you want to bake on a breezy day, you can find a virtually windless spot among the logs in the dune-like area. Shade, likewise, is hard to come by since the trees backing the shore are quite small and the shore area is level. If you are really motivated, however, you can find some shade in mid to late afternoon among the upper logs.

Beachcombing This is one of the few places along this stretch of coast where beachcombing can be combined with jogging. You might have to do a lot of light-footed leaping to avoid the large tidal pools, however, so come prepared. Those more into sauntering can still enjoy wandering by the water's edge for a considerable distance. If you head south, you will be farther away from the highway. If you head north, though, either along the shore or through the park paths, you will come to a striking spit/breakwater some 300 m long curving like a wave toward the north.

Seclusion Though this delicious spot seems generally to be ignored by the throngs, there are always several appreciative folk here during good weather. The beach may be perfect in all sorts of ways, but seclusion is not one of them.

While you're here, consider pulling off onto the shoulder of the highway about 1.5 km north, where you can get easy access to a beautiful beach comprising acres and acres of low-tide sand and tidal pools.

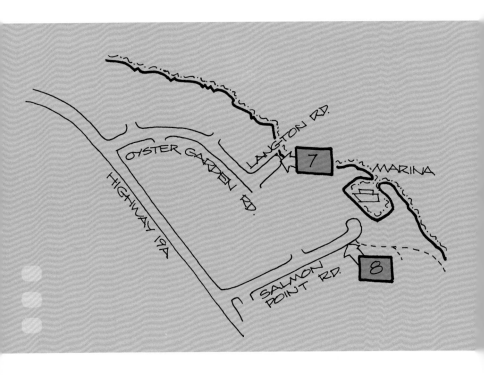

7

LANGTON ROAD

A good car-picnicking spot
perched high above the shore
and, at low tide, overlooking
an expanse of boulders

Location, signs and parking Using Ocean Resort as a prominent land-mark, turn down Oyster Garden Road beside it. After travelling just under 300 m down this curving road, you will come to Langton Road. The sign can be hidden behind foliage, but you will see a leafy lane-like gravel-and-grass strip leading toward an open area of beach grass and beach plants. Since you are likely to be the only one here, parking is not an issue, though you can find room for several cars in this gravelly area. While you can hunt down many access spots along this section of coast suitable for car picnicking, this one has the advantage of being raised a few metres above the shore, giving depth to the view. You won't see any signs, so will have to improvise the appropriate do's and don'ts.

Path An energetic local has built a solid set of concrete steps down the steep bank of jagged boulders put in place as a shore stabilizer.

Beach The beach is probably most attractive at high tide. Though logs rarely collect at the bottom of the loose-boulder retaining wall, the upper shore is largely loose pebbles, comfortable for settling a rump or two. At low tide, the sight of a 75 m expanse of barnacle-covered boulders might seem a little daunting. Still, if it's sand you want for a little castle build-ing, you can find patches at low tide by striking out a short distance in either direction. Kayakers might note, too, that because the tide doesn't go out nearly as far here as at many nearby spots, even at mid tide they can get to the water's edge without huge difficulty.

Suitability for children If you have a child or two in tow, you will prob-ably do best to choose high tide when the beach will be, in effect, pebbles. Do bring water shoes, though: a wading or dog-paddling child will discover that barnacles thrive on the submerged rocks.

Suitability for groups While this spot allows parking for several cars, it does not offer many attractions to most groups.

View The most distinctive parts of the view are the retaining wall of jagged boulders extending south and the boulder breakwater of Salmon Point Marina a little beyond. The view across the strait toward the mountains and islands is, of course, wonderful. Because of the curve of the shore, if you walk out onto the beach you can see far up the coast toward the outlying burbs of Campbell River.

Winds, sun and shade If you do choose this spot for a car picnic on a day when the strait is whipped into foam, rest assured that this is about as exposed a bit of shoreline as you are likely to find. If, however, you are seeking relief from the sun on a blistering day, you will find afternoon shade cast by a few large firs.

Beachcombing The shore is flat enough and expansive enough to allow some heavy-duty wandering. To the south, however, you will run into Salmon Point Marina. The upper beach is the most pleasant place to walk, but if you're planning a long trek, you can head out to the low-tide sand to the north.

Seclusion If seclusion is what you're after, seclusion is what you'll get here. One house, set back to one side, might register the presence of your car as you sip on your Thermos-latte. Once on the shore, though, and you will be as alone as you're likely to get.

8 OYSTER RIVER NATURE TRAILS

Known locally as the "pub to pub" trails, one of which gives access at several points to a stretch of gravelly dunes, piles of beach logs and gravel shore

Location, signs and parking You won't see any landmarks along the treed section of highway nearby, but a special left-turn lane should help you find the clearly signposted road. Salmon Point Road leads directly from the highway for about 400 m to its end at Salmon Point Resort. You will see a sign for the pub and restaurant here and, underneath it, a hand-carved wooden sign saying Nature Trail pointing to the right at the end of the public road. A wooden fence along the right side of the road bears another sign saying PRIVATE PROPERTY, and, beneath it, an arrow pointing to a gap in the fence labelled PUBLIC ACCESS. Voila! The only remaining sign tells you, "Leashing is mandatory in this park." Forewarned is fore-leashed! You will find plenty of parking along the broad gravel shoulder.

If you wish to take enthusiastic part in the "pub to pub" experience, turn off the highway farther south onto Regent Road by the Living Waters Fellowship Church and follow it over a bridge, where you will see the pub. From there you can begin your walk to the shore.

Path From the parking area (on Salmon Point Road) a broad, largely level, gravel path roughly parallel to the shore leads through an open area of grass, blackberries and occasional small firs. While the walking is easy, those who want a spot that provides them quick access to the beach won't be delighted at the enforced sauntering here. In fact, it is possible to make your way toward the beach using some narrow trails close to the trailhead, though most will want to choose one of the various established tracks farther along. If you want to explore the trails, you will find your-self swinging inland more or less by a river and, eventually, emerging at the Regent Road entrance to the park—and a pub!

Beach The upper beach is an unusually broad expanse of beach grass amid tangles of sun-bleached beach logs. At many points along this stretch, though, you will find, among the scattered logs, areas of the kind of loose, coarse sand that invites you to settle down with your basking parapher-nalia and your determination to soak in the dune-like atmosphere. In fact, you may well prefer to come at high tide to experience the beach area at its most attractive. Low tide reveals a slightly relentless stretch of small rocks, unbroken by tidal pools, large boulders or any other remarkable features.

Suitability for children High-spirited children, or those who like lots of space to run unimpeded, will enjoy galumphing along the trails and, on the beach, jumping from log to log to log before settling down with their peanut butter cookies and chocolate milk. Those who have sandcastles on the brain, though, or those who groan at the prospect of having to walk, won't be delighted and may well convey their mood to their parents.

Suitability for groups This is a great place to bring a group with a spring in their step and the desire to explore a large, natural area. The beach area, too, is so large that even a large group will barely make an impression. Be aware, though, that there are no facilities. This lack, along with the distance between cars and shore, will discourage certain kinds of groups.

View Because the shore is somewhat convex, you will find that the general orientation of the view changes depending on where you emerge from the trails. While you will find little foreground to your view, you will see such a rich array of background that, on a clear day at least, you won't feel deprived. From the southern tip of Quadra Island, sweeping south past the mainland mountains to the northern tip of distant Texada, the entire view is full of islands and peaks.

Winds, sun and shade From the northern end of the beach the northwest wind is most strongly felt. The south end of the beach, in contrast, feels the southeast wind most strongly. All along the shore, however, both winds blow with little to impede them. Behind the logs, however, you will find plenty of cover if you spread out on a towel with your SPF 50. In fact, SPF 50 is a good idea for anyone coming here on a sunny day. The only shade to be found is well back from the beach.

Beachcombing Walkers will love this spot, but those who like to comb the beach as they stride vigorously will be a little less thrilled. While the trails provide lots of easy walking, the shore, with its stretches of rocks, is a lot less easy going. If you are determined to walk long distances, be aware that in one direction your way is blocked by Salmon Point Marina and in the other by the Oyster River.

Seclusion Although a few locals make good use of the system of trails, the area is generally as empty as you are likely to find a shorefront, even on a hot summer afternoon. Whether strolling along a track or settled by the shore, you can find lots of scope to take advantage of uncluttered thoughts and uncluttered vistas.

Oyster River Nature Trails

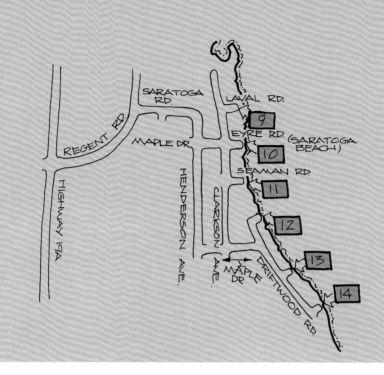

9

LAVAL ROAD

A wide upper beach of loose, white sand and logs, leading to a huge, lagoon-like tidal pool exposed by low tide

Location, signs and parking Look for the Living Waters Fellowship Church at the point at which Regent Road leaves highway 19A. Follow it for 400 m, turning right onto Saratoga Road. After 200 m, the road veers right and changes name to Henderson Avenue. Take the first left onto Eyre Road and the first left again onto Clarkson Avenue. Follow it for just under 200 m, keeping an eye out for Laval Road on your right. Follow this short road to its gravelly end in a wild-looking area of high beach grass. You will find more than enough room at the end of the road for several cars, though you are likely to have the spot to yourself. You will see no signs to prohibit you or direct you, but you will have no doubt that you have arrived at a public access.

Path The path is actually a nearly overgrown roadbed of loose sand. Walking 30 or 40 m through a broad, dune-like band of high beach grass will bring you to the beach. Although the path is level and reasonably easy for those with walking difficulties, you can find many easier alternatives in the area.

Beach You will find no other spot quite like this on the entire strip of coast. At high tide you might think otherwise, as you settle down in a gloriously wide area of loose white sand peppered with scattered beach logs. At low tide, however, you will discover that the shore drops to a broad slope of salt-tolerant green vegetation and a huge lagoon-like tidal pool enclosed by a gravel bar. It seems that Oyster River, emptying into the sea immediately north, is responsible for depositing the gravel bar and thus, over time, cutting off the upper shore from the open water.

Suitability for children Most children will be happier at Saratoga Beach, the fine stretch of sand immediately south. Their parents, however, might find good reason for bringing them here, especially if they are in search of easy parking and, to boot, a fair dollop of peace and quiet. The children of such parents will be happiest at high tide, particularly in warm weather, when their interest is getting as wet as possible as quickly and dramatically as possible. The gradually shelving beach is safe for beginning swimmers, and the large sandy area among the logs is good for barefoot scampering. Some children might find the "ick-factor" of swimming over green vegetation too much; these children would be happiest moving down the beach 20 or 30 m south where, instead of the grasslike vegetation underfoot, they will find themselves swimming over pebbles.

Suitability for groups A big family group or cluster of ravenous friends in search of easy parking and a large, empty, picnicking area among fine sand and logs might well opt to come here rather than to the more conventionally appealing and sometimes congested Saratoga Beach immediately south.

View Because the shore is slightly concave here, you will find that your view up and down the shore is a little restricted, especially by the Pacific Playgrounds area to the north. At the same time, the view across the strait is as gloriously bumpy and snow-peaked as anywhere along this stretch of coast. Those especially interested in the mysterious Mitlenatch Island will find themselves about as close to this mid-strait ecological reserve here as it is possible to get. Binoculars will give a huge boost to view lovers.

Winds, sun and shade While you might be slightly sheltered from a northwest wind, don't expect much shelter from either this wind or a southeast wind. Among the many, many logs, however, you can find yourself roasting as much as, or a little more than, you like. If you are expecting overhanging trees to give you some shelter from the UV, then you'll have to go elsewhere—or move a considerable distance up the access strip.

Beachcombing Those who like to explore an unusual bit of shore and still put a few kilometres under their heels will be delighted with this spot, particularly if they come at low tide. Although you can't go very far north without running into the marina and river, at low tide you can not only wander far out along the gravel spit across from you, but also turn your nose south to the wide expanse of Saratoga Beach and the tidal flats south of it.

Seclusion This is a great spot to choose if you want to avoid the comparatively crowded shore north at Pacific Playgrounds or south at Saratoga Beach. Sandwiched between both and yet within easy wandering distance of both, you should find yourself with a hefty chunk of unpeopled shore all to yourself or significant other selves. The only houses along the shore here, set far back on the other side of the dune area, are almost out of sight and easily out of mind.

While you're here, if you drive to the north end of Clarkson Avenue, you can visit the marina, its breakwater and the nearby sandy upper beach and lagoon.

10

SARATOGA BEACH

A large sandy beach, largely undeveloped, popular with locals but little known outside the area

Location, signs and parking Look for the Living Waters Fellowship Church at the point at which Regent Road leaves the highway. Follow it for 400 m, turning right onto Saratoga Road. After 200 m, the road veers right and changes to Henderson Avenue. Take the first left onto Eyre Road and follow it more or less to the shore. Unless you come at a peculiar time of day or a peculiar time of year, you are likely to find you are not alone. Most prominent of the many signs is an oddly commercial-looking one welcoming you to Saratoga Beach and, in the same breath, telling you that if you drink alcohol or park after 11 p.m., you are likely to run afoul of the RCMP. Others tell you not to park in the turnaround, to park at an angle only, not to collect shellfish and to muffle the decibels after 10 p.m. Those keen to know what opportunities are here, rather than what they may not do, might be interested in a commercial sign pointing to the site of kayak tours—though getting kayaks to the far distant water's edge at low tide must be a bit of a feat.

Path If you are able to get a parking spot near the end of the road, you will find that you are virtually on the beach, separated by just a few logs and a short, level area of sand. Those with walking difficulties could hardly do better than at this beach. Likewise, those with mountains of beaching devices will be pleased. In fact, don't be surprised if you see the low-tide sand dotted not just with kites and skimboards, but also shade canopies, deck chairs and the like. You might note the portable toilets cheerfully ensconced at the end of the parking area.

Beach This is one of the most gorgeous large beaches on the east coast of the Island, though little known outside of the area—in part, no doubt, because, unlike most of the others, it is not bordered by a park. In fact, except for the toilets, you will find none of the facilities one might expect at such a wonderful beach. If you don't already know what this kind of east-coast beach has to offer, expect an upper shore of bleached logs among sugary white sand. At low tide, expect 100 m of silvery sand laced with warm tidal pools full of sand dollars, tiny flat fish and clamshells.

Suitability for children No other beach for some distance in either direction is so likely to thrill children (see Oyster Bay Rest Area to the north and Miracle Beach to the south). Think sandcastles, think warm swimming water, think breakneck scampering through tidal pools and so on.

Suitability for groups In one way, this is a great place for a group. After all, the beach is huge enough to absorb even a (minor) throng. In another way, though, this is not such a great place for more than a small group, at least not on a hot afternoon in the middle of the summer. The fact is, the parking space is likely to have a couple of dozen cars taking up a high proportion of the available spaces even before your group arrives. In addition, unlike some of the big parks, this beach is backed by private residences rather than by an area of picnic tables and other facilities.

View Most visitors arriving at one of the low tides common in the afternoon during summer will be most fascinated by the sight of the beach itself. The slightly concave shoreline means, too, that on either side, but especially south, they will be aware of the outward curve of the shore. Across the strait, however, the striking array of peaks, some of them almost preposterously jagged, provide an unbeatable backdrop.

Winds, sun and shade If you are planning a beachy afternoon here, come fully prepared to be thoroughly exposed to the elements. On an otherwise warm day in early summer, a wind not noticeable inland can be chilling near the waterline. In addition, be sure you have crammed your beach bag with sunscreen, sun hats and sunglasses. You might even do what some locals do and bring a portable canopy. There is, be aware, not the slightest trace of shade to be had here.

Beachcombing If you've always loved the image of yourself running barefoot along the water's edge with your tresses in romantic abandonment, this is one of the few places where you can do exactly that. On the other hand, if you're planning a major trek, you'll have to come with sturdy beach shoes and head south. The beach, though large, does merge into a largely gravel shoreline to the south, and, to the north, grinds to a halt altogether at the Oyster River.

Seclusion Unless you creep here when all sensible folk are holed up in front of their televisions or snug in their beds, you are likely to find yourself far from alone. Take heart. Here is the chance to strut your gym-body stuff or flaunt your ridiculously expensive bikini.

11

SEAMAN ROAD

A little-used approach to the magnificent stretch of Saratoga Beach

Location, signs and parking At the Living Waters Fellowship Church, turn off the highway onto Regent Road, as if you are going to Saratoga Beach (which, in a sense, you are). Follow it for 400 m, turning right onto Saratoga Road. After 200 m, the road veers right and changes name to Henderson Avenue. Take the first left onto Eyre Road and the first right onto Clarkson Avenue; 100 m later you will see Seaman Road on your left. A short distance to the unpaved end of the road brings you to concrete barriers. From here, where you can park you car, you will see no signs to help you identify the spot, but should be able to glimpse two or three signs 20 m or so ahead, at the beach itself.

Path Though the concrete barriers prevent your driving right to the shoreline, the beach is only a short distance away across a broad and level bit of roadbed. You will have no difficulty managing the task of getting everything and everyone you want to the shore. As you approach the first of many logs scattered around the upper beach, you will see two signs. One instructs you to keep Bob the Beagle firmly leashed and, poetically, to "Stoop and Scoop" whatever Bob decides to leave. The other tells you not to camp or park overnight and to dampen the ruckus after 10 p.m.

Beach You will find yourself smack in the middle of the superbly beautiful Saratoga Beach. Unlike that at the northern part of the beach, the uppermost shore among the thickets of beach logs here is composed largely of pebbles rather than sand. While those planning to flop horizontally and pass out in the heat of the sun might prefer other, sandier parts of the beach, those who want to keep the sand out of the sandwich will see this small area of pebbles as offering real advantages. In either case, a few steps below the pebbly shore will bring you to the wide, virtually unblemished expanses of sand stretching to the low-tide line over 100 m away.

Suitability for children The beach itself, of course, could hardly be more attractive to virtually all children. From splashing in the warm tidal pools for toddlers, to dashing through the shallows with a skimboard for older children, the variety of beach activities is about as large as you're going to get anywhere. Some parents, however, will prefer the much more crowded main beach access on Eyre Road, a few minutes north of Seaman Road, for the sake of the toilets there and the sandy rather than pebbly upper beach.

Suitability for groups If you allow for the fact that the beach has no facilities appropriate to a group gathering, you can well decide that just about any group that can squeeze into a few cars can spread delightedly over this large beach. There is plenty of picnicking area among the logs, but no picnic tables. In addition, the beach is backed by private residences and, on one side, by a trailer park.

View This section of coast provides about as close a view as you are likely to get of Mitlenatch Island, but you will have to bring binoculars or a telephoto lens to get more than a distant impression of this strangely desert-like island. Otherwise, your view is made up of the sweep of shore from Oyster River estuary to the north to Black Creek estuary to the south.

Winds, sun and shade You will feel just about as much of every waft of a northwest wind as there is to be felt, though you might expect it to skirt the shore just a little. It doesn't. A southeast wind, too, seems to have nothing to discourage it from packing a wallop if it is so minded. Protection from the sun, likewise, exists only if you provide it. Bring all of the beach umbrellas, sunscreen and so on that you need—because, on a hot day, you will need it.

Beachcombing While most shores along this stretch of coast are primarily of interest to those who don sturdy shoes and set out over the sometimes challenging stretches of rock, this one is perfect for barefoot strollers, joggers or full gallopers. If you want your beachcombing to cover kilometres, though, you will have to bring those sturdy shoes. Do head south rather than north, too, since Oyster River estuary lies a few hundred metres to your north.

Seclusion While the main approach to Saratoga Beach, Eyre Road, is often busy, this approach is usually quiet or even empty. Don't be misled, however. Although fences line either side of the road, they don't actually provide much screening from the houses on one side and the trailer park on the other. Once on the beach, you will find yourself with plenty of companionship, particularly from the happy campers of the trailer park.

12
DRIFTWOOD ROAD—NORTH
A quiet and spacious approach to the south end of Saratoga Beach and the mixed level shore south of it

Location, signs and parking Look for the Living Waters Fellowship Church at the point at which Regent Road leaves the highway. Follow it for 400 m, turning right onto Saratoga Road. After 200 m, the road veers right and changes name to Henderson Avenue. Follow Henderson for about 800 m and turn left onto Maple Drive. Two hundred metres down Maple Drive brings you to Driftwood Road, where you should turn left. Drive to its northern end, where it curves sharply toward the store and grinds to a halt in a large gravel area of weeds. A little inconsistently, two adjacent signs tell you, first, that you are not allowed to park there between 9 p.m. and 7 a.m., and, second, that you mustn't play your kazoo at full volume after 10 p.m. If, therefore, you want to view the annual mid-August meteor shower, you will want to park at one of the spots immediately north (Laval Road, Eyre Road or Seaman Road). Other signs warn you against contaminated shellfish and instruct you to keep your hound on a leash and "pick up after your dog," while providing you with a helpful illustration on exactly how to do that. Dog owners shouldn't stop at reading those signs, however. Other signs, common in the Qualicum area but not north of there, tell you that during brant season, your eager retriever must steer entirely clear of the beach.

Path A barrier of jagged chunks of rock put in place to prevent erosion separates the end of the road from the shore. Still, negotiating your unsteady relatives or offspring the short distance from car to shore should be a piece of cake.

Beach This is the perfect spot to choose if you want easy access both to the large, glorious sands of Saratoga Beach immediately north and yet be a little separate from the happy crowds that you might sometimes find there. Some will prefer the upper beach here, too, for its comparative scarcity of beach logs and its mixture of sand and pebbles. Directly in front of the access spot, low tide reveals a large expanse of gravel and large tidal pools spreading south, but also, at mid-beach, a strip of sand extending a considerable distance southward.

Suitability for children If your primary aim is to delight your little ones with lots of accessible low-tide sand, you should choose Eyre Road or Seaman Road, a few minutes north. If, however, you come at high tide or want lots of easy parking and don't mind walking along the shore a short distance to a large sandy area, then keep this option in mind.

Suitability for groups The ample parking would be the chief reason for choosing this access spot, especially if your group is one that is likely to spread out in pursuit of varied interests. Your Society for the Preservation of Wizards will find plenty of room for picnicking (without benefit of facilities) immediately in front of the broad access strip, but should also be aware that private residences dot the shoreline in both directions.

View Like the view from almost everywhere along this stretch of coast, the one from this spot presents in full glory the classic array of mainland peaks and mostly distant islands. Those who have been photographing or painting the view from various spots between Campbell River and here, however, will notice that the farther south they travel, the fewer the foreground islands and the more wide open the entire view.

Winds, sun and shade All winds, northwest and southeast, are almost as frisky on the shore as they are at sea, though most strongly felt at the low-tide line. The protection from sun is another matter. In fact, this is the only spot providing access to Saratoga Beach that has some shade. During the first part of the day, your dune buggy can nuzzle into the shade on the right side of the access strip. During the afternoon you and your beach goodies can find shade a little to the south of the access strip.

Beachcombing If you want to walk off your lunchtime eclairs and fill your lungs with salty air, this is the perfect place to do it. Head north and walk barefoot on the sands, or south and, properly shod, put in a kilometre or two of exploring along the level gravel shore. Be prepared for a little wading, however, if you wish to cross Black Creek, about 1.5 km away. You might vary your walk south by walking some of the paths through the scattered woods for the last half kilometre north of Black Creek.

Seclusion Houses sprinkle the shoreline; people sprinkle the sandy beach to the north. If, however, you wander south or spread-eagle on the upper shore here, you will find lots of quiet, and, possibly, peace.

While you're here, you can follow Clarkson Avenue to its southern end and its intersection with Beach Crescent for roadside access to the north shore of Black Creek and its estuary.

13

DRIFTWOOD ROAD—MIDDLE
A nearly level access through
a subdivision to an expansive
beach of large tidal pools and
low-tide sand

Location, signs and parking Look for the Living Waters Fellowship Church at the point at which Regent Road leaves the highway. Follow it for 400 m, turning right onto Saratoga Road. After 200 m, the road veers right and changes name to Henderson Avenue. Follow Henderson for about 800 m and turn left onto Maple Drive. Two hundred metres down Maple Drive bring you to Driftwood Road, where you should turn right. After about 150 m, look for a bank of mailboxes on the left side of the road. You should see a wide, treeless area with a short, paved dip toward concrete barriers preventing you from miring yourself in the dunes. Two signs will tell you that the shellfish offering themselves to you are contaminated and that you may not stay overnight.

Path A few metres through the slip-sliding dunes and past some chunks of broken rock and scattered beach logs will bring you to the shore.

Beach The unusually extensive upper beach of dry sand and pebbles drops to a gravelly mid-beach covered by some huge tidal pools. If the tide is well out when you arrive, you will find a strip of sand extending along the low-tide line about 100 m distant, and, depending on how far the tide is out, well out into the water.

Suitability for children Feel free to let your children dash toward the shore and, if they are appropriately shod, as far down this level shore as they like. Although they could come a bit of a cropper on some of the rocks, they will, in general, find little to cramp their romping style as they splash through the tidal pools toward the tempting strip of low-tide sand. A few Band-Aids in your beach bag aren't a bad idea. High tide is best for swimming, though even at high tide, water shoes are necessary.

Suitability for groups Parking is easy for several cars, and the beach and picnic areas are large—but group facilities are non-existent.

View Bring your binoculars or zoom lens to appreciate fully the geographical derrings-do of Mitlenatch Island and the Coast Mountains, and you will find lots and lots to appreciate. Your view to the south isn't quite as expansive as that from most points along this stretch of coast.

Winds, sun and shade This shore is more protected from a southeast wind than most along this coast, though only near the upper beach. Looking for protection from a northwest wind or sun? You won't find either here.

Beachcombing This is a good launching spot for an hour or two's stride or stroll. If you want maximum flexibility in your choice of strolling terrain, however, make sure you bring shoes that are a match for barnacle-covered rocks and that you don't mind getting wet.

Seclusion You will find few other shore-goers on this bit of coast and few locals to inspect or even record your presence. While this is a residential shoreline, the houses on either side of the access spot are placed well back, their view lines set for the horizon rather than for horizontal visitors. If you walk south, within a few hundred metres you will find an undeveloped section of shoreline covered with open woods and paths. You will have to roll up your trousers and doff your shoes if you want to go much farther, as Black Creek has decided to drain into the ocean at this point.

Driftwood Road

14

DRIFTWOOD ROAD—SOUTH
Easy, level access to a beach
with a sun-baked area of coarse
sand and logs, a mid-beach of
gravel and bars of low-tide sand

Location, signs and parking Look for the Living Waters Fellowship Church at the point at which Regent Road leaves the highway. Follow it for 400 m, turning right onto Saratoga Road. After 200 m, the road veers right and changes name to Henderson Avenue. Follow Henderson for about 800 m and turn left onto Maple Drive. Two hundred metres down Maple Drive brings you to Driftwood Road. Turn right. Drive along Driftwood until you come to a huge turnaround area outside a daunting set of stone gates with a sign reading DRIFTWOOD ESTATES. Turn toward the shore. You can drive only partway toward the beach because a line of jagged boulders blocks your way. Still, you will find room for several cars in this large area.

Path You have only to walk a short distance toward the shore through a pleasant grassy area under a few firs. Fortunately, the access strip is more than road width, since the houses on either side loom large. Still, you may well feel as though you're on the beach before you get there because the last section of the approach is beckoning sand.

Beach The whole shorefront has a wonderfully sun-baked beachy feeling. You will probably want to arrive at either a very high tide or very low tide, however, since the central part of the beach is a level surface of apple-sized rocks a few dozen metres wide. The largest area of dry sand good for basking and brooding is immediately to the right of the access— unfortunately, in front of a house. Still, the whole upper beach area has plenty of space and plenty of attractively random logs, with even a few decorative fronds of beach grass.

Suitability for children Though this middle part of the beach is interesting for hunters of seashells and scuttling creatures, those who are primarily lovers of sand in either its firmly packed or its loose-dry versions will be most interested in the uppermost and lowermost beach. For the former, make sure your brood is well shod, since sand is prolific only near the low-tide line. In fact, you can paddle barefoot not just at the low-tide line but also well below it into the extensive sandy shallows. It would be an unrealistic parent who didn't make sure that the aforesaid brood were not only well shod but decked out in bathing suits before taking on the sandy parts of the shore. After all, a little water is always a prelude to more when children are involved.

Suitability for groups While you can find easy parking for several cars, you can safely trash any thoughts you might entertain of organizing a day at the beach here—unless you want to induce the ire of the close-spaced neighbouring houses.

View Bring your binoculars if you want to make as much of a journey to Desolation Sound as many will ever undertake. While your view-seeking eyes can sweep up and down the strait, if they are tuned into spectacular geography, they will naturally go directly across the strait, past tiny Mitlenatch Island, the "Galapagos of British Columbia," then past the undulations of Hernando Island and Cortes Island, to the crags around Desolation Sound and, behind it, Toba Inlet. Supplement your binoculars with a good zoom camera and come away with some eye-popping pics.

Winds, sun and shade Check the marine forecast if the day is sunny but cool. If any wind at all is forecast, you will feel it even though it will be blowing largely along the shore rather than directly onto it. Remember that you can always find some refuge tucked behind the scattered logs of the upper beach. Remember, too, that if you are only marginally warm, you don't need to worry about being further chilled by afternoon shade. There isn't any.

Beachcombing Since you are midway between two large sandy beaches, Saratoga Beach to the north and Miracle Beach to the south, each just under a kilometre distant, you may wish to set out for either. Take into account, though, that if you head south to Miracle Beach you will have to reckon with crossing Black Creek en route. On the other hand, you might well enjoy walking to Black Creek in one direction and taking some of the forest paths above the shore at least partway home.

Seclusion The bit of shore directly in front of the access route could hardly be less secluded. Houses on both sides, and for some distance in either direction, press enthusiastically forward—though some of them partially screened with firs. Since you are unlikely to find others coming to this spot, however, your low-tide wanderings will be mainly on your own. If you want further seclusion and are willing to gain it by wandering, head south. Within 200 m you will be walking by undeveloped forest and can continue to do so for the next 400 m.

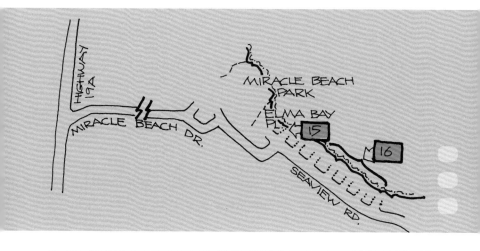

15
ELMA BAY PLACE
A secluded, treed access to the south end of Miracle Beach, a short distance from the provincial park

Location, signs and parking Midway between the Oyster River bridge and the settled area of Black Creek on highway 19A, you will see a minigolf business at a significant crossroads and Miracle Beach Drive heading toward the coast. In just under 3 km along Miracle Beach Drive, you will find yourself entering Miracle Beach Provincial Park and, understandably, will think that this is the end of the road. Not so. Peculiarly,

Miracle Beach Drive carries on right through the park, turning sharply right at one point, and so should you if you want to find your way to the "back door" of the beach. After exiting the park, follow Miracle Beach Drive until the road takes a sharp turn left and arrives at an intersection with Seaview Road and, on the left, a sign for Elma Bay Place. Park where you see a dirt road disappearing through the woods toward the shore, though you might choose to drive down this road. This track is officially called Mountain View Road, though as of yet, you will see no signs with its name. You will, however, see one sign as you approach the shore telling you that you don't want to break the law by collecting shellfish and even less do you want to suffer paralytic poisoning.

Path How far you need to walk to the shore will depend on how far you drive down the dirt track. No matter where you park, however, your route to the beach is easy and level.

Beach You emerge from the woods into a little-used area of tall beach grass, gravel and logs.

Although you may wish to sit on the logs while enjoying the view and a hamper of deli salads and buns, it is unlikely that you will want to remain here long. For many, the chief reason for coming to this spot will be to have a "private" entrance onto the large sandy beach that is shared by the provincial park a short distance north. Admittedly, from this position along the shore you don't have quite the same easy access to the sand as you would have at the park, since you have to get yourself across a few dozen metres of gravel and barnacles.

Suitability for children That Miracle Beach is a great beach for (most) children is unquestionable. What is questionable is whether this secluded approach to the shore is more suitable than that through the public park a short distance to the north. There, of course, you have the advantage of park facilities but also a narrower strip of gravel between the upper shore and the sandy tidal flats. Here, though, you have the option of driving virtually to the shore and leaving your car in secluded shade while you have a section of beach all to yourself. An experienced parent will bring crocs or water shoes so that the little ones can get over the barricade of sharp bits.

Suitability for groups Given the proximity of the large provincial park with almost unlimited parking and all the facilities that even your most high maintenance guests can demand, you would not want to come here with more than a few kindred spirits.

View Because you are on the south shore of gently indented Elma Bay, your view along the coast is of the graceful curve of the shoreline north to the Black River estuary, and, beyond that, the distant promontory of the Oyster River estuary. If you have brought binoculars or chosen a particularly clear day, you might be able to pick out half a dozen islands, ranging in size from tiny Mitlenatch Island in the north-central part of the strait to Cortes Island looming behind it.

Winds, sun and shade Northwest winds, the bane of many clear-weather beach days early in the summer, can blow intemperately onto and across the shore, particularly toward the low-tide line. A southeast wind, too, can be a little more energetic than you consider desirable, but it blows roughly parallel to the shore. While you cannot adjust the amount of wind you are feeling, you can choose the amount of shade you are getting, particularly in the afternoon when, if you prefer, you can confine your visit to the now shady upper beach.

Beachcombing It would be close to criminal to come to this beach without leaving the upper beach and heading across the rocky mid-beach and onto the long stretches of low-tide sand. Do be prepared either to get sand between your toes or, at the very least, get wet feet, since part of the pleasure—and an unavoidable pleasure—is wading through the extensive sandy tidal pools.

Seclusion One of the points of coming to this spot rather than to the nearby adjacent park is the possibility of having this little bit of shore all to yourself. The impression of seclusion is amplified by the solid growth of firs lining the shore in either direction for almost 100 m. Don't be misled, though, for you will find houses lurking beyond these patches of wood. Sad to say, too, these woods may have a short lifespan. The low, level land on either side is slated for residential development.

16 SEAVIEW ROAD

A series of gravel tracks
through open woods to a low,
level shore with a broad upper
beach of pebbles and a lower
beach of rounded rocks

Location, signs and parking Turn onto Miracle Beach Drive from the highway. Two kilometres will bring you to Miracle Beach Provincial Park, and an additional kilometre will bring you through the park and toward the shore. At the first intersection turn right onto Seaview Road. For the next 2 km along Seaview Road, several dirt tracks, each about 100 m long, run between Seaview Road and the shore. It is possible to drive down almost all of them, though some of them are rougher than others. On some you can drive right to the edge of the beach for a great foul-weather car picnic or easy kayak launch (at mid to high tide). While 8 of these have been designated roadways, and all of them have been given names (Anchor, Franklin, Woodbine are three), none of them has a road sign and not all of them are equally cleared. Using house numbers, therefore, as your guide, you will find the best tracks opposite 1409, opposite 1503, beside 1523, between 1528 and 1536, beside 1566, and opposite 1609. While these are similar, you might wish to begin your explorations with the route opposite 1609 because the track to the shore is particularly easy to drive and because at this end of the beach, you are within easy striking distance of Miracle Beach itself. On the other hand, fishers might wish to begin at the southern end, since that is the spot most favoured by locals casting for pink salmon during the late summer run.

Path At some points you might like to park on Seaview Road itself, or partway down the tracks toward the shore. Nowhere, however, will you find a route that isn't easy, level walking. Kayakers will be particularly interested in those spots where the "path" is shortest, of course.

Beach No matter where you walk onto the beach, you will see a broad upper beach of pebbles and fine gravel. At low tide you will see about 75 m of gradually sloping, rocky shore, home to the almighty barnacle and the teeming world beneath the rocks. The most discernible differences among the various spots are that beach logs accumulate more along the southern section of the beach and that the northern end of the beach is closer to Miracle Beach.

Suitability for children Getting onto the beach could hardly be easier, since you can drive virtually onto it. While the beach doesn't have the areas of sand required by many children, most inventive and curious children can spend a happy hour or two devising all sorts of play. Where sea life is to be investigated under rocks, seashells are to be collected, bright pebbles are to be sifted through, and logs are to be climbed, a good afternoon's play awaits. That the upper beach of loose pebbles is unusually broad at many points encourages play in this area. Still, this beach is not well suited to all children. If your children are saddened by a lack of sand, stop at Miracle Beach Park rather than carry on here.

Suitability for groups The main reason for bringing a small group here is to treat them to a slice of shore where you are likely to be the only visitors. Whether for a Good Talk or a private picnic, these spots are chiefly attractive for their isolation. Stop at Miracle Beach Park if you want facilities and a large sandy beach.

View Since you can park right by the shore's edge at some of these tracks, you can enjoy the view in any weather. Bring your binoculars and zoom lens to enjoy all the nobbles and bumps across the waters. Island spotters will be able to pick out tiny Mitlenatch Island in the middle of the strait and Cortes Island looming behind it. A little farther south, they will spot the pyramidal shape of Mount Addenbroke on East Redonda Island. At 1,591 m, it is the highest North American mountain on an island (excluding Vancouver Island). Farther south look for the sandy cliffs of Savary Island, another curiosity of the northern strait.

Winds, sun and shade Winds tend to blow parallel to the shore rather than directly onto it, though at times all parts of the shore can feel windblown. Those planning to spend a long, hot afternoon on one of these spots will be pleased that enough Douglas firs dot the shoreline that finding a shady spot on the upper beach in the afternoon is usually easy.

Beachcombing Many will content themselves with prodding and peering around the low-tide line. Those who want to stride out, however, can easily head in either direction, at least if they are prepared for sliding a little in loose pebbles. Long-distance walkers can choose to head north, where they will come across Miracle Beach, or south, where, within 2 km, they will find Williams Beach.

Seclusion Almost every lot on this shorefront subdivision has a house on it. Unlike some property owners—around Nanoose, for example—who try to replicate the prairies by stripping their land of vegetation, those here have left groves of trees. The result is that even though you are never far from a house, you will never feel thrust into the middle of a suburb.

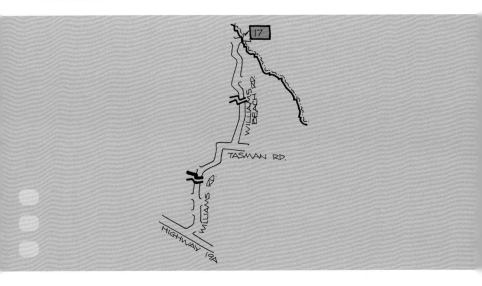

17
WILLIAMS BEACH
A quiet approach to a large sandy beach with a few patches of gravel and huge tidal pools

Location, signs and parking Williams Road leaves the highway along a straight wooded section without any obvious landmark other than a sign advertising second-hand goods, auctions and paintball. Follow Williams Road for nearly 3 km, noting that its name changes to Tasman Road at a right-angled corner. After a few hundred metres on Tasman, turn left onto Williams Beach Road and carry on for about 3 km until the very end of the road, immediately next to the shore. You will find plenty of easy parking for several cars here, but only one sign, in this case telling you any (unlikely) plans you might have had to park overnight will have to be trashed. Notice, by the way, that since you can park immediately behind a few beach logs, you might well want to return to this spot when a wintery sou'easter is creating havoc so that you can sip on your Thermos of mulled apple cider and enjoy every car-rocking gust of gale-force wind.

Path Before you hurry off to the beach, take a minute to look at the eroded side of the parking area and the clear evidence of an ancient Native midden, or debris pile. After contemplating the nature of "pre-contact" life here, turn toward the end of the parking lot and the very few steps needed to get through a gently sloping bit of sand onto the beach.

Beach If you haven't already figured out how to read tide tables, make sure you do before coming to Williams Beach. Missing low tide amounts to missing the beach. Admittedly, the upper beach, amid an area of beach logs, is a hugely appealing place to sprawl or perch to lose yourself in the view or in your laptop. Still, it is the lower beach that is most striking. In fact, you will immediately notice that the largest stretch of sand, some 200 m of it at low tide, is not directly in front of this access road but a little to the south, in front of a rustic resort. You clearly have the option of making your way over the intervening rocks to the smaller area of sand close by or investigating the huge expanse there. In either case, you won't want to miss exploring the large bars and interspersed wading areas that create wildly convoluted shorescapes.

Suitability for children This beach should rank high among the beaches children love most. If you can cope with the fact that there are no park facilities and that you might have to walk down the beach a little to get to the best sand, you can sit back and watch your child get up to every activity that a child faced with a magnificent sandy beach and lots of warm water is likely to get up to. One factor you might want to note, though, is that horse riders occasionally bring their steeds here for a bit of shorefront wandering.

Suitability for groups The big drawback to bringing a dozen or two effusive aunts, sticky cousins and troubled in-laws to this beach is the complete lack of facilities. If you are prepared for that, you can invite just about any beach- or picnic-loving group here. Not only can you toss aside worries about intruding into a quiet residential neighbourhood, but your group can also find lots of space to picnic or paddle, toss Frisbees or fall fast asleep.

View Since you are near the northern tip of a shallow bay, your view is largely of the gentle curve of the shore to the south, rising to a forested bank nearly 50 m high toward the end of the bay. You should be able to make out Harwood Island off the northern tip of Texada Island and, directly across the strait, Savary and Hernando islands in front of Malaspina Peninsula. If you have brought binoculars, you will be able to see tiny, treeless Mitlenatch Island nature reserve in the middle of the strait.

Winds, sun and shade You will have absolutely no difficulty telling the direction of the wind. You will feel all winds, though not their full force—for good or ill. You won't find any protection from sun, either. Considering that you and yours are likely to linger at this gorgeous spot, make sure you have all the sun protection creams and devices in your repertoire.

Beachcombing Those who are less interested in immersing themselves in sand and water than in exploring a virtually untouched section of coast will want to make a special point of coming to this spot. While walking is good in both directions, though not always easy, the shoreline is more interestingly shaped to the south, and the stretch of completely untouched shore much longer.

Seclusion Welcome to a little-used entrance to one of the most secluded stretches of shore on the entire east coast of Vancouver Island! Even on a hot summer's day, not many people seem to come to this access spot (except those who are guests at the resort next door).

Even the resort is discreet. Rustic cabins are set far back from the shorefront at the back of a huge meadow. Beyond the resort, you will see virtually no shorefront buildings for many, many kilometres. This is one secret spot you may just want to keep secret.

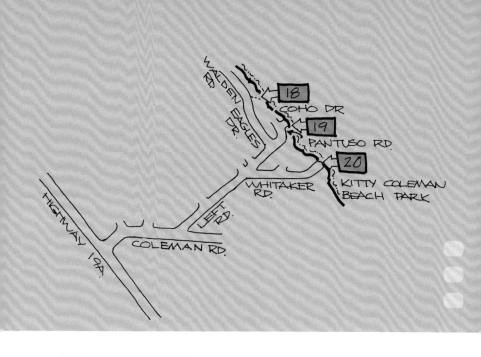

18
EAGLES DRIVE PARK
A spectacular wooden staircase down a steep forested bank to a secluded beach of sand and rock

Location, signs and parking Look for the landmark sign advertising Wolf aluminum boats along a straight section of treed highway about 6 km north of Courtenay. Turn down Coleman Road and continue for just under 2 km until you see Left Road on your left. After about 2 km on Left Road, take another left onto Eagles Drive. Just past the point where Eagles Drive merges directly into Walden Road, you will see a large carved sign announcing the name of the park and a parking area for several cars. Another sign warns you to stay out of the park during high winds and to be aware that the trail may be slippery after rains.

Path Part of the attraction of this spot is the walk to the shore, and all the more because you will find nothing quite like it north of Qualicum. The trail, about 200 m long, drops approximately 30 m down a beautifully forested bank. Beginning as a groomed gravel track, the trail leads to a magnificently structured staircase of some 90 steps. Don't be daunted by the prospect of facing such a long flight, however. The stairs not only turn as they pass landings but also are interrupted by a resting platform with a bench, perhaps even more welcome on the return journey!

Beach The trail leads out from overhanging firs onto an upper shore of pebbles and fine gravel among several beach logs. This is a reasonably inviting area for pausing and possibly refreshing yourself before exploring further. The lowest tides expose about 75 m of rocks and boulders. Both in front of the access trail and for a considerable distance in either direction, a curious sequence of long, narrow tidal pools runs down the centre of the beach.

Suitability for children You won't have to ponder the pros and cons of this beach for very long before realizing that many children won't be delighted with either the long staircase or the rocky shore.

Suitability for groups Obviously this beach is not suited to low-energy groups who merely want to ooze from their vehicles onto a patch of baking sand. With the easy parking, however, and the enormous isolation of the whole area, a group of nature lovers could well meet up here for an unusual adventure into a section of near wilderness.

View You can't help but be impressed by the high treed bank behind you running along a straight shore for a great distance in either direction. Look out to sea, though, and you will be struck by the opposite kind of view, one of large expanses and great distances. While the southern strait will seem to disappear over the horizon, across the strait you will see beautiful contours and crests of islands and mountains. Standing out through the blue haze of distance are the sandy cliffs of Savary Island and, farther north, those at the south end of Denman Island.

Winds, sun and shade If a wind is up to its usual tricks, it will be blowing roughly parallel to the shore. That means that the farther you go toward the waterline, the more wind you will catch. While you can't do much, therefore, to time your visit around winds, you will certainly want to time it around sun and shade conditions, if you plan to stay for any time. Want sun? Come during the morning. Want shade? The upper shore is swathed in shade for the entire afternoon.

Beachcombing The attractions of this spot as the beginning of a beach-combing expedition result less from the shore itself than from the seclusion. Head north at low tide confident that if you watch your footing over the generally rocky shore, you will face no significant obstacles and will see interesting tidal pools.

Seclusion For the select few who prize a well-hidden beach and a profound sense of untouched nature, Eagles Drive Park will become a favourite destination. Not just the walk to the shore but the shore itself for almost 4 km north is probably the most nearly untouched section of forested coastline between Campbell River and Cowichan.

19
PANTUSO ROAD
Quiet shorefront parking, good for car picnicking and launching kayaks

Location, signs and parking About 6 km north of Courtenay, turn onto Coleman Road. After about 1.5 km, head left onto Left Road for another 2 km. Left Road morphs into Coho Drive where it turns sharply left near the shore. Within a few metres you will see Pantuso Road clearly marked. It is only a few metres long and ends, happily, virtually on the shore. Apart from the prohibition against overnight parking or camping, no signs are posted here. While you will find lots of parking along the shoulder of the road, only two spots provide a good view of the sea if you have come with an appetite for storm watching and devouring your shrimp-and-brie panini with hot tea.

Path For kayakers and toters of unwieldy easels or unwieldy family members, being parked virtually on the shore is a major advantage. A few gradually sloping steps, and you are in an area of pebbles and logs.

Beach You can find a small area of coarse sand amid the logs if your inclination is to while away an hour nibbling at *War and Peace* and cashews.

Most of the upper shore is loose pebbles and logs, though, so bring a beach blanket for a little padding. Kayakers and parents in particular should note that low tide exposes about 75 m of boulders and their little friends, the barnacles. A few large tidal pools await exploration.

Suitability for children Few parents would make a point of singling out this beach from among the sandy alternatives. Once here, however, a child can be amused with the kinds of pleasures that local children are adept at managing— pebble collecting, log scrambling, crab and starfish prodding and the like. At high tide, too, as any realistic parent knows, watery play to the point of total immersion is almost inevitable, even in cool weather. Come prepared.

Suitability for groups The parking is limited and the neighbouring houses crowd close. Take your cast of thousands elsewhere.

View Dozens of diverse geographical lumps and bumps decorate the distant shores of the strait. Among them, you might single out curiously pale Mitlenatch Island in the middle of the strait and looming behind it, Cortes Island. Another curiosity is the triangular peak in the mountains to the south of Cortes. East Redonda Island is the location of Mount Addenbroke, at 1,591 m the highest mountain off mainland North America (excluding, of course, Vancouver Island.)

Winds, sun and shade Although the northwest winds that accompany warm weather can sometimes be a little too refreshing for comfort, you can find a little shelter among the logs and beside the heaped bank reinforcement of jagged boulders to the left of the entrance. Since you won't find even a morselette of shade, make sure you have the hats, creams and glasses you need to ward off the rays.

Beachcombing Shore-walking enthusiasts who have come prepared to brace their ankles while managing some of the lumpier sections of shore will probably find the most interesting part by turning north. Here the rock-and-boulder lower beach is varied with a curious sequence of long, narrow tidal pools. Within a few hundred metres walkers will find themselves beneath virtually untouched forested banks.

Seclusion The only seclusion you are likely to experience without walking north is in being the only visitor. As for not wanting to see neighbouring houses or be seen by them, don't expect much.

20

KITTY COLEMAN
PROVINCIAL PARK

A full-facility park with shorefront meadows under firs by a
broad rocky beach

Location, signs and parking About 6 km north of Courtenay, turn onto Coleman Road. After 1.5 km, take Left Road on your left, and after another 1.5 km or so, turn right onto Whitaker Road for just over 1 km, where it ends at the beach in Kitty Coleman Provincial Park. Once in the park, assuming that you have come for day use rather than camping, you can, if you're lucky, find one of the parking spots with a view of the ocean. A large notice board tells you to abandon all plans of wrestling succulent clams from their sandy homes: they are contaminated. Drift-wood collectors' note: find your lamp bases and candle holders elsewhere. In this park, what's on the beach stays on the beach.

Path Unusually for a provincial park, this one has some parking so close to the shore that those with walking difficulties can get to a seaside park bench, picnic table or even a seat on beach logs within a few metres. Kay-akers who want to be able to drive right to the water's edge can manage that trick at virtually every tide. Be prepared to pay a fee, however: the yearly rate is $40.

Beach Some will find a trace of irony in the fact that the 600 m of beach-front in this park is among the least varied or interesting stretch of beach anywhere nearby. Except for the minor estuary created by Coleman Creek, it is, at low tide, a virtually unbroken 100 m wide strip of rocks and boulders. No beach is without its charms, though. The shore is rich in the scuttly and clingy-oozy sorts of sea life, and the strip of beach logs makes for plenty of picturesque perching.

Suitability for children This is hardly likely to be a top choice as a place to treat deserving children with a day at the beach. Still, if you have a large group of children to amuse and the weather is iffy to the point of precluding swimming, you might consider the attractions here. You will find not just lots of facilities in the form of picnic tables and washrooms, but also lots of grassy area for tag and British bulldog. Log running, crab hunting and stone skipping just might be enough to keep the wee folk happy. Even during warm weather you might want to come here, knowing that, with water shoes in place, swimming and wading can be warm and safe.

Suitability for groups This is a valuable option to keep in mind for a group whose chief interests are in having a beautiful seaside backed by fields dotted with coastal firs as a place in which to picnic and wander. The facilities are a clear asset to a group of any size.

View Since the Strait of Georgia is wide here, your general sense will be of the expanse of the inland sea coming to be known as the Salish Sea. Bring your binoculars, however, and you will be able to spot such islands as Hernando, Savary, Harwood and the north part of Texada. The sandy cliffs of Savary are probably the most immediately noticeable feature.

Winds, sun and shade The beach itself is exposed to the northwest winds and southeast winds that bustle up and down the strait. Under the trees, however, you can get a little protection if the wind is chilling rather than refreshing. On a hot day you have lots of shady options, since the scattered trees provide many patches of shade, some of them on the upper beach in the afternoon.

Beachcombing If you are comfortable walking among loose pebbles and enjoy long walks, you can stroll a long distance in either direction along this level, unbroken expanse of shore. To the south you will have to manage to cross Coleman Creek, but can cut inland and cross the park bridge if you prefer. In fact, in your walk to that end of the park you may want to hunt down the 500-year-old giant Douglas fir protected by the park.

Seclusion Although this is a provincial park, it is managed by the community and thus is without the exposure—or crowds—of some other large provincial parks. You are unlikely to find more than a few others wandering the shores or launching boats.

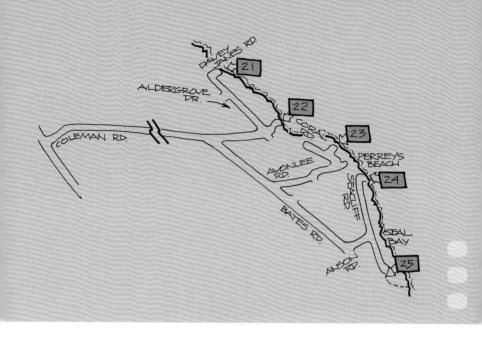

21 DAVEY JANES ROAD

A well-hidden, leafy path down a bank to a secluded shore with a sandy upper beach amid logs and a lower beach of rocks and large tidal pools

Location, signs and parking From the highway turn left onto Coleman Road, using the Wolf aluminum boats business as a handy reference point. Drive for about 5 km before turning left onto Aldergrove Drive and follow it for about 1 km until you see the sign for Davey Janes Road and a narrow, treed road heading a short distance downhill. You might be intrigued to see in tiny print under the name of the road a set of dates, "August 5, 1912–July 2, 2002," and speculate that Davey Janes was the name of a local settler. On the other hand, if you look at an official land management map of the area, you will find that the name of the road is Davey Jones, not Janes. The fact that all the other branch roads off Aldergrove have a maritime theme suggests this is the correct version. Thus mulling, you can park in the only space available to you on the grassy shoulder of the road and turn toward the shore down what appears a leafy roadbed.

Path You will drop about 10 m over the course of the increasingly narrow path that is sometimes overgrown with thimbleberries and snowberries.

Beach The sort of beachgoers who are looking for a pretty space of sand dotted with handy logs so that they can spread out a beach blanket and get lost in a biography of Michael Jackson will feel they have found heaven. If, thereafter, our beachgoers wish to take a dip, they will feel considerably less in heaven unless they arrive at high tide, when the rocks and boulders of the lower beach are covered. On the other hand, the sort of beachgoers who prize seclusion above all and enjoy not just a period of meditative indolence but also exploring a virtually untouched bit of shore will be delighted at any tide.

Suitability for children A little knowledge of your children's likes and dislikes will go a long way to ensuring that your children, and thus you, have a happy afternoon. Does your child like to play in a sunny area with lots of dry sand, seashells and driftwood, creating roadways and burying toy trucks? What about using beach logs as pirate ships? Or making crab cities among the rocks for scuttling citizens? If the answers are positive, and your child is happy with a bit of a tromp up and down a bank, then by all means, choose this secluded spot. If, however, your child is bent on sandy swims and sandy architectural projects, Davey Janes should go near the bottom of your list.

Suitability for groups If you are looking for a lovely picnic site with the impression of forested isolation, half a dozen office buddies would congratulate you on your choice of beach. For large numbers, though, and beachgoers with conventional expectations, go to adjacent Kitty Coleman Park where you will find lots of facilities and space.

View Since the shore is parallel to the axis of the Strait of Georgia, you will find yourself looking more or less directly across the strait at one of its widest points. On a clear day you will be able to pick out basically three layers of view: a chain of islands, the low hills of the mainland and the Coast Mountains.

Winds, sun and shade Both common winds run largely parallel to the shore, though both have a habit of stirring up a lot of active air. Expect to be refreshed on a hot day and chilled on a cool day. On the other hand, don't expect too much in the way of shade except in the afternoon and on the uppermost beach.

Beachcombing Turn south if you want the most interestingly varied shore with tidal pools and spits. Turn north if you want the most isolation, though you will have to be prepared to cross Coleman Creek. In either case, brace your ankles against some twists and turns.

Seclusion To some extent, the profound sense of seclusion you will feel here is an illusion. But, if you have a romantic temperament or simply need to forget the rest of humanity, it is a glorious illusion.

22 COLEMAN ROAD
A well-hidden spot with shorefront parking and access onto a mixed shore with 100 m of gravel, tidal pools, and patches of sand

Location, signs and parking Although your destination is a good distance from the highway, the directions for reaching this spot could hardly be easier. Simply turn onto Coleman Road at the well-signposted intersection where you see a Wolf aluminum boats business. Once you've found your road, drive to the end of the road, some 5 km distant. You will find a large gravel turnaround area where, if you've planned ahead and come with a stuffed hamper and a full Thermos, you can position your car for a great car picnic. You'll find room for several cars here, but no signs alerting you to dangers and prohibitions. To one side you will find a park bench, though most visitors will make a beeline for the shore.

Path The turnaround borders on a short, steep bank of jagged rocks put into place to prevent erosion. Getting down this short drop is a breeze, though, since a few concrete steps are there to aid you.

Beach Although the upper beach has no sand, it does have a strong beachy feel because plenty of convenient and picturesque beach logs have collected in a nearly level area of loose pebbles and fine gravel. In fact, typically the logs are pushed into useful configurations by beachgoers who come to this spot. The rest of the beach has a bit of everything. Extending to about 75 m at low tide, it comprises small patches of sand, gravel, boulders and a few large tidal pools.

Suitability for children If you have a checklist of what your child enjoys doing at a beach, you can skip right past the activities involving sand. If your checklist has on it molesting shore life on a beach rich with starfish, sculpins, sea snails, hermit crabs, limpets and the like, or if it has on it using beach logs as jungle gyms or hunting for magically coloured pebbles, then you might consider this spot. In any case, since any decent checklist has picnic yummies on it, the suitability of the upper shore for picnicking is a key feature.

Suitability for groups While you might be amused bringing several like-minded friends to this little-known spot, the locals will be less amused. The houses on either side are set far enough away that a small, discreet group could picnic without feeling intrusive—but only a small and discreet group.

View This access spot is located on one side of a gently curving bay. As a result, your direction of view is basically along the high wooded banks behind a shore dotted with houses. Turn your head a whit, though, and you have a full view of the strait lined with mountains and islands, Texada and Lasqueti islands prominent among them.

Winds, sun and shade Because of the angle of the shore, you will be reasonably well protected by the northwest winds endemic to good-weather mornings along this coast. The barricades of logs can give you even more protection if you are in sunbathing mode. Even the logs can't give you much protection from a southeast wind, though. Here's where the possibility of a car picnic might come into play if the day is cool. On the other hand, if you're marginally warm, you don't need to worry about being plunged into shade to cool you further. There isn't any.

Beachcombing Set your sails for a southern venture if you're interested in the most varied shore. Large tidal pools and peculiar sand and gravel bars await you. Make sure your ankles are braced for some unevenly rocky surfaces, though, and be prepared to get wet feet if you walk along the low-tide area.

Seclusion You won't find throngs of people or phalanxes of beachfront houses either at this access spot or farther along the beach. You will, however, almost certainly see a few folk dotting the beach or, at least, sitting behind their front-room windows.

23 CORAL ROAD
Shorefront parking on an exposed beach with lots of sand on the upper shore and, after a band of gravel, the extreme lower shore

Location, signs and parking From the highway turn onto Coleman Road, using the Wolf aluminum boats business as a handy landmark, and carry on more or less straight for just under 5 km. Turn right onto Bates Road for 300 m and left onto Avonlee Road for 200 m. A sharp left onto Coral Road will bring you to Jasper's Seaside Resort and immediately north of it, a gravel road leading almost to the water's edge. This is technically Pebble Road, but as yet is unsignposted. After reflecting that this would make a perfect spot for unloading a kayak, an overstuffed cooler or three bumptious children, take note that, whatever else you might bring here, shellfish-collecting tools should not be among them. The clams are contaminated. A second piece of good news, on the other hand, is that this makes just about as perfect a car picnicking spot as you'll find anywhere.

Path There is no path. You are already on the shore, or as close as you can imagine getting.

Beach This is one of those "sandwich" beaches where the bread is sand and rocky gravel is the filling. Fine-tune your timing so that you arrive at high tide if you plan to spend an hour soaking up sun or munching grapes among the dry sand and logs before a delicious swim. Alternately, arrive at an extremely low tide for more than a 100 m of beach, the last 50 m of it sandy tidal flats, great for wading or splashing.

Suitability for children As with adults, so with children: an extremely low tide or high tide is more likely to please than a mid tide. While the activities will vary, involving, we all know, more energy from children than from well-baked adults, the attractions of the dry upper beach sand or of the low-tide shallows are likely to be paramount. In your packing, consider kites and Frisbees if you have managed to arrange a perfect low tide for your young 'uns.

Suitability for groups Since parking is not likely to be a problem and you will find lots of space on the broad beach, you could lead a small cavalcade of two or three cars here for an hour or two of picnicking before getting wet and sandy. Remember that you will find no facilities, however, and that you are right beside a large resort.

View Binocular enthusiasts can spend a lot of time picking out many geographical features across the strait. Among those easiest to spot with or without binoculars, though, are the sandy cliffs of low-slung Savary Island, more or less straight across from you, and right behind this island, the breaks in the mountain line that indicate the approaches to Desolation Sound and East Redonda Island. The curious fact around this island is that it features the highest mountain in North American not on the mainland—and excluding Vancouver Island (1,591 m).

Winds, sun and shade Exposure, exposure and more exposure is what you will find here. With no protection from wind or sun, you will have to bring your own—though, to be absolutely accurate, it is true that most winds blow from either side rather than directly onto the shore.

Beachcombing You can set out for a gentle stroll of about 100 m or a trek of several kilometres if you are prepared to brace your ankles on some uneven surfaces and get wet feet on low-tide routes. Beachcombers are likely to be most interested in heading south, since there they will find not only some weird and wonderful sandbars at Perrey's Beach, but also considerable natural isolation at the foot of some high wooded banks.

Seclusion While you are hardly likely to see many people here, don't forget that you are in the middle of a subdivision and right beside a resort. If you do yearn for a little private time, you can find considerable isolation within a few hundred metres south, where the wooded banks start rising higher and higher.

While you're here, if you drive to the north end of Coral Road you will find a small trail through high grass and trees leading to an interestingly varied shore with attractive areas of low-tide sand.

24
PERREY'S BEACH
A secluded but popular beach on an amazingly convoluted shoreline with bars of low-tide sand

Location, signs and parking Your route starts with a turn onto Coleman Road from the highway, where you will see a well-marked intersection with a separate left-turn lane. Wolf aluminum boat builders is a handy landmark. Drive for almost 5 km and turn right onto Bates Road when you see a triangular intersection. Follow Bates for about 1.5 km. Anson Road, the only left turn for many kilometres of treed road, leads to a T-junction with Seacliff Road, your destination. Turn left and follow it to its end, preparing yourself for the fact that the last part of the road is a narrow, roughly paved descent down a high bank. You will find a paved turnaround and an unofficial-looking sign welcoming you to Perrey's Beach and asking you to help keep it clean. That's it! Every other guiding principle is left to your good sense.

Path The wide dirt path slopes for two or three dozen metres down a small bank. Only those with extreme walking difficulties will have a rough time getting onto the beach.

Beach This is one spot where you will miss most of the pleasures of the beach unless you come at low tide. Why? At low tide you will find exposed not only a beautiful area of sand interspersed with a few huge boulders but also a 100 m long gravel bar angling away from the shore and creating a fascinating area of shallows for wading. Beyond the shore, too, the shallows are dotted with more huge boulders and, if your timing is right, dozens of canny great blue herons wading gingerly among their hors d'oeuvres. The middle part of the beach, in contrast, is made up of a swath of rounded rocks. As for the supratidal area among the dozens of beach logs, this part of the beach, unusually, is mostly fist-sized rocks with only small areas of pebbles and coarse sand for lounging and picnicking.

Suitability for children Comb through your tide tables until you find a day with low tides. You won't regret it—nor will your children. While the beach might not be perfect for the smallest children, for the fleet of foot and curious of mind this is an unusual opportunity to wade through huge areas of shallows and dash around swaths of firm sand. As for the absence of comfortable picnic areas in soft sand, given the plethora of logs and, no doubt, the perfection of your peanut butter sandwich recipe, nothing should stop you from putting together a great afternoon at an unusual beach.

Suitability for groups Many small groups with a range of interests and expectations could easily be accommodated here, in large part because the beach is big and secluded. Keep your group to just a few cars, however, and warn them that they will find no typical park facilities.

View Because you are on the northern tip of Seal Bay, your eyes will naturally be drawn to the curving shoreline of the rest of the bay and the high wooded banks, most of them completely natural. Lovers of wide-open views will want to walk a few dozen metres to the north and round the corner of the little headland. Suddenly opening before you will be not just the whole sweep of the northern strait, but also the curving shoreline leading to Kitty Coleman Park.

Winds, sun and shade Since you are just a dozen or so metres south of a headland, you can more or less adjust your exposure to wind, depending on whether you want it turned up or down on your wind-o-stat. A northwest wind will feel stronger if you move north, while a southeast wind will feel as strong as it's going to feel if you stay put. Up to a point you can adjust your shade level as well. While you will find that patches of shade start to creep onto the shore in mid afternoon, if you wish to remain in full sun you should stay immediately below the largely treeless access path.

Beachcombing Probably the most interesting beachcombing is to be done right in front of the access point, especially if you have brought shoes suitable for wading. If you really want to work off those Nanaimo bars, though, you can do so by heading in either direction, since the shore is walkable for many kilometres. Most will want to direct their steps south, where they can walk below the wooded banks of Seal Bay Park and, at low tide, doff their shoes for at least part of their trip.

Seclusion Even though you are next door to a seaside resort, a buffer of woods and the curve of the shore give this spot a considerable sense of seclusion. In the other direction, too, a buffer of woods running along the slope of the 25 m high bank will amplify the sense of seclusion. You are unlikely to be alone on the beach, though, so don't abandon all codes of civilized dress or behaviour!

25 SEAL BAY

A large wilderness park with a network of trails and access down a forested ravine to a secluded beach with low-tide sandbars

Location, signs and parking You can start walking (or jogging—or horse riding!) along the many kilometres of trails in Seal Bay Nature Park from more than a dozen points located on several different roads. To gain the quickest access to the beach, however, drive directly to the park entrance at the end of Seacliff Road. Your route starts with a turn onto Coleman Road from the highway, where you will see a well-marked intersection with a separate left-turn lane. Wolf aluminum boat builders is a handy landmark. Drive for almost 5 km and turn right onto Bates Road when you see a triangular intersection. Follow Bates for about 1.5 km. Anson Road, the only left turn for many kilometres of treed road, leads to a T-junction with Seacliff Road, your destination. Turn right onto Seacliff Road and follow it to its end, about 100 m later. Here you will find parking for a few cars in the circular turnaround and, at the entrance to the trail system, several signs, some hand-carved into venerable wooden slabs. The first sign is a map of the park. You may want to study it a little. None of the other signs is likely to affect your planning unless you have arrived with a bicycle or horse—although both are permitted on other trails. Your beach hound is permitted, but only if leashed.

Path You may wish to begin your exploration of this forest by taking the Coupland Loop Trail, signposted here, but, if getting to the shore is your priority, then head straight for the trail with the simple wooden sign To Beach pointing down a handrailed track. Be prepared for a nearly 40 m descent—and, even more, a 40 m ascent. The path, down the side of a small ravine, passes mostly fairly large but second-growth fir, hemlock and maple with an undergrowth of swordferns, salmonberries and salal.

Beach The beach has a bit of everything. The upper shore, some of it overhung with alders, is a soft bed of pebbles and coarse sand among several beach logs. A mid-beach section of rounded boulders is followed by several metres of sand dotted with tidal pools and patches of rock. In front of this access spot, the tide exposes only a little over 50 m of intertidal zone, but the beach is considerably wider both to the north and to the south.

Suitability for children The obvious—and considerable—feature to be factored into your planning is the compatibility between your child and trails down high banks. As for the compatibility between your child and the offerings of this beach, you should have no concerns.

Come at low tide, though, if your child is to find on offer the full buffet of beachy pleasures. Most, of course, will make a beeline for the low-tide section of sand. Here they will find a great place for dashing around in barefoot abandon between fits of excavation and construction of sand edifices. Don't forget the water shoes or crocs, though, since the rocky section of the mid-shore can be a real barrier.

Suitability for groups The spot is not suited to a group whose chief interests are indolence and gastronomy. A group interested in walking, nature observation or photography, however, could be easily accommodated in this huge park. Parking for more than a few cars is limited on Seacliff Road, but even then is manageable. Some groups might be interested in starting their walk from one of the many distant entrances to the park.

Even the main entrance on Bates Road provides more walking, more parking and, partway to the beach, a washroom. You can find a downloadable trail map on the Comox Valley Regional District website: http://www.comoxvalleyrd.ca/.

View Seal Bay Park, unsurprisingly, borders on a bay. Although the bay is only slightly concave, the high wooded banks and curving shoreline mean that you will not have the same wide-open sense of space as at some other access spots. Merely look across the extensive reaches of this northern section of the Strait of Georgia, however, and you will immediately sense the scale of the geography. A chain of islands runs down the coast of the mainland in front of Malaspina Peninsula and, behind it, the skyline of the Coast Mountains.

Winds, sun and shade You won't find much protection from either of the prevailing winds along this northeast-facing shore. Since the winds run largely parallel to the coastline, however, and since the high wooded bank acts as a bit of a buffer, both refreshing breezes and icy blasts aren't as strong here as they are even a short distance offshore. Shade can be a significant factor in your planning if you are expecting to picnic or sunbathe. During the first half of the day the beach is in full sun, but during the afternoon the shade on the upper beach becomes increasingly dense. Even during the first part of the day you can escape burning rays by finding a protected spot under one of the overhanging alders.

Beachcombing If walking is your desire but forest walking is not, then you can march straight toward the beach and begin a great bit of beachcombing in either direction. You should come at low tide, though, since the low-water strip of sand can make for the most pleasurable striding. You do have a bit of a dilemma, even then. If you put your priority on easy walking and would like to explore a fascinating sandbar extending into the strait, head north. If you want silence and solitude, head south.

Seclusion Because the park is huge and the forested banks are high, you will find many different places to find solitude. The park never seems to be crowded. Even when the numbers are highest, many choose to walk the forested trails at the top of the bank rather than undertake the beach trail down, down, down.

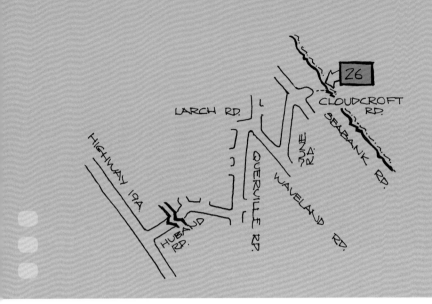

26 CLOUDCROFT ROAD

A thoroughly "secret" beach, sandy near the upper shore and rocky on the lower shore, reached via a narrow trail down a steep, wooded bank

Location, signs and parking You can approach this truly hidden spot from three directions off the highway. Probably the simplest, if not the shortest, starts with a turn off the highway at Huband Road, about 1 km north of Courtenay. Follow it for just under 4 km. Turn left onto Querville Road and, after about 1.5 km, turn right onto Larch Road until, after a very short distance, you come to a T-junction with Waveland Road. Turn right onto Waveland for less than 1 km and left again onto June Road for just under 1 km. Cross Seabank Road and, almost straight ahead, onto Cloudcroft Road. One hundred metres will bring you to the end of the road at the top of a densely wooded bank. You will find easy parking on the grass shoulder. At first you will see no signs, but en route to the beach you will discover it is closed to gathering chowder ingredients. You may be happy you don't have to lug a heavy bucket up the steep bank.

Path Leave your flip-flops at home. While you're at it, leave your beach umbrellas and coolers at home. This is not a path for the ill prepared. The uneven dirt track drops steeply 20 m down a beautifully treed bank. The fact that a kindly (or desperate?) local has tied a hand-height rope between trees for the last part of the path tells you something about what you will be facing.

Beach It is, of course, the truly lovely parts of the beach that make the treasure-hunt approach worthwhile. Most appealing is the large area of soft, silvery sand above the high-tide line. Dotted with a few logs suitable for lounging against or sitting on, the broad swath of sandy beach extends well beyond the access point in both directions. This is the kind of shore you have been looking for if your desire is to spend a delicious few hours of utter seclusion in a bed of pristine sand, pebbles and seashells. The beach will strike you as most attractive at high tide, be warned, since the intertidal zone—all 150 m of it—is almost entirely rounded rocks and boulders. One interesting feature you would miss coming at high tide, though, is a huge tidal pool, almost 100 m long, a short distance to the south.

Suitability for children This is not a beach for little children unless you feel comfortable toting them. Even then, you will want to quadruple-check that you have everything you need from your car. Older children, especially those with lots of energy and a sense of adventure, might well love the challenging trail to the beach. Once there, they might equally enjoy exploring the huge tidal pool and the furtive life under the rocks. Even so, bring children to this beach only if your main purpose is to find a "secret" spot for yourself rather than a perfect beach for your child.

Suitability for groups Theoretically, several cars could park on the shoulder and lots of beach folk could arrive at this beach with no fear of overwhelming either the beach or the locals. It is hard to imagine, however, the kind of group that would want to come to a beach whose chief merit is its scarcity—or absence—of people!

View The shore is virtually straight here and runs parallel to the main axis of Vancouver Island. As a result, though you can see up and down the wooded shore for some distance, your tendency will be to direct your eyes across the wide expanse of the Strait of Georgia. If the day is clear, you will be able to make out the distant humps of Lasqueti Island to the south and, to the north, Cortes Island. For the most part, though, your view will be of four islands across the strait: Hernando, Savary, Harwood and northern Texada, and the mainland mountains behind them.

Winds, sun and shade The prevailing winds from both directions, which should run essentially parallel to the shore, can in fact riffle the pages of a magazine or bring relief on a hot day. This is one of the few beaches along this stretch of coast where you should choose your time of day in accord with your desire for shade or sun. The morning is sunny; the afternoon— at least on the upper beach—is shady.

Beachcombing Keep to the upper beach if you plan to walk any distance along the shore. Even then, be prepared to slide around a little among loose sand and pebbles. In either direction, you will be walking below high wooded banks and, at low tide, by a broad expanse of rocky shore. To your north, though, the banks are lower, though the convolutions and pools in the shore are more pronounced.

Seclusion You have the 20 vertical metres of thick trees to thank for the seclusion you are almost certain to find here. This is the perfect spot to scheme how to achieve world peace or how to get revenge on your neighbour. The chances are high that you will have the whole shore to yourself, not just below the access spot, but for a considerable distance in either direction, and especially south.

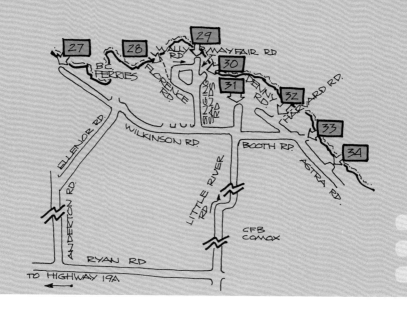

27 WILKINSON ROAD

An isolated route to a secluded beach of sand and gravel along the northern shore of the Little River estuary

Location, signs and parking You can choose many different trajectories through intersecting roads that take you far from the highway to this remote bit of shore. You probably will find most convenient, however, the route that starts at the Ryan Road intersection at the north end of Courtenay's commercial area, as the highway enters town. Turn up the broad road past Canadian Tire and carry on for about 4 km to Anderton Road. Turn left onto Anderton and, after about 1.5 km, when Anderton turns left, keep right on Ellenor Road for an additional 1.5 km. Turn left onto Wilkinson Road and so to your destination at the end of the road. Immediately outside a gateway of vertical logs, you will see parking for several cars in a gravel area overlooking the shore. Four prominent signs assert that there are four forbidden activities, two of them that might cramp your style, two of them unlikely to do so. You may be saddened that you may not collect shellfish or light fires but are unlikely to suffer much grief from not being allowed to park overnight or dump "refuse."

Path Much to the satisfaction of avid car picnickers, you could hardly find a spot with a shorter path than at this bank-edge parking spot. Indeed, that you are slightly above the beach makes this an even better car-picnicking spot than some other great spots along this coast. A slightly awkward but, for most, perfectly passable track leads through big chunks of bank-reinforcing rock onto the shore just below.

Beach Your impressions of the beach will depend much on the level of the tide when you arrive. Come at high tide, and you will be pleased that immediately in front of you is a broad expanse of soft, silvery sand stretching many forest-fronted metres to your left. You won't find a huge number of all-purpose beach logs here, but, depending on what antics the winter storms have been up to, you are likely to find at least a few to use as backrests, wind shelters or park benches. If you arrive at low tide, you might be a little daunted by the expanse of rounded boulders between you and the waterline, almost 100 m away. In fact, the intertidal zone is narrower here than farther south; the closer you get to the mouth of the Little River to the south, the broader the low-tide shore.

Suitability for children Given the vast preference most children have for sand over boulders—and for water over boulders—you will probably see most smiles if you bring your little ones at or near high tide. It is true that the many pleasures of sifting and mounding sand into roadways and caverns are available no matter when you arrive. Still, few are the children who aren't bent on getting as wet as possible as quickly as possible. That they can do so at high tide without slithering over boulders is bound to win approval. If you do arrive at low tide, though, don't overlook the interest children can have in exploring the nether world of intertidal shore life, much richer among rocks than on sand.

Suitability for groups Three features of this section of shore make it well suited to two or three cars crammed with like-minded friends or unlike-minded relatives: the easy parking, the comparative solitude and the sandy picnic and sprawling area. Even so, if your group wants park facilities, a softball game or the like, you are better off taking them to one of the large parks in the area.

View The most prominent and eye-arresting element of your view is the ferry terminal along the shore to your right. A fortuitous flurry of geographical activity has created this largely natural spit extending into water deep enough for a ferry as large as the one that plies the waters to Powell River. At this broad part of the Strait of Georgia, you will have an extensive view of distant landforms, especially if your gaze swings north, where the geographical features seem to recede into the distance. Of the various islands that line up along the opposite shore of the strait, Harwood Island is the closest. Behind it and against the skyline, you may be able to single out Mount Porteous. North of Harwood Island, across Shearwater Passage, lie first Savary Island and then Hernando Island, both equally low, and behind and above them, Malaspina Peninsula.

Winds, sun and shade Whether you welcome a refreshing breeze or shiver under the effects of a chilling wind, you will feel lots of air along this shore. At the same time, most winds do not hit the shore directly but run roughly parallel to it. On a steaming day, at least in the afternoon, you can find refuge from the heat in the shade of trees along the upper shore to the left of this access strip.

Beachcombing Boulder walking can require strong ankles and some patience. If, therefore, you want to walk any distance, you are probably best off keeping to the uppermost beach, where you can usually find sand or pebbles (though not immediately to the right of this access spot). Obviously, if you want to cover any distance you won't want to walk south, since the ferry terminal and Little River constitute considerable obstacles.

Seclusion Surprisingly, perhaps, it is only the proximity of the beach to the roadside parking area that prevents this spot from being wonderfully secluded. While houses dot the shore in both directions, screens of trees and the distant placement of the houses bless this beach with a strong feeling of seclusion. If your hair has been far too up for far too long, you can, with great confidence, let it down here.

28 FLORENCE ROAD

A groomed, crushed-gravel path through gardens to a quiet shore of fine gravel with patches of sand, looking north toward the Powell River ferry

Location, signs and parking The distance from the highway is considerable, but the number of access beaches near each other is more than enough to make your foray rewarding. From the major intersection at the north end of Courtenay's commercial district, turn onto Ryan Road. Plow ahead for 6 km until a junction with Little River Road at the edge of Canadian Forces Base (CFB) Comox. Turn left and stick with Little River Road, trying not to be thrown off by a profoundly wild zigzag midway. After about 2.5 km, take a left turn onto Wilkinson Road for about 200 m, then right onto Singing Sands Road for about 300 m until, just over a small bridge, you see Florence Road on your left. About 100 m down Florence, just as it starts to curve toward the shore, you will see a prominent sign on the left reading Public Walkway. While you won't find a special parking area, the shoulder of the road is unusually wide here.

Path A well-groomed walkway of crushed gravel makes a gentle S-curve as it leads about 100 nearly level metres toward the shore. En route you will find yourself passing gardens. As you approach a three-storey, multi-family building, your path curves around the shaded side of the building. The last few metres onto the shore can be a little overgrown with tall grass and beach vegetation.

Beach Unlike most beaches along this section of coast, this one begins not with coarse sand but with fist-sized, well-rounded rocks. Only a few beach logs line this stretch of shore, in part, it seems, because the shore slopes quite steeply. For many metres in either direction, the shore is almost a smooth slope of fine gravel, pebbles and coarse sand, never more than 30 m wide. While you can find a pleasant place to sit on one of the few beach logs, you will notice that the beach is particularly attractive at high tide, when it is nearly perfect for swimming. While water shoes might be helpful if your feet are particularly tender, you don't really need them since, within a few steps, you can be in water deep enough to get ducked.

Suitability for children This is not a great beach for toddlers to do much more than make a quick visit. For older children, though, and especially those who can swim well, the beach has some real attractions. Since the shore is comparatively steep, children, like adults, can swim within a short distance of shore. Even when swimming is not on the agenda, older children could well enjoy skipping rocks, looking for the most magically coloured pebbles, and, of course, getting far wetter than their parents consider desirable.

Suitability for groups This is far from a good choice for a group of more than five or six. The limited parking and the proximity to the densely built area to the right are clear drawbacks. Still, don't rule out the spot altogether for a few friends. Since the land to the left of the access is undeveloped for more than 200 m, your small group can easily explore a virtually empty piece of shore.

View This is one of the few pieces of shore on the coast that faces northwest. One result is that this is a good viewing spot for sunsets. Another, unique to this spot, is that you will be looking more or less away from the northern strait, and primarily toward the BC Ferries terminal and, behind it, the sweep of high wooded shore below Waveland Road.

Winds, sun and shade You would be hard pressed to find a beach for many miles that feels so thoroughly the full brunt of a northwest wind and accompanying waves. Remember the well-rounded rocks and well-polished pebbles? From a southeast wind, however, the beach is largely protected. While you will find a few small firs backing the shore to your left, they don't cast shade because they are separated from the beach by a band of vigourous beach grass.

Beachcombing You will probably feel tempted to wander along the empty bit of shore to your left, but, of course, cannot go very far without bumping smack dab into the ferry terminal. The angle of the shore can give an odd twist to your gait. One of the advantages of heading in the opposite direction is that within a few minutes you will be rounding a headland and thus gaining a whole new section of view down the southern strait.

Seclusion In some ways, the spot could hardly be less secluded, especially since the path to the shore is squeezed up against a large multi-family building. Still, as the somewhat overgrown nature of the path suggests, few people use this access. In addition, a short wander to the left will take you away from the binocular-wielding dwellers of the three-storey building.

29
SINGING SANDS ROAD
A road-end strip of pebbles to a fine gravel beach on a small headland with views of the Powell River ferry terminal

Location, signs and parking Like most spots on the coast immediately north of Comox, this one involves many kilometres of back roads. From the major intersection at the north end of Courtenay's commercial district, turn onto Ryan Road. Drive for 6 km until a junction with Little River Road at the edge of CFB Comox. Turn left and stick with Little River Road for 2 km, trying not to be thrown off by two sharp turns midway. After about 2.5 km take a left turn onto Wilkinson Road for about 200 m, then right onto Singing Sands Road for about 300 m, until it passes Wally Road on your left (Google Maps calls it Florence Road). At this point you will see that you can drive straight ahead to an open, road-width parking area in sight of the shore. Two signs affect your parking strategy, one reading Angle Parking, the other telling you to abscond overnight. Another two signs tell you that fires are not permitted. As for consuming alcohol in a public place, you probably already know the law. You will find room for plenty of cars but are unlikely to see any others.

Path Although the end of the road is close to the shore, it is not as close as some other spots in the area. Fences on either side further limit your vision. You are better off at nearby Florence Road if you want to picnic in your car. In any case, winter storms have created something akin to a dune of gravel and logs immediately in front of the road's end. Still, the shore is only two dozen steps away through a gradually sloping area of loose gravel and a gap in some jagged boulders.

Beach The slightly undulating upper beach is a broad area of fine gravel with a few logs suitable for perching. For sunbathing or lounging, though, you would probably want a plush towel for padding. While the beach is composed almost entirely of pebbles and egg- and fist-sized smooth rocks, to your right you can find a small area of firm sand at low tide. The shore slopes fairly quickly to the low-tide line immediately in front of the access spot, but, to the right, at the tip of the headland, it extends about 100 m to the low-tide line.

Suitability for children This is not the kind of beach you would go far out of your way to find if giving your children beach fun is your main goal. At the same time, the beach is safe and easy enough for children to negotiate that at virtually any level of tide they can create watery havoc. At low tide, too, they will be drawn like little magnets to the patch of firm sand a short distance to the right of the access point.

Suitability for groups A minor cavalcade could find easy and ample parking but little else to draw them to this spot, unless it be part of an itinerary of visits to several beach spots in the area. In that case, the broad sweep of the view from this small headland and the proximity of the waterline—and bobbing shorebirds—could be prized features.

View You won't find many spots in the area—Cape Lazo is the closest— where you can get as many compass degrees of sea view as here. While most of the features are distant, if you come equipped with skookum binoculars, you will be able to pick out all the geographical bits and pieces that strew the view from Cape Mudge in the north to Texada's receding southwest shore in the south. In the foreground, though, if your timing is right, you will have an interesting perspective on the plying to and fro of the Powell River ferry.

Winds, sun and shade Because of the convex nature of the low shoreline, it is exposed to both southeast and northwest winds. You can walk along the curving shore in either direction to increase or decrease your exposure to the wind. If the weather is such that you have a significant proportion of your skin exposed, come prepared. You won't find a shade tree anywhere near the shore.

Beachcombing Strolling is comparatively easy in either direction, but obviously you can't go very far in the direction of the ferry terminal without life becoming a little awkward. Remember, too, that gravel and small rocks, particularly when sloped, can require a special technique of strolling.

Seclusion You won't get very far from the sightlines of the houses that pepper the low, treeless shore. At the same time, the fences of the adjoining houses and the boulder retaining walls along the bank help you feel you are finding your way through a secret channel rather than stomping through locals' front yards.

30 MAYFAIR ROAD

Shorefront picnic tables and park benches improvised by locals, next to a beach with a large area of coarse sand on the upper beach and gravel on the lower beach

Location, signs and parking You need to be braced for more than a short nip off the highway, but your route is reasonably straightforward —at least until the end. From the major intersection at the north end of Courtenay's commercial district, turn onto Ryan Road. Plow ahead for 6 km until a junction with Little River Road at the edge of CFB Comox. Turn left, then stick with Little River Road, trying not to be thrown off by a profoundly wild zigzag midway. After about 2.5 km take a left turn onto Wilkinson Road for about 200 m, then right onto Singing Sands Road for about 250 m. As soon as you cross a little bridge (over Little River), take the first right onto unsignposted Mayfair Road, which ends on the shore. The only sign you will see is one telling you to park at an angle. You will find parking for several cars, some of it with a good view over the beachfront logs to the open ocean. The most remarkable features of this road end are the picnic tables and park benches put into place by locals who obviously cherish this access spot.

Path For those with difficulty walking, this spot is gem. A few metres down a slight incline will bring you onto the shore, though some with real difficulties might want to stop at one of the two commemorative benches.

Beach Many will want to go no farther than the upper beach if their primary reason for visiting is to catch some rays or finish off a particularly salacious novel. This broad expanse of coarse sand has surprisingly few logs but enough for those who like these convenient backrests. The lowest tides expose no more than about 50 m of shore, though the lower beach is largely gravel and small rocks. Swimming is obviously best at high tide, though even then, water shoes make life a lot easier.

Suitability for children The child who loves the pleasures of the sandbox or burying her little brother up to his obliging neck in soft, warm sand will be cheerfully occupied for as long as it takes the tide to rise over the hot rocks and water play to begin. If your child really yearns for some hard-packed damp sand for castle construction, you can walk along the beach to your left at low tide, where you will find a small sandbar.

Suitability for groups This is very much an access spot for the neighbourhood. While a few visitors will no doubt be welcome, many more than that will be intrusive.

View Because the shore is slightly concave here and angled toward the southeast, your view is primarily of the wide open strait, with most of the features appearing like distant undulations. One of the interesting close-range sights, though, is the ferry to Powell River, its terminal tucked out of your line of vision a little more than a kilometre to the north.

Winds, sun and shade This whole stretch of coast is exposed and open, in part because of the low shoreline, in part because of the lack of trees. Thus, while the winds don't blow directly onto the shore, you will feel lots of wind if there is lots of wind to be felt. Bring protection against the sun on a clear day, since the only shade is that created by beach umbrellas.

Beachcombing The beach invites strolling in either direction. Choose north if you want a short walk around a small, low promontory and a new view opening up toward the north and the ferry terminal. Choose south if you want to walk a long distance. Make sure you bring sturdy shoes with good ankle support, though, since the gravelly parts of the shore can be a little uneven and soft underfoot.

Seclusion You won't feel even remotely secluded at this spot, because the treeless shore is so level and also because houses are built along the shorefront on both sides of the access road.

31
LITTLE RIVER ROAD
Secluded shorefront parking with a good view and lots of soft sand on the upper beach

Location, signs and parking Though the distance from the highway is significant, the route is simple. First find the Ryan Road intersection at the north end of Courtenay's commercial area as the highway enters town. Turn up this broad road past Canadian Tire and carry on for about 6 km until a junction with Little River Road in front of the Air Force Museum. Turn left onto Little River Road and follow it until its end—being careful not be thrown off by its two right-angled corners en route to the shore. Oddly, a fence now slices across the paved end of the road. Still, you can drive to the end of the road and get an excellent panoramic view of the sea and its splendours without budging from your car seat. Keep this location in mind for those winter days when your soul needs some energizing but your body really doesn't want to get wet and cold. If you've arrived with a trunk full of marshmallows and hot dogs, betake yourself elsewhere—beach fires are not permitted here.

Path Considering the fact that you are—literally—within spitting distance of the shore, you can obviously arrive here with all of the picnic hampers and artists' easels your heart desires and your trunk can accommodate. Watch your footing, however, since you will have to get over a dip between you and the beach.

Beach Those who love sprawling in oodles of soft white sand amid a scattering of beach logs will be toe-wigglingly delighted by the dune-like undulations of the uppermost beach. These are the folk who might well plan to come at high tide, when they can gain quick access to the turquoise waters without having to cope with more than a few minor patches of gravel. Low tide reveals about 100 m of shore with sand and a few tidal pools begging to be explored.

Suitability for children Because you can park so close to the shore and because you will find so much soft sand in the high-tide area, choose this beach if it will suit your child's particular play requirements. If those requirements include lots of sand to push into fortresses and roadways, seashells and pebbles to collect and logs to leap around, then consider yourself to have done the right thing by your child. You will probably want to come at high tide, though, if you also want to provide the easiest access to water play.

Suitability for groups You can find parking for several cars (though watch out for the driveway on the left) and lots of beachfront, particularly on your right, where you are buffered by about 100 m of shorefront between you and the next house. You won't find any facilities, of course, but if your Save the Albino Sloth Foundation members are dispirited and need a shorefront picnic to inspire them, you could do a lot worse than bring them to this pretty spot.

View Your eyes can sweep up and down the great distances and many islands of the widest part of the Strait of Georgia. If you look directly across the water, however, you will be looking through Algerine Passage between smallish Harwood Island to the north and the northern end of gigantic Texada Island to the south. On a clear day you will be able to make out Westview and bits of Powell River.

Winds, sun and shade Check your marine forecast if you want to avoid wind. If either a northwest or southeast wind is a-howling, you'll feel it here. Considering that both winds blow more across the shore than directly onto it and that you can hunker down behind some of the beach logs, don't be put off by a cool breeze.

Beachcombing Head north for the more interestingly varied shoreline, rounding headlines and changing views. You will have to watch your footing and be prepared either to get wet feet occasionally or keep to the sometimes awkward upper beach.

Seclusion While the apparent seclusion is a bit of an illusion, at least it's not a delusion. You will see a well-wooded shorefront and are unlikely to find more than the occasional curious basset towing his owner along the beach. Wander very far, however, and you will find plenty of houses in both directions, all eager to get their money's worth of shore-gazing out of their high property taxes.

32
HARVARD ROAD
A truly "secret" beach with lots of high-tide sand and driftwood, approached by a wooded trail on a dead-end road

Location, signs and parking Your route to this hidden bit of shore begins most conveniently at the major intersection at the north end of Courtenay's commercial district. Ryan Road, the wide, straight road leading uphill past Canadian Tire, is your route for the next 6 km or so. When you spot the Air Force Museum at the junction with Little River Road, turn left. Follow Little River Road almost to its end, trying not be thrown off by the right-angled zigzags partway along. After about 650 m, turn right onto Booth Road for about 300 m, then left onto Denny Road. Prepare yourself for a little surprise. Within 100 m, you will see a perfectly positioned road sign for Harvard Road—but no road! Still, this is the spot you are looking for. Pull over onto the shoulder, since you will see no other area to park, or, indeed, any other signs—until you reach the shore, where you will see two intriguing ones.

Path The path is part of the pleasure of this beautiful spot. About 30 m of this generally level, gently undulating trail takes you through an airy grove of firs toward a shorefront pine thicket of yarrow and beach vegetation. Immediately to the left of the path, nailed to a short barricade of creosoted pilings, you will see two signs, both clearly homemade. One venerable sign declares (defiantly?) this to be PUBLIC ACCESS. The other, new but hand-scrawled, goes further, insisting PARKLAND, CVRD 2010 PLAN. One can only guess at the local politics that lie behind these signs.

Beach Like many other spots in the immediate area, this one is most appealing at high tide, when the wide expanse of soft, silver sand dominates the shore. Convenient and attractive beach logs—one of them strikingly long—further embellish the beach. If you haven't caught up on the latest Booker Prize fiction, this is the perfect place to settle down for an afternoon of bliss, and you are not likely to be disturbed. At low tide the shore is more limited in appeal, since then you will see almost 100 m of barnacles and small rocks. Still, it has its own charms if you enjoy prodding and poking along the kind of shore that seethes with scuttling and oozing life.

Suitability for children Although you will have to manage toddlers on the short walk from the car, once on the sandy part of the shore, you can deposit even the littlest ones with few concerns that they will get bored or get up to anything worse than eating fistfuls of sand. Picnicking, decorating mounds of sand with shells and dried seaweed, and climbing around logs can amuse slightly older children. Since the sand can get hot and the barnacles can get up to their usual lacerating tricks, make sure you bring water shoes. Choose high tide if your children want to demonstrate their dog-paddling technique for you, since they will then be close to the towels and home base.

Suitability for groups The parking and length of public shorefront are both limited, so you wouldn't want to bring more than two or three cars' worth of eager shore-goers. Still, on the shore itself you have enough space and enough relative privacy that up to a dozen picnickers could devour Greek salad and falafel without intruding overmuch. Don't forget, however, that Kin Beach Provincial Park is only a few minutes' drive to the south.

View Like other spots along this stretch of coast, this one looks out across large distances over the northern part of the Strait of Georgia. Thus you can see a low set of islands, the slightly higher rise of Malaspina Peninsula, and, against the skyline, the Coast Mountains. To the north you will see a graceful curve of shore leading past Little River to the headland at the end of Singing Sands Road.

Winds, sun and shade Neither the northwest winds typical of settled weather nor the southeast winds most commonly associated with unsettled conditions blows directly onshore here. Even so, the shore is exposed enough that, unless you hunker down behind some logs, you might feel a little chilled on a breezy day. On the other hand, the trees are far enough back from the shore that you won't be further chilled by heavy shadows. Do, however, bring sun protection.

Beachcombing For some, the best beach walking area is directly in front of the access spot, where they can search out the shelled and unshelled creatures there. For those happy to ignore the slightly crunchy and lumpy surface of the rocky beach, the most enjoyable walk is to head out along the shore for many kilometres. If you are the latter type, you probably would be happiest heading south, where you can find not only a section of unpeopled shore, but, after an hour's walking, Kye Bay, with its huge sandy beach that fills the whole bay.

Seclusion Even though this is a thoroughly subdivided and settled section of coastline, this particular access spot allows you a surprising degree of seclusion. Not only are you completely screened from the neighbouring houses; they are also set so far back from the shoreline and so scattered among the evergreens that you will feel even more secluded than you actually are. Searching for a spot for the perfect picnic à deux, followed by a wedding proposal? You just might have found it.

33

BOOTH ROAD
Level, easy access to an upper
beach of loose sand and scattered logs and a lower beach
of rocks and tidal pools

Location, signs and parking Your route begins most conveniently at the major intersection at the north end of Courtenay's commercial district. Ryan Road, the wide, straight road leading uphill past Canadian Tire, is your route for the next 6 km or so. When you spot the Air Force Museum at the junction with Little River Road, turn left. Follow Little River Road almost to its end, trying not be thrown off by the right-angled zigzags partway along. Turn onto Booth Road for about 250 m. You will come across an odd roadside with arrows, one pointing to Booth Road on your left and another to Astra Road on your right, though Astra seems like a continuation of the main road and Booth Road seems to be a minor offshoot, turning as it does into a gravel track. Drive to the end of Booth Road and park virtually on the shore, trying not to be disconcerted by the feeling you may be more or less in the front yard of the house on your left. A Private Property sign has been nailed onto a tree at such an angle that you might at first think it applies to your little dirt track. It doesn't.

Path Though you are close to the cottages on both sides of this access spot, you could well find this to be a near perfect spot for car picnicking during a storm from the southeast. Needless to say, those with walking difficulty will have no difficulty whatsoever making their way the few paces necessary onto the shore.

Beach Your impressions of the beach will vary enormously depending on whether you arrive at high or low tide. Most, it has to be said, will prefer the beach at high tide. Saunter onto the shore then and, particularly during the first half of the day, you will find a gently sloping beach of sand and shell fragments with exactly the right number of beach logs. At low tide, about 100 m of rocky shore are exposed, though a small channel cuts into the rocks slightly to the left of the beach. It would be possible to launch a kayak here, but you would probably want to choose neap tides, when the tide remains at least partly in for several hours.

Suitability for children The lovely area of sand and logs is perfect for a toddler who is tired of the backyard sandbox and would love to push mounds of sand around. For other beaching activities, though, remember that the almighty barnacle is to be reckoned with, particularly at low tide. The proximity of the neighbouring houses might make you feel less than totally relaxed if your child is a candidate for Ritalin.

Suitability for groups Forget it. The spot is much, much too confined for more than a few people.

View The orientation of the shoreline is such that your gaze will most naturally fall on the north end of Texada Island and Surprise Mountain, near its southwestern shore. In fact, however, you can see not just Harwood Island to its north, almost obscuring Powell River, but also all the islands and peninsulas of the northern part of the Strait of Georgia.

Winds, sun and shade While the shore faces directly into neither of the two most common winds, it is exposed to both, and especially a south-east wind. Though more or less in full sun during the first half of the day, this spot is one of the few in this area that has some patches of afternoon shade. On a blistering day, this may be exactly what you want and need.

Beachcombing The beach is level though rough underfoot for a long distance in both directions. If you have strong ankles and determination, you can head south and, within two kilometres, come across Kin Beach. Another kilometre takes you to Kye Beach. For many, though, merely exploring the shoreline nearby and looking for seashells will be the most attractive sort of beachcombing.

Seclusion You won't find throngs of visitors coming to this spot. Indeed, you may well be the only visitor. On the other hand, you will find local houses. Lots of them.

34

ASTRA ROAD

A large upper beach of loose sand and logs leading to over 100 m of low-tide rocks and tidal pools

Location, signs and parking Your route to Astra Road and the other beaches in the area begins most conveniently at the major intersection at the north end of Courtenay's commercial district. Ryan Road, the wide, straight road leading uphill past Canadian Tire, is your route for the next 6 km or so. When you spot the Air Force Museum at the junction with Little River Road, turn left. Follow Little River Road almost to its end, trying not be thrown off by the right-angled zigzags partway along. Take Booth Road on your right almost to its end, and follow Astra Road for about 600 m until you see Seal Road on your right. Almost opposite Seal Road, you will see what looks like a gravel driveway toward the shore. Drive partway down and, if you like, park in the shade. The indication that this is a public access is the sign pointing out that you are not to park overnight or camp—though it is hard to imagine who would choose this close-packed residential area to do either.

Path If you are feeling nervy or desperate, you can probably drive nearly to the shore along a level grassy area at the end of the road proper. Wherever you park, you will find the route onto the beach to be level and clear, requiring only a short walk. En route, notice the strikingly gnarled and heavily pruned fir on your left. Kayakers could easily get their colourful craft onto the shore, but will want to come at high or neap tides if they want to avoid a long trudge over gravel and small rocks.

Beach The majority of visitors will find the beach most appealing at high tide, when turquoise wavelets lap at the edges of a broad area of loose sand and conveniently arranged beach logs, backed with a thicket of beach grass. This is the kind of beach that invites a little sun worship or novel reading. At low tide, with the water more than 100 m distant over an expanse of barnacle-covered rocks, the beach has some interest, but mostly for the investigators of the dark and wet world of life under the rocks.

Suitability for children Come at high tide if your child is bent on splashing, throwing rocks, setting driftwood afloat and the like. Searching for bright-coloured pebbles and plowing car tracks through the coarse sand are the kind of thing that will amuse a child on the upper beach. At low tide a child will be kept happy only if hunting for creatures and seashells among the rocks are considered fun.

Suitability for groups While there is no reason a small group couldn't be accommodated here, it would be a peculiar group that would choose to come to this spot when Kin Beach Provincial Park, with all of its space and facilities, is right next door.

View If you remember to bring your binoculars, your visit will be that much more interesting. One of the features you might want to focus your lens on is Westview, a town on the mainland visible between the north end of Texada Island and Harwood Island to its north. Farther north, past Shearwater Passage, you should be able to pick out Savary Island and, fading into the distance to its north, Hernando Island. If you want to focus on closer features, you will immediately notice the bizarre line of concrete blocks cutting across the beach 200 m south.

Winds, sun and shade While both prevailing winds run roughly parallel to the shore here, you are likely to feel both winds if they are blowing with any strength. While you can park your car in the shade (depending on the time of day), you can't find any shade on the beach. Trees line the shore, but are all well set back from the exposed grassy banks.

Beachcombing This is a good beach for strolling considerable distances, though you will have to choose between walking along the generally sandy but loose upper beach and the firmer, but more irregular, lower shore. In either case, be sure to bring sturdy shoes, and, ideally, ones that can get wet.

Seclusion Don't even think about coming to this spot if your goal is to get away from civilization and to immerse yourself in nature. You are in the middle of what amounts to a subdivision. Still, take heart. The houses on either side of the access spot are set well back from the shore and, on one side at least, with a high hedge that partly screens the access spot.

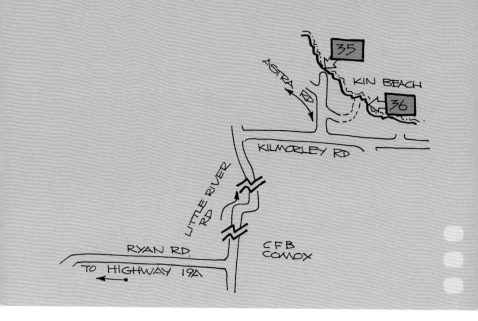

35 KIN BEACH PROVINCIAL PARK—NORTH

Campsites and a day-use area by a seaside meadow leading to a dune-like upper beach, scattered with beach logs, and a lower beach of rounded boulders

Location, signs and parking Your journey to the distant shores of this stretch of coast begins most conveniently at the major intersection at the north end of Courtenay's commercial district. Ryan Road, the wide, straight road leading uphill past Canadian Tire, is your route for the next 6 km or so. When you spot the Air Force Museum at the junction with Little River Road, turn left. After about 1.5 km on Little River, turn right onto Kilmorley Road for about 1 km until you see Astra Road on your left. Drive about 150 m down Astra Road until you pass the main entrance to Kin Beach Provincial Park, its name prominently carved into a log. This main entrance leads to a day-parking area and may be of interest chiefly to those wishing to camp at the park, or as a marker along the way to the next access point (Kin Beach Provincial Park—South). For the northern access, continue another 100 m farther along Astra. There you will see a roadside parking space by the edge of a huge grassy meadow in clear sight of the shore beyond. Along the parking area lining the meadow, you will see many, many signs pointing you to the different areas of the park and, among other things, stating the open hours. From April through September, the park is open from 7 a.m. to 11 p.m. The winter hours are 9 a.m. to 6 p.m. Some of the prohibitions are familiar to all beachgoers: your retriever can do no retrieving here unless you gallop after her on the other end of her leash. Likewise, abandon any plans to have a beach fire. You will find two prohibitions here that you are not likely to find on any other beach on the island. There is to be no golfing, and metal detectors can be used only on the beach. Who would have thought? The day-use parking lot at this end of the park has room for about two dozen cars.

Path Depending on your inclination and which side of the park you leave your car, you can approach the long strip of shoreline from several different ways. All approaches, though, require no more than a few dozen metres of level walking across a sun-bleached meadow and weathered shore firs. Among other facilities you will note are pit toilets, picnic tables, a slightly exhausted-looking playground and a massive, covered barbecue.

Beach Most visitors are likely to find that the uppermost part of the beach is by far its most attractive feature. Here they will find a broad, sun-baked area of coarse, loose sand scattered with hundreds of beach logs. This part of the beach is broad enough and the logs are scattered enough that you can easily find a section of beach among the logs to make your own. This area is great for picnicking or contemplating the strange life of gulls as you lean against logs or sit on them. The lower section of the beach is made up almost entirely of rounded rocks and small boulders. Since this part of the shore is fairly sloped, the water never retreats more than a few dozen metres. Primarily of interest here are a few large tidal pools, the critters that lurk under the rocks, and a line of huge concrete blocks marching toward the low-tide line. Most visitors will probably find the beach most attractive both for gazing and for swimming if they come at high tide.

Suitability for children The park facilities, the playground and the soft dry sand above the high-tide line are the most child-friendly elements of this park. Running along, over and around logs can be as much fun for some children as pushing the sand into piles or burying their fathers' legs. Children are most likely to enjoy trying to tame their inflatable dolphin or practise their duck diving at high tide. At low tide, though, they can equally enjoy collecting multicoloured shore crabs and hunting for seashells with which to decorate their sandcastles.

Suitability for groups This a great park for handling the entire Bobbins family reunion. Given the huge meadow for tossing Frisbees, the long shoreline and all the park facilities, almost any large group should be able to enjoy themselves without crowding other visitors. In fact, because Kin Park is so well hidden at the end of a labyrinth of roads, it seems to attract only a small number of day visitors.

View Bring your binoculars to enjoy the view at its best. Thus equipped, you will be able to pick out the northern tip of Texada Island and, slightly north, the low rounded shape of Harwood Island, behind which lurks the town of Powell River. Mount Porteous and Mount Mahony are two of the higher peaks on either side of and behind Powell River.

Winds, sun and shade The shore is more or less exposed to the prevailing breezes and gales making their way up and down the strait roughly parallel to shore. On a sunny day when the breeze is a little cooler than you find quite perfect, remember that once you are behind one of the barricading logs, and particularly if you are spread-eagled in the sand, your temperature will shoot up.

Beachcombing If you are feeling inspired and wish to walk many kilometres, you will probably most enjoy heading southeast. Within half a kilometre you will be walking along a quiet section of shore with little more than a campsite used by military families to break your solitude. In another half kilometre you will be rounding a curious little headland to find yourself at the bottom of the high bank at the sea side of the Comox airfield. Here you can shed your shoes and walk along a sandy shore all the way into Kye Bay beach.

Seclusion This is a public park. It is not a hidden path to a secret cove. On the other hand, it is one of the quietest public parks you are likely to find anywhere. People watching is not likely to be very satisfying, if that, rather than a quiet day at the beach, is your priority.

36 KIN BEACH PROVINCIAL PARK—SOUTH

A dirt track leading through Kin Beach Park to a beachfront parking space south of the park with good options for car picnicking or using the sandy upper beach

Location, signs and parking The route to and location of this access spot are peculiar. The access spot is distinctive enough both in location and features, however, to make it a good "secret" alternative to the Kin Beach Park access immediately to the north. To find this little-known and little-used spot, follow the general directions to the previous entry (the northern access to Kin Beach Provincial Park), but this time enter the park at the main entrance, marked by the horizontal log sign. Continue along the dirt track right through the park until it takes a sharp turn toward the ocean along the southern boundary of the park. Drive through an open grassed area past some abandoned tennis courts until you find yourself in a small parking area with good views of the open strait and a few signs to give spice to your seafront adventure. These tell you that you mustn't park overnight or camp and what you shouldn't have to be told—not to dump refuse. Another more cheerful sign tells you to be "sun smart" and lists ways in which you can be exactly that.

Path For those with walking difficulties or those who are looking for an isolated spot to gaze on the winter storms from the comfort of their car, this is a perfect alternative to the park immediately north. In fact, since you can park right behind the beach logs on the upper beach, the only real impediment you face in getting yourself onto the sun-baked picnicking area are the beach logs jostled by winter storms.

Beach Like the beach in the adjoining park (this beach appears to be outside park boundaries), the beach here will probably appeal most to those who love a dunelike atmosphere in a large upper beach of loose sand and pebbles, all amidst jumbles of beach logs. A high-tide visit means not only that the water is close by for a delicious dip but also that your beaching experience is essentially a sandy one, with just odd patches of

Kin Beach Provincial Park

loose pebbles and egg-sized rocks. On the other hand, low tide reveals a few interesting features, including a large tidal pool, an odd pile of large boulders, and, of course, the mollusks, crustaceans and echinoderms busy about their watery lives.

Suitability for children The great merit of this beach for children is the close proximity of the car and all of the bits and pieces some children need. The upper beach will be huge fun for children who love sandboxes—with the additional features of seashells and bits of driftwood. While the lower beach can cause a few stumbles among the rocks, well-shod children who have finished jumping and climbing around the jumbles of beach logs can find lots of shore life scuttling or oozing under the rocks.

Suitability for groups The severely restricted parking is the major draw-back to this as a destination for any group that doesn't fit into a car or two. Most groups are much better accommodated at the park immediately beside this spot.

View Since the shore is slightly convex here, you will have an expansive view up and down the whole northern part of the Strait of Georgia. The mountains and islands north of Texada Island taper off toward the distant horizon and the barely discernible southern tip of Quadra Island, off Campbell River.

Winds, sun and shade Although you essentially are on the sidelines of the winds that blow parallel to the shore in either direction, you will nevertheless feel both breezes and storms. If you want to bake a little, though, you need only nestle into one of the hidey-holes among the logs. No shade falls onto the beach, meaning that, for good or ill, you will never feel the cooling effects of shorefront trees.

Beachcombing Although you can walk for a considerable distance in either direction, if you walk north you will find yourself before long at the BC Ferries terminal. If you head south, not only will you find the walking over the uneven surface easier the farther you go, but also you will soon be on an isolated piece of shore beneath the high banks separating it from the Canadian Forces Base airfield.

Seclusion To one side lies a little used section of Kin Beach Park and to the other, a private house, 100 m away across an open grass area. As a result, the chances are high that you will be able to focus on the wheeling of gulls rather than the goings-on of fellow humans.

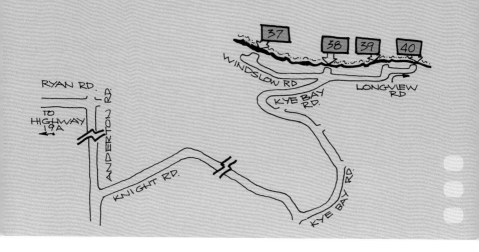

37 WINDSLOW ROAD

A little-used route through a grove of firs to a large area of soft sand and logs leading to the northern end of the main part of Kye Bay beach and its acres of sand

Location, signs and parking From the major intersection at the north end of the commercial area of Courtenay, turn left past the Canadian Tire store and uphill along Ryan Road for more than 4 km. A right turn onto Anderton for just over 1.5 km should bring you to Knight Road on your left. Stay with Knight as it curves past the Comox Valley Airport until, near the shore, you finally come upon Kye Bay Road on your left. You're not there yet. Follow Kye Bay Road along its twining course for several kilometres until it drops down from a high bank and delivers you to Windslow Road running along the upper edge of Kye Bay beach. Turn left onto Windslow Road and follow it about 400 m to its northern end. While two other strips of public access land lead to the shore along this stretch of cottages, you will find it difficult going down either without feeling that you are intruding into someone's yard. Although parking isn't extensive at the end of the road, you should be able to park discreetly on the shoulder or ease forward into a grassy area under the trees on the shore side of the road. You won't see any signs at this spot but can expect the signs posted farther along the beach prohibiting fires and collecting shellfish to apply equally here.

Path The path under the patch of large firs is level and only gently undulating, but after two or three dozen metres you will find yourself wading through a broad stretch of soft sand dotted with occasional logs.

Beach This little used access brings you to a part of the beach that, in some ways, is more attractive than the main park-side access at the other end of Windslow Road. Although mid tides don't expose quite as much sand here as they do farther along the beach, you don't have to walk far to get lots of sand underfoot at any but the highest tides. Furthermore, there is no murky lagoon behind the shore here as there is at the other end, and the area of loose, white sand for spread-eagling is significantly larger. Large tidal pools and a striking sandspit are enticing features of this end of the beach.

Suitability for children The beach itself could hardly be better for children. The large supratidal area of soft sand is a great, if gritty, place to spread out all your beach wares and blankets so that toddlers can toddle and scamperers can scamper—in the latter case, off over the sand and through the tidal pools. Whether this particular access to the beach seems better than the public park 400 m along Windslow Road will depend on if you prefer on having a spot more or less to yourself here or, by the public park, having picnic tables, washrooms and a playground close at hand.

Suitability for groups Only a small group of people who want a sandy picnic and lounging spot all to themselves would come here. By far the majority of groups would be happier with the facilities of the public park.

View The curving shore of Kye Bay, some 3 km broad, dominates your foreground view, framing your perspective on the strait. Across this northern section of the Strait of Georgia, you will see three layers of landforms: first a chain of islands, then Malaspina Peninsula and, against the skyline, the Coast Mountains.

Winds, sun and shade Northwesterlies, whether breezes or gales, are a little less strong here than on the main public part of the beach to the southeast—but not much. On the other hand, southeasterlies, never fully felt here, are a little stronger than at the public end of the beach. If you are nursing a sunburn or hope to avoid having to nurse one, you can find some shade on the uppermost band of dry sand in the afternoon.

Beachcombing This is a glorious beach for the barefoot crowd. Whether running decoratively by the water's edge or slouching pendulously through tidal pools after a megapicnic, you can get several kilometres' worth of sand under your bare feet. Do, however, be aware that you will have to wade through several tidal pools and that in some areas sharp bits of shell can lurk. The dramatic sandbar that, at low tide, juts into the strait to your left is an obvious destination for beach walkers.

Seclusion Although the access path brings you to a relatively secluded bit of upper beach, the tidal flats themselves are just as likely to be dotted with other beachgoers at this end of the beach as at the other. A guest lodge on one side and cottages on the other make sure of that. Still, the beach, at low tide, is huge, and the density always low. In addition, to the northwest of this access spot you will find no houses for about 3 km. Within a few minutes, you can find yourself intoxicatingly alone.

38 ELKS AND ROYAL PURPLE PARK—WINDSLOW ROAD
A dozen or so picnic tables in a treed grassy area beside a playground, with access to hectares of low-tide sand in Kye Bay

Location, signs and parking Like finding other access routes to Kye Bay beach, tracking this one down requires lots of gumption and patience. Worth it? Absolutely! From the major intersection at the north end of the commercial area of Courtenay, turn left past the Canadian Tire store and uphill along Ryan Road for more than 4 km. A right turn onto Anderton Road for just over 1.5 km should bring you to Knight Road on your left. Stay on Knight as it curves past the Comox Valley Airport until, near the shore, you finally come upon Kye Bay Road. You're not there yet. After a left on Kye Bay Road, follow it along its twining course for several kilometres until it drops down from a high bank, delivering you close to the shore and the prominently marked Elks and Royal Purple Park at the intersection with Windslow Road. Here you will find parking in a lot that holds about two dozen cars, but, on a busy day, you can find spots along the nearby shoulders. You will see many signs intended to make sure you don't misbehave while beaching. Among the behaviours that you must contain are camping or parking overnight, burning open fires and collecting shellfish. Your dog doesn't get off scot-free, either. Wolfie must stay out of the playground area altogether and, in the rest of the park, must stay leashed. Washrooms, incidentally, are located across the road from the park.

Path If you happen to be able to nab one of the parking spots close to the shore, you can be wiggling your toes in the sand or perched on a log within a dozen or so metres of horizontal strolling. Because Elks and Royal Purple Park is, understandably, the most popular access to a relatively popular beach, upon reaching the shore you almost certainly will want to stagger under the burden of your beaching paraphernalia along the upper shore until you find the perfect spot.

Beach Children, at least, will be quick to aver that this is one of the best beaches to be found anywhere. At low tide, with all of those vast expanses of gleaming, fine sand and warm tidal pools, how could the beach be improved? Adults will largely concur but will notice that there are a few patches of gravel that have to be reckoned with, and that there is an unappetizing quasi lagoon between the beach and the playground. Note that while this kind of wide beach produces bathtub-warm water near the edge of an incoming tide, finding deep enough water to actually swim in can require lots of wading toward the horizon.

Suitability for children Most children will be ecstatic with the options of building castles and excavating water channels, throwing Frisbees, flying kites and coming a cropper with skimboards. Dashing barefoot for great distances and thrashing about in warm turquoise water over soft sand are the most obvious draws of the beach. Parents will likewise be aware of the washrooms and easy walk to the family car but should be a little wary that a non-swimming child might get into an awkward situation on an incoming tide. A blissfully oblivious child might, for example, be standing in waist-deep water on a submerged sandbar and, floundering toward shore, suddenly find herself in chest-deep water and panic.

Suitability for groups Although groups will find lots of parking, they won't find enough for a whole jamboree. A dozen or two frolickers should be easily accommodated, though, given the plethora of picnic tables, the presence of washrooms and the vast size of the beach.

View As the name suggests, Kye Bay is indeed a bay and therefore has a less expansive view than do some spots nearby. Most striking, perhaps, is the long sandspit projecting across the beach from the north end of the bay. The more distant views are of Malaspina Peninsula and, in front of it, Hernando Island to the north, leading southward to Savary, Harwood and the north end of Texada.

Winds, sun and shade One of the qualities of this beach that makes it good for kites has to be factored in when you arrive for a few hours of beach fun with lots of exposed skin. A northwest wind, sometimes soothingly warm, can be chilling here, especially mid morning. Sunbathers amid the logs of the upper beach are much less likely to feel it fully than those wandering the shore. Southeast winds, less common during sunny weather, are generally little felt, especially on the upper beach and especially near the southeast end of the beach. Make sure your beach bag is well stocked with sunscreen, sun hats and sunglasses.

Beachcombing Those who love the idea, and possibly even the reality, of running barefoot by the water's edge will find their big chance here. Do watch out for some sharp shell fragments, however, particularly in some of the tidal pools. The beach is also great for barefoot sauntering, not just because it is large but also because it has considerable variety. Particularly intriguing for many will be the long sandbar, exposed at low tide, leading from the northwest end of the beach.

Seclusion If you use the standards of most local beaches, you may find this beach can get crowded. If you use the standards of most of the world, you will find it almost always nearly empty. If you've been working on those beach abs, this is one of the few beaches along this coast where you're likely to win even a small number of appreciative fans.

39

LONGVIEW ROAD—WEST

A short, forested track to an upper beach of interesting boulders and a broad, lower beach of expanses of fine sand

Location, signs and parking Like other access spots near Kye Bay tucked below Comox Airport, Longview Road requires hefty levels of determination and treasure-hunting skills. From the traffic lights on the north side of Courtenay's commercial area, turn up Ryan Road for 4 km, then right onto Anderton Road for about 1.5 km. Turn left onto Knight Road and follow it for about 5 km until, near the shore, you see Kye Bay Road. Follow this tortuously twisting road until it takes a slight jog left and changes name to Longview Road. Here you can pull over onto the shoulder, the only place to park, and note two telltale signs, one stating No Open Fires, the other warning you that the area is closed to shellfish.

Path The prettily winding path leading from a grassy area can be a little overgrown. The good news? Not only is it level, it is also secluded. After several metres the path comes to a slightly awkward patch of shore vegetation and logs. While most visitors will not even notice the irregularities in the path, those for whom walking is a challenge will be better off at the access immediately west on Kye Bay Road.

Beach Your access path brings you a few metres beyond the sandiest part of Kye Bay beach. Immediately in front of the trailhead you will find a patch of small beach logs and an area of beautifully marked boulders. Depending on what tricks the winter storms have been up to, you may or may not find a small area of coarse sand in which to settle down with your laptop and picnic bag. To enjoy the best features of the beach, you will probably want to arrive at low tide so that once you have picked your way through the deliciously rounded boulders and rocks, you can step onto the huge expanse of firm sand and tidal pools that extends more than a kilometre to your left.

Suitability for children If solitude is your chief goal rather than treating your child to the greatest possible beach fun, you can still come to this spot assured that your child will have relatively easy access to acres of sandy bliss. Do, however, remember the crocs or flip-flops so that the tender-footed can make their own way over the area of boulders to the sand.

Suitability for groups Given the proximity of other access routes where the parking, facilities and picnicking area are much better, you would choose this spot for a small group only if you needed a shady area among the logs in which to hatch a conspiracy theory or plan your next singalong.

View Island lovers will be pleased at the neat order in which the islands of the northern Strait of Georgia march purposefully toward the northern horizon. From the northern tip of Texada on your right, the islands in sequence to the north are Harwood, Savary, Hernando and Cortes. If you have brought your binoculars, you will also be able to make out Mitlenatch in the middle of the strait; Marina, tucked in to the west of Cortes; and Cape Mudge at the southern tip of Quadra.

Winds, sun and shade Be warned—this spot can get a little breezy during the early part of a sunny day if the characteristic northwesterly is up to its usual antics. On the other hand, it is fairly well protected from a southeasterly. While the upper beach is shady during the afternoon, you can easily get more than enough sun by wandering out onto the sands, or simply enjoy the protection, dished out by the shorefront firs, from the sun's burning rays.

Beachcombing Come at low tide to enjoy the greatest variety in walking options. At low tide you will find not only hectares of firm white sand on which to wander, but also striking spits thrusting out into the strait. For long-distance exploring, be sure to bring sturdy shoes and, possibly, a water bottle. While you can walk for a long way even at high tide, most of the interesting features will be thoroughly submerged.

Seclusion The main reason for coming to this access to Kye Bay, rather than choosing one of the others that lead more directly to the sandy beach, is seclusion. Few people come down the trail to the shore here, and you are also fairly well removed from the houses on either side. Don't expect too much, though. The main part of the beach, a hundred metres away, is almost always busy with happy beachgoers.

40

LONGVIEW ROAD—EAST

A rarely visited access to the even less visited sandy cliffs, and a rocky spit extending far out into the strait

Location, signs and parking Like other spots off Kye Bay Road, this one requires real dedication to find. The good news is that once you have made your way from the highway to Kye Bay, you have several spots open to you to visit, all of them interesting, some of them wonderful. From the traffic lights on the north side of Courtenay's commercial area, turn up Ryan Road for 4 km, then right onto Anderton Road for about 1.5 km. Turn left onto Knight Road and follow it for about 5 km until, near the shore, you see Kye Bay Road. Follow this tortuously twisting road until its very end, where it takes a slight jog left and changes name to Longview Road. The access route is not hard to find. Simply drive as far as you can, until your way is blocked by a row of boulders separating you from a flat area of gravel a dozen or so metres from the shore. No signs tell you anything about the various prohibitions on your beach behaviour, but you can guess what they might be, especially considering the proximity of the new house at the end of the road.

Path You won't find much of a path so will have to make do with finding your way down a rough track to the shore about 2 m below the end of the road.

Beach The upper beach might have been appealing at one point, but it isn't particularly appealing now, since a tumble of rough boulders pushed into place by excavators covers the upper beach. Immediately to the right, a barricade of pilings prevents the road's end from further erosion. All of this is to say that picnicking close to your car should not be your goal in coming here. Come at low tide, though, and you will see a long narrow spit extending an amazing 300 m into the strait. Immediately to the left of your access spot, too, you will see some sandbars emerging from the tidal shallows.

Suitability for children This isn't the best place to bring toddlers, given the scramble onto the shore and the lack of an attractive spot to spread out beach blankets and beach toys. Children primed with curiosity and energy, however, should be as intrigued as their parents by the long spit exposed by low tide. They no doubt will also enjoy creating watery havoc in the shallows of the nearby sandbars.

Suitability for groups Certain kinds of small group could well come to this secluded spot to explore an unusual and striking area. Take birth-day parties and family reunions elsewhere. Reserve this spot for walkers, explorers and naturalists, without fear that they will be intruding or jamming up a busy residential road.

View The most immediately attention-grabbing parts of your view are in the foreground, not just the long spit revealed by low tide but also the sandy cliffs curving out of sight around Cape Lazo. Across the strait, you will be able to make out Powell River between Harwood Island and the north end of Texada Island. To the north, Savary, Hernando and Cortes islands recede into the distance. Bring your binoculars to admire the more distant landforms.

Longview Road—East

Winds, sun and shade The spit is especially exciting to explore if either a northwest wind or southeast wind is blowing, since it is exposed to both. On the other hand, if you want to escape wind you can easily do so. Head along the upper shore to the west and you will soon be out of a southeast wind. Head along the shore to the south and you will find a northwest wind is much reduced, if not altogether absent. The whole area is pretty much in full sun as long as there is sun in the sky.

Beachcombing As you might have gathered by this point, walking is the main pleasure of this spot. While the spit exposed by low tide is the most obviously striking feature, the whole shore to the south around Cape Lazo to Point Holmes beach has remarkable sand and gravel bars. Head the opposite direction, too, and you will come not just to the beautiful low-tide sands of Kye Bay but also its dramatically extended sandbars.

Seclusion You are unlikely to see anyone very much at the shore immediately below the access spot, and you are also unlikely to see anyone at all if you walk below the sand cliffs. If, however, you head toward Kye Bay beach, you will find lots of opportunity to practise your people-watching skills.

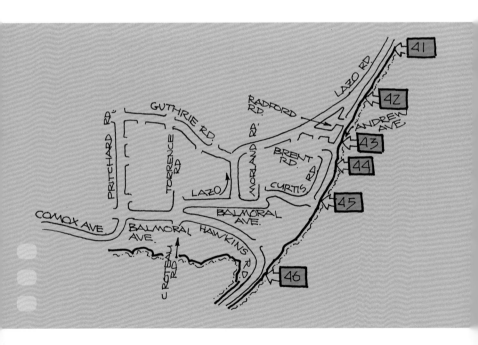

41
POINT HOLMES
Launching ramp, fire rings and picnic shelter at the northeast end of a three-kilometre-long beach

Location, signs and parking From Comox Avenue in central Comox, follow the rather complex directions for the Andrew Avenue entry (43), but stay on Lazo Road until it runs immediately next to the shore. A little more than a kilometre's drive along this beautiful shorefront road will bring you to a picnic shelter and several signs on the shoulder of the road. Since you can park in full view of the shore, remember this spot during winter weather when you need a little salty stimulation—from the comfort of your car. Here you will see parking for two or three dozen cars on the strip alongside the road, park benches, a picnic shelter and a waste bin, along with signs admonishing you not to park overnight (without the risk of being towed) and not to collect shellfish. Two signs concern fires. Prepare yourself for a little bafflement. One asserts that fires are to be built only in "designated rings" and are to be "extinguished by 11 p.m." The other is a little less expansive. It reads No Fires. Since it is posted at 90 degrees to the other, however, you might be right in concluding that it refers to the section of shore in the direction of Cape Lazo. About 100 m north of the picnic shelter, you will see an astoundingly long concrete launching ramp that, at low tide, extends more than 100 m down the gradually shelving shore.

Path Although you can make your way onto the shore from virtually any spot along the hundred or so metres of parking area, if you are toting picnic hampers or tiny picnickers, you will find the easiest routes near the picnic shelter and near the launching ramp.

Beach The first thing that will strike you about the beach here, if you have visited other access spots to the same strip of beach closer to Comox, is how much farther the tide goes out here and how much more diverse the beach is. Extending more than 100 m, the low-tide area is made up of patches of gravel, some solid rock ridges and a few huge boulders, and some large level patches of sand. Slightly to the northeast, the tide goes out much farther, revealing almost 200 m of mostly gravel. The uppermost beach, in contrast, is fairly consistently the same stretch of coarse dry sand, pebbles and mounded tangle of beach logs that characterizes the whole 3 km stretch of beach. The short version? Avoid arriving at mid tide. Both high tides and low tides offer attractive versions of a beautiful beach. Mid tide gives you the impression that the beach is mostly rough rock. In winter, choose a particularly frenetic southeast storm and come here for a great show.

Suitability for children The advice to arrive either at high tide or very low tide is particularly relevant to children. At the lowest tides, the large swaths of sandy shore are great for the barefoot splashing and castle building most children love. At the highest tides, children can easily and safely leave their play spot amid the soft sand of the upper beach and drag their inflated caterpillar to its watery fate.

Suitability for groups Though well used by locals, this is a great spot for a group outing. Even when others are busily enjoying the area, your group of duck spotters or lunch munchers will find lots of parking and a huge area of beach on which to get up to whatever is on their minds. Be mindful, though, that you won't find washrooms and that other facilities are limited.

View To the north, or left side, you will see your view framed by the high shore of Point Holmes leading to Cape Lazo. A stretch of mainland mountains leads to Texada Island and two of its main features, Surprise Mountain and the slightly less appealing mining scar. Lasqueti Island looks tiny tucked up beside Texada and considerably farther south. To the west of the open strait, Hornby Island hulks to the left of and slightly behind Denman Island.

Winds, sun and shade When beachgoers at virtually all other beaches on the east coast of Vancouver Island are buffeted by a northwest blow, people along this stretch of beach might feel only the occasional breeze. The flip sides are, unsurprisingly, that this beach can become oven hot and that southeast storms lash the beach—and account for the presence of so many beach logs. The only shade to be had, other than that provided by your beach umbrella, is under the picnic shelter, an additional reason to expect this beach to be warmer than many.

Beachcombing Those who come to this beach several times without dedicating at least one of those to walking along the shore are missing out on one of the most interesting aspects of this beach. While you can walk in both directions and at any tide, you will find the shore most interesting if you come at low tide and head north. Within a few hundred metres you will find a huge anvil-shaped gravel spit extending far into the deep waters around Cape Lazo. Continue your exploring and, as you round the high sandy cliffs of Cape Lazo itself, you will come across another long narrow spit, equally striking. Not only will your view up the strait change dramatically but also that of the shore. Suddenly, in front of you, will spread the vast low-tide sands of Kye Bay.

Seclusion If you are planning to confine your beach pleasures to the roadside, don't expect to feel much in the way of solitude, unless, perhaps, you come during a winter storm. Long-distance beachcombers, however, will find, in all likelihood, they have to share the beach with only the occasional preoccupied gull.

42

LAZO ROAD
Roadside access to park benches amid dunes, and a long curving shore of sandy upper beach and gravelly lower beach.

Location, signs and parking From Comox Avenue in central Comox, follow the directions for the Andrew Road entry (43), except stay on Lazo Road until it drops parallel to and immediately beside the shore. You will see a gravel parking area for half a dozen cars and two signs. Planning a beach-fire encounter session? Go elsewhere. No fires are allowed here. One of the signs reminds you not to consume alcohol, though, of course, that prohibition applies to all public places.

Path Only a few metres separate the parking lot from the beach, but for some people, these can be a tricky few metres. The loose sand track can be little slip-slidey as it drops down a short, though considerable, slope through the dune and mounds of beach logs. The roadside area of dunes, thick with beach grass, is also dotted with several park benches. Those who have walking difficulties might prefer to find the perfect viewing and gourmandizing spot on one of these benches rather than the beach.

Beach This access brings you more or less to the centre of the 3-km-long beach between Cape Lazo and Willemar Bluffs. Like most of the beach, the large area at the beginning of this section is dry sand and beach logs. Visitors have created some teetering stacks of logs leaning on each other—fun to look at, but perhaps dangerously unstable. This upper beach area is exactly the kind of place most visitors will find perfect for laying out their full arsenal of beach paraphernalia. At low tide, swimmers or waders will have to cross a band of small, rounded rocks to get to the water, though this band is narrower here than immediately to the north. To the south, at extremely low tides, a section of low-tide sand emerges from the wavelets.

Suitability for children This is a great beach for children who love to push around piles of soft sand and decorate them with seashells and seaweed—though remember that on a hot day, this sand can sear little feet, so tote along flip-flops or crocs. The beach is not quite so perfect for riding inflatable hammerheads and crocodiles, except perhaps at high tide, when the rocks are mostly submerged. If there is a northwest breeze, too, note that it can gust offshore, taking a bobbing child with it.

Suitability for groups Of the various spots along this long beach suitable for groups, this one is probably second-best for groups. Although this spot lacks the facilities of Point Holme, to the northeast along Lazo Road, it does have plenty of parking for several cars and a wide strip of public land on either side of the access track. If your pack of picnickers is happy to sit in the sand or lean against logs, they will find plenty of space to enjoy themselves.

View Because the shore dips in slightly here, you cannot see the full sweep of the beach as you can at some other access spots to the south. Still, you will have the same wonderfully varied view of the Coast Mountains to the north of Texada Island, and the sequence of other islands to the right of Texada: Lasqueti, Hornby and Denman, with tiny Sandy Island barely discernible off the northern tip of Denman. Beaufort Range, on Vancouver Island, tapers north toward the distant bumps of Mount Arrowsmith.

Winds, sun and shade One of the features of this beach that makes it good for children is that it is well protected from the northwest winds that usually accompany sunny summer weather. Storm watchers will love the fact, however, that southeast storms charge up the whole length of the Strait of Georgia before battering this shore. In the absence of trees or high banks, beachgoers will have to be prepared both to provide their own shade and to be happy with finding the beach swathed in cooling shade.

Beachcombing Properly shod and properly determined, beach walkers can conquer several kilometres in either direction. In both cases, a kilometre or two will bring them to high sandy bluffs.

Seclusion From one perspective, seclusion is the last feature you would expect from this spot, smack in the middle of a heavily built-up strip of shore-gazing houses. From another, though, the seclusion is much greater than you might expect. This comparative seclusion arises from two factors. First, you will find no shorefront houses for a considerable distance to your northwest, since the road borders the shore. Second, a mound of dunelike sand and vegetation separates the road from the upper beach. Come prepared to walk a short distance from the access path, therefore, and find more seclusion than you might have bargained for!

While you're here, if you want an even quieter approach to much the same beach, turn down Hutton Road just where Lazo Road turns away from the shore and find secluded parking overlooking the shore.

43

ANDREW AVENUE

A well-hidden and little-used
access to a long sweep of beach
with a wide upper beach of loose
sand and logs and a lower beach
of rounded gravel

Location, signs and parking Like the other access routes to this long beach, this one involves advanced map-reading skills, not least of all because the roads that lead to this beach don't interconnect close to the shore. You will have to retrace your route a considerable distance inland if you want to arrive at an access spot one or two hundred metres along the shore. To get to Andrew Avenue from downtown Comox, drive through the main street of this pretty town, swinging left onto Pritchard Road as you leave the downtown section. The simplest, but not the shortest, route is to stay on Pritchard for about 2 km until a significant intersection with Guthrie Road. Turn right and follow your new road for about 1.5 km until it arrives at Lazo Road. Turn left here, and, just under a kilometre away, turn right onto Radford Road. A T-junction at the end of Radford allows you to turn right onto Andrew Avenue and follow it to its southwest end. Here you might be a little taken aback by the apparent lack of access to the shore. In fact, immediately to the left of imposing gates at the end of the road, you will see two huge boulders and a sandy track leading toward the shore. In the absence of a special parking area, you can fit into the spot by the boulders or along the shoulder on the approaching roads. The only prohibition posted for this beach you won't see until you reach the shore, where you will be instructed on the dangers of contaminated shellfish.

Path A sandy track leads about 30 m to a section of tall, thick beach grass and a pick-up-sticks tangle of beach logs. Those with walking difficulties or 30 cm long legs would probably be better off going to one of the access routes to the same beach immediately off Lazo Road to the north.

Beach This is the perfect beach for hours of basking and lunching amidst a wealth of dry, soft sand and beach logs. It is also a good, but less perfect, beach for cooling off with a dip. If your intention is to polish your freestyle or simply dampen your tootsies, you will probably want to come at high tide, when the water is warmest and when the barrier of rocks is narrowest.

Suitability for children While this is not the beach to choose for building castles from wet sand and running over sandy tidal flats, it nevertheless can be appealing to children. The upper shore is a kind of never-ending sandbox, with lots of seashells and pretty rocks close by to enhance play in the sand. For many children, too, log jumbles are the next best thing to the jungle gym in their local park. Parents keeping an eye on the chaotic strokes of beginner swimmers will be pleased that the water is never far away and that no drop-offs lurk beyond the water's edge.

Suitability for groups The narrowness of the access strip between neighbouring houses and the lack of a separate parking area are the chief limitations of this spot. The beach itself is great for spreading out a small group and providing lots of opportunities for wandering and wading. Still, most groups will be much better off selecting an access to the same beach directly off Lazo Road, a short distance north.

View While this spot has a view that is nearly identical to that from the other access spots along this shore, the one from here is strikingly different from the vast majority of views along this coast. Facing essentially south, the shore here invites the appreciative collector of views to run eyes past Cape Lazo to Texada Island and then to distant Lasqueti Island. The open horizon of the southern strait leads in turn to Hornby Island and, tucked in front of it, Denman. The skyline of Vancouver Island itself begins with distant Mount Arrowsmith and leads to the undulating humps of the Beaufort Range.

Winds, sun and shade One of the features of this beach that makes it great for children is that it is so well protected from the northwest breezes typical of sunny mornings in summer. At the same time, be prepared for the lack of shade: if you're not careful, your little ones can be sizzled to a crisp in no time. The flip side of the protection from the northwest winds, unsurprisingly, perhaps, is the full exposure to the southeast gales of winter.

Beachcombing Walking can be a little awkward in the soft sand of the upper beach or the loose gravel of the lower beach. If you are not intent on making speed, however, you will feel tempted to stroll for a good distance in either direction, perhaps as far as the sand cliffs at either end of the beach.

Seclusion The access strip is sandwiched between treeless waterfront houses and beyond them, more and more waterfront houses. Nevertheless, below the dune of beach grass and jumble of beach logs, you can expect to find a considerable sense of seclusion and, most likely, no other beach visitors.

44

CURTIS ROAD—EAST

A quiet access to an upper shore with a large upper beach area of sand, pebbles and logs

Location, signs and parking From Comox Avenue, follow the driving directions for the next entry, Curtis Road—West (45), except that when you reach Curtis Road, follow it to its northeastern terminus after its junction with Brent Road. You will find lots of easy parking for several cars in the partially paved turnaround area at the end of the road. The only sign directed toward visitors is visible only when you have made your way to the beach. If you are planning a beach fire, you should note that this sign, issued by the Comox Fire Department, tells you that you must first get a fire permit.

Path A wide sandy track climbs 20 or so metres over the dunelike crest at the end of the road and crosses a strip of dune vegetation before dropping, through increasingly loose sand, to the shore.

Beach This is an access to a long beach with much the same features as are found from other access routes to it. A gently curving sweep of shore is thick with a tangle of beach logs and loose sand, the result of winter storms from the southeast. The tide drops only a short distance, revealing a band of gravel and egg-sized rocks near the water's edge.

Suitability for children High tide is the best time to come for perfecting splashing technique or dog-paddling speed. Not only is the water warmest then, but also the water's edge is close to the broad sandy band of the upper beach. Low tide nevertheless provides lots of opportunities for both getting wet and finding squidgy creatures under the rocks.

Suitability for groups A few cars' worth of family, friends or like-minded beachgoers can find easy parking and access to a section of beach with uninterrupted sun and a sandy picnic area. More than that, however, would probably be intrusive, since houses line the shorefront on either side of the access spot.

View The view along the shore, with its tangle of mounded-up beach logs stretching into the distance, is one of its most striking features. If you want to tick off islands, from left to right across the southern strait you can clearly distinguish Texada, Lasqueti, Hornby and Denman. Above the sweeping shore of Vancouver Island looms the Beaufort Range and its highest point, Mount Joan.

Winds, sun and shade Like other access spots on this stretch of shore, this is a great one to choose if the day is sunny but cool: the beach is in full sun throughout the day and well protected from a northwest breeze. On a hot day, though, beware the furnace-like conditions that can result. When a southeast storm is charging up the strait, this is a good spot to experience the wind and waves at their most histrionic.

Beachcombing The distant perspectives along the beach invite a shorefront tromp, but you may be a little frustrated that the going isn't quite as easy as it looks. The soft sand of the upper beach may lead you to reflect on the advantages of being a camel. The rocky lower beach may make you feel weirdly lopsided. Persevere, however, and in both directions you will come to dramatic sandy cliffs and a convoluted shoreline, about 1 km away if you turn right and 2 km if you head left.

Seclusion You are unlikely to see many other visitors at this access point. You are highly likely to see locals and be seen by them. Unsurprisingly, houses crowd forward along this (treeless) strip of choice waterfront.

45

CURTIS ROAD—WEST

A little-known route to the western end of a huge sweep of significantly sloping sand and gravel shore

Location, signs and parking Brace yourself for finding your way through a truly weird and wonderful labyrinth of roads. If you start from downtown Comox, follow Comox Avenue east through town until it swings left onto Pritchard Road. Two blocks later, turn right onto Balmoral Avenue. When you see Torrence Road, go left for one block, and then right onto Lazo Road. This is the point at which peculiarities in road names can throw you off if you're not careful. Follow Lazo for about 700 m. You will come to an intersection where, oddly, Lazo Road is the left turn, and even more oddly, the continuation of your road, formerly Lazo, now reverts to being called Balmoral Avenue! After 300 m down Balmoral, turn left onto Morland Road and then take the first right onto Curtis Road, a long winding road that takes you down from the top of a bank toward the southern end of a long sweep of beach. Once at the bottom of the hill, watch for a gravel track that leads to a barricade of boulders just past the driveway numbered 448. On a telephone pole you will see three signs, all of which you should know about before you make specific plans for this beach. Unfortunately, two of the most relevant to some beachgoers contradict each other. Planning a feast of s'mores and hot dogs? One sign tells you that you can have a beach fire only if you get a permit from the Comox Fire Department. The other, drat the luck, says no fires are permitted. As for the consumption of alcohol or the collecting of shellfish, these, too, should not be on your repertoire of expectations.

Path You need only a few steps to bring you to the shore down the small bank, but you will need to climb over an impressive tangle of beach logs before reaching the sand.

Beach The beach has much of the feel of an open-ocean beach, in large part because of the pounding it gets during winter storms from the southeast.

The amazing mess of logs and large swath of dry, loose sand above the summer high-tide level make for exactly the kind of sandy lounging that many have in mind when heading for a beach. If swimming is on your agenda, you are best off coming at high tide, since at low tide you have to negotiate a barrier of fist-sized, rounded rocks before you can cool off.

Suitability for children If you can manage your children over the tangle of beach logs, you can set them free to romp. Beach shoes are a good idea, though, since the upper sandy beach can be scorching hot on bare feet, and the lower gravel beach can be more than a little uncomfortable.

Suitability for groups As long as obeying the signs doesn't cramp their style, minor hordes of beach-going enthusiasts will find the parking space and picnicking area they need to have a sun-baked, sandy afternoon at the beach.

View The sweep of the long beach toward the east ends with Cape Lazo. From there you will find that you are essentially looking southward down the Strait of Georgia, past Texada Island toward Denman and Hornby islands to the southwest. Dimly discernible is Mount Arrowsmith and, forming the skyline above the western shore, the Beaufort Range and its highest point, Mount Joan.

Winds, sun and shade Like this whole stretch of beach west of Cape Lazo, this spot is unusually well protected from northwest winds, the most common hot-weather wind. The heat that can be generated by a summer sun—especially given the complete absence of shade—is exactly what you might expect.

Beachcombing This is the kind of beach that invites long-distance wandering. Admittedly, walking isn't exactly easy because of the soft sand on the upper beach and the slope of the lower beach. If you plan only a short walk, you may prefer to head west, since to the east you will soon be walking immediately below the seaside road. If you are planning a long-distance walk, you will be rewarded in both directions by seclusion, dramatically high cliffs and striking low-tide shore configurations.

Seclusion Although you will encounter few other visitors at this spot, you will not find much seclusion on this densely residential shoreline. Long-distance walkers, however, will be virtually alone at the bottom of high sandy cliffs.

46
GOOSE SPIT
A beautiful and striking spit
with several hundred metres
of beach-side parking

Location, signs and parking Various routes can take you through the web of streets to Goose Spit. If we assume that you can find your way to Comox Avenue in Comox, the route that requires fewest turns starts with a left on Stewart Street, and after three blocks, a right onto Balmoral Avenue. Keep straight ahead across Croteau and Torrence roads, though now you will be on Hawkins Road, the very road you want to take you to Goose Spit Park, a few downhill winds and dips later. You can choose between the two main parking spots, one at the beginning of the spit, the other at the end of the public area, just before the Department of National Defence land. Three signs, two of them unique to this park, could significantly affect your plans for an outing here. Hoping to chainsaw some beach logs for firewood? That's not allowed here. Hoping to have a gourmet wiener roast? You may—but from May 1 to September 5, you must use the rings provided. Hoping to stay overnight in your Monstrobago? It will be towed if it's found there between 11 p.m. and 5 a.m.

Path Since your parking is virtually on the beach, you can come laden with all of the umbrellas, chairs, coolers, hibachis and blisteringly ugly beach hats you want. Be aware, though, that the logs and loose sand or gravel can be a little bit of a struggle for those with difficulty walking.

Beach The shore is composed of areas of rounded egg-sized rock and large bands of fine white sand. If you want to sit on gravel and avoid sand in your sandwiches, choose the first parking lot and find a spot along this end of the beach. At the farthest end of the spit, you will be picnicking in the sand, though you will have to cross a band of gravel when you want to take a dip. In fact, taking a plunge is comparatively easy here, since the tide does not drop very far. If plunging is, indeed, what you have in mind and you find the water a little nippy, you can cross the road to the lagoon, where the water is likely to be warmer. Few people use this beach, however, perhaps because of the slightly murky feeling, in part because of the shorefront vegetation and the quality of the sand. If you are after a broader swath of beach than is exposed along the spit itself, choose the first parking lot and walk east (to your left) for a short distance.

Suitability for children Most children love coming to this beach. Most parents love bringing their children to this beach. Easy access from the car, safe, sandy swimming, protection from northwest winds, and, as a bonus, masses of beach logs for scrambling and jumping all conspire to make this a wonderful beach for children. Be aware, however, that you won't find washrooms or other big-park facilities.

Suitability for groups While you can find oodles of beach on which to accommodate oodles of friends or relations, you should build into your reckoning the fact that this is a popular spot with locals on a hot summer's afternoon. Don't expect to have the beach to yourself or find easy parking for many cars. Don't expect to find tons of picnic tables, either.

View The view will rank high among connoisseurs of the best view spots on the island. Immediately behind and above you, the white sandy cliffs of Willemar Bluffs extend along the curving shore toward Cape Lazo and, just to the south, the northern end of Texada. Rising to the highest point on the north part of Texada is Surprise Mountain, and, you might note a little less enthusiastically, a mining scar. Far in the distance, Lasqueti Island and, closer, Denman and Hornby islands embellish the central strait. Perhaps most striking, though, is Comox Glacier and the adjoining mountains in this part of Strathcona Park, The Red Pillar and Argus Mountain among them. Come during early summer when the mountains are still snowclad, and you will find your camera hand exhausted.

Winds, sun and shade One of the unusual features of this beach is that it is almost entirely protected from a strong northwest wind. When beach-goers elsewhere along the coast are donning sweatshirts, those here can be basking and baking. Even if the wind is from the southeast, as it occasionally is on a sunny day, it is possible to tuck down out of it simply by heading to the beach on the lagoon side of the spit. There is not a whiff of shade to be found, so the beach can be scorching hot. Don't forget your bathing suit!

Beachcombing The combination of striking geography, sand and the ridiculously scenic view makes this a great beach for walking long distances. Remember, though, to walk east, in the direction of Cape Lazo, rather than toward the tip of Goose Spit. The military folk who own this chunk of prime real estate don't take kindly to intruders.

Seclusion The park is well loved and well used by locals. While this might not come as a surprise, what might is that if you are are willing to set out with your beach bag along the shore, you will soon find yourself—or selves—alone.

While you're here, consider visiting some of the roadside stops along Comox Road where it borders Courtenay River as the latter enters the sea. One particularly attractive view spot is opposite the I-Hos Gallery. For picnic tables and kayak launching, try nearby Dyke Road Park.

View from Comox Road

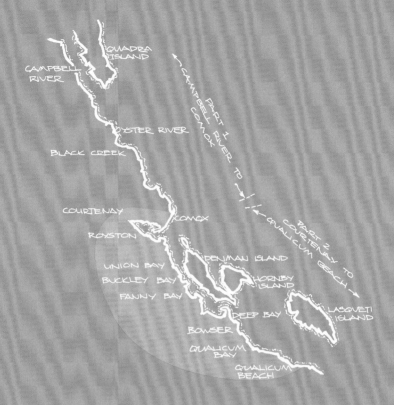

QUADRA
ISLAND

CAMPBELL
RIVER

OYSTER RIVER

BLACK CREEK

PART 1
CAMPBELL RIVER TO COMOX

COURTENAY

COMOX

ROYSTON

UNION BAY

DENMAN ISLAND

BUCKLEY BAY

FANNY BAY

HORNBY
ISLAND

PART 2
COURTENAY TO QUALICUM BEACH

DEEP BAY

LASQUETI
ISLAND

BOWSER

QUALICUM
BAY

QUALICUM
BEACH

PART 2 Courtenay to Qualicum

THE SECTION OF COAST FROM COURTENAY TO QUALICUM
begins near Royston, where the estuary-dominated shoreline of Comox
Harbour starts to take on the character of the seashore. Even so, the shore
from Royston to Deep Bay is distinctive because it is protected from the
action of large waves by Denman Island. That, in combination with the
number of streams entering the shore and the generally low coastline,
produces many seaside areas of salt-tolerant vegetation and broad areas
of sea meadows. The sheltered character of this section of coastline no
doubt accounts, too, for the intriguing vestiges of a rich coastal history
dotted along it.

From the south end of Denman Island, though, and all the way to
Qualicum, the coast takes on a markedly different feeling. Exposed
to the wind and waves of this open part of the Strait of Georgia, the
shoreline often feels both sun-baked and wave-washed. While wind
and waves have created no large sandy beaches, they have created many
small ones. This is a shore of sandy refuges amongst beach logs, strangely
sculpted gravel bars and huge tidal pools. Rarely is the coastal highway
far from the shore, either. When the time comes for a picnic or a splash,
you usually have only a short way to go from the highway before you are
savouring both your sandwiches and the view.

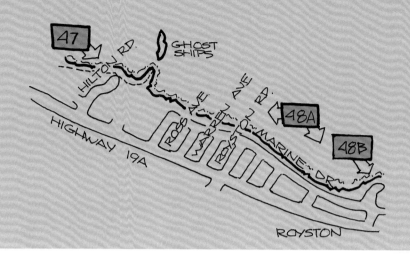

47

HILTON ROAD

The closest public access from which to view the "ghost ships" of Royston and the historic breakwater near them

Location, signs and parking The Hiawatha Evergreens business makes a good landmark for finding Hilton Road along this treed section of highway a few minutes south of Courtenay. Hilton Road winds toward the shore for just over 200 m and comes to an end in a large gravel turnaround area. Here you will find parking for more than a dozen cars. Three battered signs reinforce much the same basic point—stay away at night. One tells you that you cannot park there between 11 p.m. and 7 a.m.; one that you cannot park or camp overnight; and the third that you should be quiet after 10 p.m. Point, one thinks, made.

Path A wide gravel path, bordered with a log, leads the few steps necessary to get from the parking area to the shore. Those with walking difficulty could hardly have it easier getting onto the beach—though they will not have it quite so easy if they want to make their way out to the breakwater itself.

Beach Two particularly long logs lie across the upper beach, separating an area of wild grass from a broad band of coarse sand and pebbles. The tide drops about 20 or 30 m, revealing a patchy shore of uneven gravel and ostrich-egg-sized rocks. Intriguingly, some energetic visitor has arranged a cleared strip to the low-tide mark. The upper shore to the west side has some patches of tall shore grass. The whole shore is tucked behind a breakwater to the east, creating a protected little bay. Most visitors will come here to view the broken hulks of ships. If you are one such visitor, don't overlook the fact that the beach at high tide makes for pleasant and protected lounging and picnicking.

Suitability for children If your main purpose in coming here is to see the almost Gothic peculiarity of the shipwreck breakwater, you will want to bring only older children capable of appreciating the experience and capable of walking along the shore or paths to the breakwater itself.

On the other hand, if you want merely a pleasant pebbly beach protected from the wind and close to a vehicle, then bring virtually any child. Come at high tide, however, for the most attractive and comfortable beach experience.

Suitability for groups If you are looking for a picnic spot for a group, you could come here confident that you will find plenty of parking and shore area. Most picnicking groups would be happier where they can find park facilities. A group looking for a place to walk, photograph or paint will want to make this spot a priority. What anthropologists call the "culturally modified" elements of the site are guaranteed to provoke curiosity at the very least and, with any luck, full-blown fascination.

View Last on your checklist of criteria for choosing this place should be distant views. Though can see around the curve of the shore past Royston, through Courtenay and most of the way out to Comox, it is unlikely that you will notice or care. This is a place for close-up "oohs." The configuration of breakwater (in two chunks), broken hulks of ships, and minor forests of pilings are the most likely to clamour for your attention.

Winds, sun and shade The spot is protected only slightly from a northwest wind, but from a southeast wind it is well protected, not just because of the curve of the bay but also because of the treed promontory leading out toward the breakwater. You will find a little shade around noon if you need it, but after noon the shade moves along the shore to the right of the most comfortable part of the beach.

Beachcombing A strip of public land stretches along the waterfront for a considerable distance to the west as well as out to the breakwater. Called variously "Breakwater Esplanade" and "Royston Greenway," the strips of public land are well tramped, but not nearly as fully developed as some would like. You can also walk along the beach itself, either out to the breakwater or toward Courtenay, past patches of shore grass and stands of pilings. Wear protective footwear, since the going can be a little challenging.

Seclusion Although there are many houses littered around this whole section of coast, from the end of Hilton Road you will find yourself screened in virtually all directions by thickets of trees. You may well find a few other visitors at this special site, but could equally well be alone, especially if you explore the breakwater itself.

While you're here, you may want to turn off the highway 2 km north of Hilton Road onto Millard Road and drive straight ahead for a good car-picnicking spot overlooking the sea meadows and tidal flats.

Also while you're here, you may want to turn down 31st Street on the southern outskirts of Courtenay for one of many access spots to the Courtenay Riverway, a well-maintained shorefront walking and cycling route running toward the centre of Courtenay.

48A
MARINE DRIVE—WEST
A series of roadside facilities for picnicking and viewing historic sites and wildlife

Location, signs and parking If you are approaching from the north, look for the road sign for Marine Drive along a straight section of treed road on the southern outskirts of Courtenay. If you are approaching from the south, however, look for Hayward Avenue beside Royston Mini-Mart.

In either case, just over 100 m of driving will bring you to the shore-side section of Marine Drive. While you can park and wander along any part of this kilometre-long section of road, those looking for picnic facilities will find them between Warren Avenue and Ross Avenue, while those wanting the best parking area and a viewing platform should seek out the end of Royston Road. Note the sign, surely irrelevant to virtually all visitors, threatening tow-away for overnight parking. The most interesting signs give you fascinating historical information on the main draw of this area, the "ghost ships of Royston." You will also find directions to the Courtenay Riverway and Millard Nature Park, a few minutes' drive in the direction of central Courtenay.

Path It is possible to walk along the side of Marine Drive for its entire length, but for most of the way you will find no developed path.

Beach Your reason for visiting here is very unlikely to be to engage in typical beach activities, but, rather, to look along the shore from the viewing platform or from the grassy strip along the road. At low tide the water retreats for over 100 m toward the west end of the shore, but considerably less in the centre part of the bay. At a few spots, gravel strips lead to the waterline, though most of the shore is covered with a band of salt-tolerant vegetation.

Suitability for children This is a good place to bring older children who are interested in the history of the "ghost ships" or have their eyes firmly fixed on the picnic tables and the events that are likely to transpire there. It is not a good place to bring children who want to play in the water.

Suitability for groups If you are looking for a destination not only with lots of picnic tables but also a large stone barbecue, you don't have to head for a public park—you will find all of these facilities within a few metres of your roadside parking. Be aware, however, that you won't find public washrooms.

View The main reason for visiting Marine Drive is to enjoy the view, partly of the sweep of the bay with its tidal flats and distant estuary, partly of the hulks of the so-called "ghost ships" to the north. If your main reason for choosing this spot is to see these historic relics, however, do make sure you bring binoculars or zoom lens. In addition, think of including in your plans a visit to Hilton Road, where you can get a closer viewing spot for the ships than you can get here.

Winds, sun and shade This strip of northeast-facing shore is not the exposed piece of coastline you will find at some nearby beaches, but it nevertheless feels windy if there is wind to be felt. You can find a few patches of shade toward the west end of Marine Drive, but not in the picnic or viewing areas, where you are likely to linger. On a cool day, therefore, you can plan a picnic without worrying about being further chilled by shade.

Beachcombing Most visitors who enjoy shore walking will probably choose to walk the kilometre or so along the grassy shoulder of the road. More adventurous shore-goers can walk along the shore itself but will want to come at low tide and wear boots. If you wish to walk to the breakwater and ships, you can do so, but approaching from Hilton Road is much easier.

Seclusion This fascinating area receives few visitors, presumably because only locals know of its existence. At the same time, it is very much in the middle of a thoroughly developed residential area, so don't expect to lose yourself in the bosom of Mother Nature.

View south from Millard Road

48B

MARINE DRIVE—EAST
A seaside drive with paths through level areas of salt-tolerant shore plants to broad expanses of estuary

Location, signs and parking In the "centre" of Royston, look for Royston Mini-Mart and Hayward Avenue. Drive straight down Hayward just over 100 m until a T-junction with Marine Drive. You can choose either or both trailheads leading from this end of Marine Drive, one of them just to the left of the T-junction and one in the turnaround area 100 m to the right. Some signs provide guidance about proper shorefront behaviour, at least if you have a frantic hound bounding around you or a bucket and spade in hand. In the former case, unsurprisingly, you are told—by means of a wonderful little cartoon drawing—to "leash and clean up after your pet." As for the latter, note that the area is closed to gathering shellfish.

Path You can choose among two or three routes to the upper beach, though the two most cleared routes are from the turnaround at the east end of the road and via a gravel track cutting toward the water slightly to the left of the T-junction. Paths are level and a few metres long.

Beach Come to this spot for a striking estuary area. The Trent River, slightly to your north, spills into Comox Harbour, in the process creating a huge area of complexly patterned channels and bars stretching almost 400 m to the water's edge. The upper shore is pleasant for walking and provides a perspective on a fascinating piece of geography. The whole strip of shore fronted by Marine Drive should be high on the must-visit list of any through-and-through shorefront explorer, but this is hardly a beach for picnicking or swimming. You will probably be happiest with your visit if you choose low tide, when the bars and bays of the estuary are fully visible—though, of course, the waders and quackers are likely to be most distant then.

Suitability for children If you think of this as an exploratory outing rather than a day of conventional beach activities, then high-energy children could well enjoy accompanying their parents. Keep in mind, though, that most children are likely to be chiefly interested in the features of the northwest end of Marine Drive, about a kilometre distant.

Suitability for groups The northwest end of the shorefront drive has the space, facilities and historical curiosities that are most likely to suit a cavalcade of like-minded beachgoers. This end of the drive, however, with its large estuary area and shorebirds, is an enticing add-on.

View Your eyes will most likely be fixed on the curves and patterns of the large sweep of the bay in which you find yourself. If you lift your eyes, however, you will notice that from here you get the full panorama of the Courtenay and Comox shorefront. The odd blip along the waterfront to the east of Comox is Goose Spit, though from here you can see only the section with military buildings and not the expanse of public shore.

Winds, sun and shade While both a southeast and a northwest wind can produce breezes and blusters, for the most part this northeast-facing bay is fairly protected from both. The lack of shorefront trees ensures that you will be in sun as long as there is sun in the sky.

Beachcombing If you are feeling either intrepid or curious, you may want to venture far out onto the low-tide estuary. Rubber boots are the footwear of choice. Most walkers, however, will be happiest not walking on the beach itself but along the roadside next to the shore.

Seclusion The whole bay is lined with houses, few of them screened by trees. Though this is usually a quiet area, not visited by throngs, it is intensely residential.

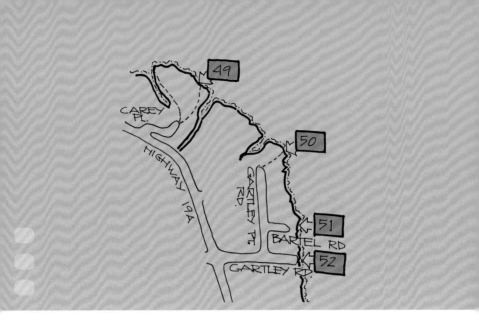

49

CAREY PLACE

A long trail starting by the banks of the Trent River and leading through estuary meadows to a shore of gravel and salt-tolerant plants

Location, signs and parking Near the southern end of Royston, and about 100 m north of the Trent River, turn down Carey Place. This road runs parallel to the highway for a distance, then dives toward the coast and comes to an end in a broad turnaround. Here you will find plenty of parking for several cars, though you have to be careful not to block driveways. That this is one of the few spots in the area with signs posted suggests that visitors are expected here. Both signs might affect your planning. First, if you are hoping to concoct your prize-winning chowder, don't expect to get your ingredients here. The shellfish are contaminated, so don't collect them here. Second, if you and your frisky four-legged friends are looking for a romp, make sure you arrive with leashes. It is imperative that your dogs don't chase shorebirds, though it is not explicit that they be leashed. You are also asked to arrive with several used plastic shopping bags, one to take with you for cleaning up after your dog, the others to leave for those who arrive without plastic bags.

Path The pleasures of the path are probably the main reason most visitors come here. Largely level and about 350 m long, the path is easy for most of its length but not without surprises. Beginning as a narrow track through a patch of bushes, it takes a short dive across a gravelly dip that can—be warned—be full at high water. Most of the trail is through a meadow of tall grasses and shore plants, beautifully varied in colour and texture. At some points, however, the vegetation can be a little overwhelming. Depending on the time of year and the numbers who have used the trail, you may find yourself pushing your way through waist-high thickets. With this in mind, you probably will want to avoid using the path after a heavy dew or a soggy downpour. Nothing is guaranteed to soak you faster than wet vegetation.

Beach The land slopes so gradually that plants thrive almost to the low-water mark. Still, you may be surprised to find something very much like a strip of beach around the high-tide line, near the so-called "swash" zone. This strip of coarse sand and pebbles, embellished with the occasional log, makes a surprisingly appealing spot to picnic or set up with your binoculars or easel. In fact, from this spot, you probably will feel little temptation to push through the intertidal salt-tolerant vegetation all the way to the low-water line of gravel.

Suitability for children Think of this as a good place for a family walk rather than a family day at the beach. That being said, if you do arrive at high tide and play your gastronomic cards right, you could mastermind a great picnic at a comfortable picnic spot.

Suitability for groups This area is tailor-made for those groups who like exploring unusual shores and fixing their binoculars on water birds. Parking is adequate for a few cars at least, and the vast meadow area will allow several wildlife seekers or photographers to string out.

View Your appreciative gaze will naturally tend to be trained on the foreground. Take the time to notice, however, some of the unusual distance views. In fact, from various parts of the trail, you will have an especially stunning view of Strathcona Park mountains, a view not possible from most shore spots in the area. You can look across Comox Harbour to Courtenay and Goose Spit, but your view is confined to the military end of the spit. Cape Lazo is tucked around the corner of Comox from this angle.

Winds, sun and shade On these exposed estuary meadows, you will find no shelter from sun or winds.

Beachcombing Because you are to the north of Trent River, you might think you can walk for a considerable distance north. While you can, indeed, walk over 300 very enjoyable metres along the pebble and gravel high-tide line, you will come across a deep channel cutting you off from the rest of the shore. At this point you can, however, make your way along the edge of this channel and end up near the starting point of your original trail.

Seclusion Although the trail starts in the middle of an established subdivision, within seconds you will be out in meadows far away from the mere mortals who have insisted on spending their afternoon on a crowded public beach.

50
GARTLEY POINT ROAD
A long, level path through a meadow of estuary plants to a broad gravel shore with intertidal salt-tolerant vegetation

Location, signs and parking About 1 km south of Royston, you will see a large intersection at the Grassi Point Farm Market. Take Gartley Road and follow it 200 m until Gartley Point Road. Turn left and follow Gartley Point Road until its end. As yet, no signs have been posted telling you what you mustn't do and when you mustn't do it. The absence of signs is probably irrelevant to most visitors except, possibly, a few pooches who have hounded their housemates for a little salty sniff and stroll. Though not capacious, the gravel parking area at the end of the road is big enough for the few cars that are likely to be found here.

Path You will see a wide path of crushed gravel leading first to a bridge and then to an intriguing treed ridge extending north across the salt meadows. The path you want, however, turns right from the right corner of the parking area. This interesting path is one of the main reasons for visiting this spot. Although fairly narrow, it is usually well beaten and level as it meanders gently over 100 m to the usual high-tide mark. Depending on the season and tides, the path passes large pools or vegetated depressions.

Beach This estuary area is so level and low that you will find little distinction between the supratidal zone and the intertidal (or littoral) zone. Thus you will find the path brings you to a sloping band of loose rocks that seems, more or less, to be the high-tide zone. Below this zone, however, more flats thick with estuarine vegetation like glasswort and alkaligrass extend for dozens of metres toward the low-tide area of exposed gravel.

Suitability for children This is a good place for a family walk. The level path makes going easy, even for those stubby of leg, and the various pools and interesting variations in vegetation add points of interest. It is not, however, a good place to head for the beach. Most children would be very, very hard pressed to call what they see a "beach."

Suitability for groups The same features that make this a good spot for a family walk make it a good spot for a small group. The kind of group that would like to refresh their senses at this spot is the kind that enjoys not just walking but also photographing or viewing wildlife. The varied textures of grasses in the meadows, offset against the treed ridge and, in the distance, the mountains behind Courtenay, make for some wonderful and rarely seen compositions.

View It is not just the views over the meadows and back toward Vancouver Island that distinguish this area. From here you can get interesting perspectives on Goose Spit and the sandy cliffs near Cape Lazo to the north and, to the south, the overlapping mounds of Denman and Hornby islands.

Winds, sun and shade Winds from all directions do pretty much what they want on this exposed, treeless bulge of shoreline. Just as you will feel the wind on a windy day, so, too, you will feel the sun on a sunny day.

Beachcombing The most pleasant, though fairly confined, walking is along the trail to and from the shore. If you don't mind a little slogging over rounded rocks and through patches of vegetation, you can head south and find enormous variations in shoreline on your way. Your walking to the north is considerably more limited, since you come across a striking channel cutting into the shore and leading more than 100 m into the estuary.

Seclusion While your walk begins well within a subdivision, by the time you have gone a few steps you will have gained considerable seclusion and, with each step, will gain more.

51

BARTEL ROAD

A quiet, little-used approach to an unusual shoreline made up of gravel, shorefront vegetation, small inlets, and a large offshore sand-and-gravel bar

Location, signs and parking Less than a kilometre south of Royston, look for a well-developed intersection with left-turn lanes and special yield lanes. Grassi Point Farm Market is a useful landmark. Turn first onto Gartley Road and follow it about 200 m until Gartley Point Road branches to the left. Follow Gartley Point Road about 100 m until the first right, Bartel Road, a short road running close to nearby houses. You will see no signs, but at the end of the road you can park to the side in clear sight of the low shore ahead, beyond an area of grass and low bushes.

Path To get to the shore across the grass, look for a narrow but well-defined footpath curving a short distance onto the shore. The path is largely level and fairly smooth underfoot, manageable even by those with walking difficulties.

Beach The beach will please those collectors of beach experiences who pursue novelty. It will be less pleasing to those who arrive encumbered with a beach bag and stack of celeb mags—this spot isn't comfortable for lounging. The former will be struck first by the chaotic tumble of butter clamshells, beach logs, gravel and shore vegetation on the steeply inclining upper beach. They might speculate, approvingly, on the possibility of using the logs and smallish area of loose sand as a roosting spot. Then they will find themselves intrigued by the way the shoreline seems to have been given a good shakeup. Large areas of shore plants are intersected by deeply scooped-out gravel inlets, and at low tide the whole arrangement is embellished with a large sand-and-gravel bar.

Suitability for children If you are bent on finding a little-visited and unusual bit of shore and find yourself in the company of your children, build into your planning two facts. First, remember that there is a pleasant spot among the logs for a thoroughly delicious little picnic. Second, remember that the shore can be rough going and does require a bit of enthusiastic determination to be explored properly. Leave your toddlers with your parents-in-law, but bring their eager and sure-footed older siblings.

Suitability for groups Mostly because the approach is cramped between neighbouring houses, but also because you won't find much picnic area, even a small group would be much better off picnicking and walking at nearby Gartley Road.

View Your view is framed by Gartley Point to your north and by the sweep of a kilometre-long bay to your south. Across Comox Harbour you can see much of the peninsula extending to Point Holmes and Cape Lazo and, behind it, a short but dramatic section of the coastal mountains and the northern end of Texada Island. Denman Island is the large land mass a few kilometres to your south.

Winds, sun and shade The shore is cooled a little by a northwest wind, though you won't feel it directly. A southeast wind is less circumspect about blowing directly on you. If you are picnicking or mulling on the logs, you don't need to worry about being roasted beyond recognition, but you might need to worry about being a little chilly. During the afternoon, the shadows cast by a few tall trees crawl along the upper shore.

Beachcombing Walking along the unusually configured shore—or drinking in the view—is probably the main reason for choosing to come here. While the uppermost shore, in spite of being given to sliding away underfoot, is easiest, you will want to investigate the water's edge to experience the beach fully. Expect to have to circumnavigate or even wade through some thickets of shore vegetation.

Seclusion You will be forgiven for feeling a few qualms about squeezing between the neighbouring houses en route to the shore. Once there, however, you might be surprised how the slope of the upper beach and the enthusiastic vegetation behind it give you a real sense of seclusion.

52

GARTLEY ROAD

A small, protected bay with easy access from the car, a pebbly upper beach, and a sandy lower beach

Location, signs and parking Less than half a kilometre south of Royston, look for a major intersection with left-turn lanes and yield lanes. Grassi Point Farm Market, looking like a small red barn, is a clear landmark for the intersection. Simply drive to the very end of Gartley Road, about 300 m from the highway. Though the road turns to gravel after it crosses Gartley Point Road, it is well maintained and widens to a broad parking area for at least a dozen cars.

Path You would be hard pressed to find a spot where the term "path" is less appropriate. In fact, from one side of the gravel parking area, you can park virtually on the shore. Needless to say, those with walking difficulties or lugging monstrous picnic buffets could hardly choose a more convenient spot.

Beach This is probably the prettiest beach for many kilometres in either direction. The upper beach is the potpourri of logs and pebbles common to the best beaches on the east coast of the island. While the tide drops no more than 30 or 40 m, it does reveal a lovely band of firm, silvery sand, perfect for barefoot wandering or playing. If you are in quest of this sandy part of the beach, head south where it extends a considerable distance. To the north, the intertidal zone is overgrown with salt-tolerant vegetation and the sand disappears altogether.

Suitability for children Ask any local beach-wise children and they will tell you that this is the best beach for many kilometres around. While low tide does not create a huge sandy area, what it does reveal is perfect for almost every sandy activity an eager child or coaxing parent can imagine. One of the advantages of the tide's not dropping a huge distance, of course, is that at this beach, unlike some of the more spectacular public beaches, a child can splash and cavort at any time of day, at any tide, without facing the prospect of having to walk toward the horizon to find enough water, or, indeed, any water at all. The only drawback of such a small access is that you find no washrooms, picnic tables or the like.

Suitability for groups If a picnicking gaggle of extended family members is prepared for the lack of facilities, they can come to this beach confident that they will find both parking for several cars and comfortable picnicking space among the logs and pebbles for several great-uncles and second cousins twice removed. At low tide, too, especially by heading south, they will find more than enough space for a little high-stakes Frisbee throwing or warm-water swimming.

View To the north, Comox Harbour is largely tucked out of sight, but the tip of Cape Lazo is visible. To the south, the mainly wooded foreshore curves elegantly out to frame the northern tip of Denman Island and at low tide, the spit extending to Sandy Island, known locally as Tree Island. On a clear day, a small but dramatic section of coastal mountains rises behind and to the north of Texada Island.

Winds, sun and shade The most swimmable weather is usually accompanied by a northwest wind, so it is fortunate that this highly swimmable beach is somewhat protected from that wind. When a southeast wind is whipping up whitecaps and raising goosebumps, however, you will not receive much protection. If you want to picnic in full sun, you are best off coming in the first part of the day. If you want to be able to lounge with a stack of newspapers without risk of becoming thoroughly sizzled, come during the afternoon, when large areas of shade, cast by the firs behind the beach, crawl along the upper beach.

Beachcombing You can walk in both directions along this fairly narrow shore. In both directions, too, the shoreline is interestingly indented and varied. To the north, however, expect to find large areas of beach vegetation and, about one kilometre away, expansive shorefront meadows. The Trent River to the north, cutting across the shore, makes walking difficult for more than two kilometres, though. To the south, the going can be rough underfoot unless you stay near the upper beach. Even then, expect to give your ankles a bit of a workout.

Seclusion Unless you come at an absurd time of day or year, you are not likely to be alone at this spot. The charms of the beach have not gone unnoticed by many locals. The picnicking area of the upper beach is largely screened from the house on the left, and the house on the right is set back far enough that you won't feel like an intruder. To the south, the foreshore is wooded for 100 m or so; to the north, houses line the shore.

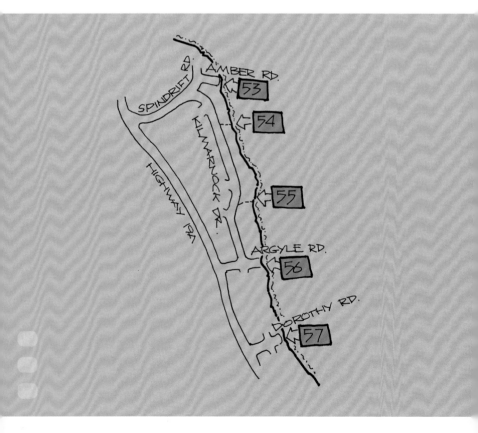

53
AMBER WAY
A bank-top spot with a view toward Sandy Island and information about the Amber Way Biofiltration Wetland

Location, signs and parking Turn off the highway onto Spindrift Road about 4 km south of Royston and 5 km north of Union Bay. After about 250 m you'll come across the intersection with Kilmarnock Road and, almost immediately after, Amber Way, clearly signposted. (If you are using Google Maps, be warned: Amber Way is shown as coming directly off the highway about half a kilometre north of where it actually does.) Unlike many other access spots in this area, this one is instantly obvious as a way to the shore. Drive the 70 m to the end of the road and park in one of the several spots in the gravel off the side or end of the pavement. Of the three signs posted here, two of them might not arouse huge interest, one of them prohibiting staying overnight and one ghoulishly warning of the dangers of contaminated shellfish. The third, however, sadly weather-worn, is a detailed, illustrated guide to the Amber Way Biofiltration Wetland.

Path Although you can park virtually on the beach, actually getting yourself onto the shore 3 m below you can be a bit of a trick. A kind or determined soul has chopped some rough steps into the steep dirt bank. As long as these are not slippery with mud, they are easily manageable for most but could be a significant difficulty for those less agile.

Beach The uppermost section of beach is the most conventionally attractive. A pod of beached logs, nestled among loose gravel, makes an attractive spot for sitting and spending a little time. Come at high tide, though, if you want to experience the shore at its prettiest. At low tide, a tiny streambed of gravel and boulders winds through patches of salt-tolerant beach vegetation to an indented shoreline. The tide does not expose a large section of shore, but an interesting gravel bar extends southward toward deeper water.

Suitability for children It is not impossible that a curious and nimble child would enjoy coming here with adults to explore this unusual bit of shore. Most children, however, would see this as a diversion, not a day at the beach.

Suitability for groups This is a good spot for an interesting stop, not for a lengthy visit. The comparatively easy parking, unusual shoreline and informative poster could make for a refreshing stop on an afternoon of beach exploring. Wildlife viewers, especially at high tide, could well appreciate the slight vantage point given by the elevation of the bank.

View It is amazing how even the few metres' elevation of the small bank gives depth to the view. The foliage and inset shore, however, mean that your view is largely confined to the north end of Texada and a few of the coastal mountains to its north. To the south, you can gain an interesting perspective on the north of Denman Island and off its tip, Sandy Island Marine Park.

Winds, sun and shade Because you are tucked into a small dip in the shore, from the upper beach, at least, you will feel reasonably protected from the winds scooting by a short distance away. You won't find much shade here but are unlikely to stay long enough to bake.

Beachcombing The shore is level in both directions for many kilometres. If you are interested in a broad swath of it at low tide, head south. If you do plan to investigate this little-visited section of coast, be prepared to cope with the lumps and bumps of an uneven—though unthreatening—surface.

Seclusion You are unlikely to bump up against other visitors. This is not an area of coast that attracts lots of sand-loving beachgoers. At the same time, you will find houses dotting the shore no matter how far you wander.

54
KILMARNOCK DRIVE—NORTH
A pretty, wooded path to a level shore of beach logs, tall grass and rounded boulders

Location, signs and parking In the absence of any striking landmarks along this straight, wooded section of highway, look for Spindrift Road about 4 km south of Royston and about 5 km north of Union Bay. After about 300 m along Spindrift, take the first right onto Kilmarnock Drive. Look for a house numbered 4617 and, nearly opposite, a wooded lot. This spot seems to be designated as "Harby Road" on the local zoning map, but as yet it is only a strip of undeveloped land. You will see no welcoming or prohibiting signs, just a narrow but well-beaten track.

Path The path leads about 40 m through a roughly level treed lot of wild roses, swordferns and large firs. Although the path is easy going, be prepared to climb over a barricade of beach logs to get onto the shore itself.

Beach The cluster of logs along the upper beach invites perching while you whip out your binoculars or sketch pad. Don't expect to find any other comfortable spot to picnic, though, since beach grass and boulders of various sizes and colours cover the entire upper beach. The tide does not withdraw nearly as far here as at nearby access points to the south.

Suitability for children Adventurous children could well enjoy a short visit here if the alternative is spending an afternoon shopping for school clothes. They might be less than enthusiastic, though, if the alternative is going to a "proper" beach. If you decide to have children accompany you while you visit this spot, make sure they are sure-footed enough that they can bounce from boulder to boulder without coming to grief. You might also want to remind them of the pleasures of hunting out wary critters.

Suitability for groups It would be possible to bring a small group here, but it's not obvious why you would want to.

View from Kilmarnock

View The view directly in front is dominated by the north end of Texada Island, at this point comparatively low and undulating. This view, however, is framed on the north by the bluffs of Cape Lazo and to the south, the intriguing combination of Seal Islets, Sandy (Tree) Island, and the low-tide spit leading to Denman Island.

Winds, sun and shade Winds from both the northwest and the southeast can knock your easel about but, since they blow more across the beach than directly onto it, you won't feel their full brunt. If you arrive in mid afternoon and ensconce yourself on a log on the upper beach, you are likely to find yourself, for good or ill, dappled with shade. Otherwise, expect full sun.

Beachcombing Don't imagine for a minute that you can stride comfortably along the water's edge. You can't. What you can do, however, is prod around among large boulders near the low-tide line, or, by the high-tide line, stroll the 100 m or so north that allows you to round the peninsula, where the view along the coast suddenly opens up before you.

Seclusion Because the access path arrives through a robustly overgrown flurry of bush, you will find considerable privacy on the upper shore. Since the shore in both directions is dense with houses, however, don't come here looking for the experience of a wilderness beach.

55

KILMARNOCK DRIVE—SOUTH
A well-hidden route to a little-visited rocky shore with views of Comox, Cape Lazo and Sandy Island

Location, signs and parking Since Kilmarnock Drive runs parallel to the shore, you can reach its northern end by turning off the highway onto Spindrift Road or its southern end by turning off the highway onto Argyle Road. In either case, you will have to keep your eyes well peeled along a wooded section of highway about 5 km north of Union Bay, since you will see no other obvious landmarks to indicate that you are close to either turnoff. This particular access spot is located beside the house numbered 4702. You will see a car-width grassy path leading through the woods toward the shore, but no signs indicating that this is public access. You will have to park along the shoulder of Kilmarnock Drive, since you will find no other clear parking spot.

Path A level and compacted gravel-and-grass track leads about 60 m toward the shore. Near its end, it opens out a little to a grassy area so that you can view the shore through the frame of small, overhanging maples. Getting onto the shore itself can be a little less easy, depending on conditions, since you might have to beat a track through thickets of driftwood and knee-high vegetation on the upper shore.

Beach You won't find many picnicking or sitting possibilities here. For many metres the upper shore is covered with salt-tolerant vegetation. At low tide the water recedes more than 200 m, revealing a stretch of gravel and pebbles, and surprisingly few barnacles, interspersed with a few patches of vegetation and occasional boulders.

Suitability for children If you come to this spot, it will be to explore a little-visited section of shore and take a few photographs of a very pretty view. Thus, with a child in tow, you are best off planning this as just a stop on the way to another, more child-friendly spot. Wandering out toward the low-tide line or along the shore looking for interesting pieces of driftwood or shell, prodding under rocks and the like will divert a curious child. For a while.

Suitability for groups Although space along the shoulder of Kilmarnock isn't capacious, a few cars can find spots there. While most groups—and that means picnickers, sunbathers and swimmers—will find little point in coming here, those interested in exploring an unusual piece of shore with lovely views might come for an hour or two of wandering or sketching.

View From the vantage point of this section of coast, midway between the tip of Denman and Cape Lazo, you will find your eye drawn not just to Willemar Bluffs to your north, but also to the lovely contours of Sandy Island (aka Tree Island) directly across. Unlike spots farther south for many kilometres, this one also provides, in clear weather, a great view of a dramatic slice of coastal mountains.

Winds, sun and shade A wind from the northwest scoots along the shore more or less parallel to it. While southeast winds often seem less strong here than at many points farther south, they are not buffered by any protective trees or banks. On a hot day, you could find a shady spot under the shorefront maples to set up an easel, but you shouldn't come to this spot expecting shade to bathe the shore.

Beachcombing Any visitors to the spot will find most enjoyment if they come prepared to wander along the shore. Although walking is easy immediately in front of the access spot, it can be a little lumpy in either direction, so bring appropriate footwear. You will probably find walking to the north most interesting because the shoreline in that direction is more varied.

Seclusion You don't need to worry about feeling as if you are intruding into a local's front yard as you come through the trees to the shore. You will find, though, that as you walk down the beach you are in the middle of a strip of shorefront houses, only occasionally screened by patches of trees or vegetation.

56

ARGYLE ROAD
A car-width compacted gravel
track leading directly onto
a gravel shore, used for
launching boats

Location, signs and parking In the absence of obvious landmarks along this straight stretch of wooded highway, you are best off taking your cue from Union Bay, just under 5 km south. The Argyle Road sign is more or less clearly visible from the highway. Drive straight ahead, crossing Kilmarnock Drive, and park in one of several spots available at the paved end of the road. Be careful not to block the gravel track at the end of the paved area, since this track is clearly used by occasional vehicles visiting the spot. In fact, you might want to make use of this track yourself if you happen to have a pair of brightly coloured kayaks on your roof. Of the two signs posted here in the middle of a robust blackberry patch, the one telling you not to dump refuse is likely to be less relevant to your activities here than the one telling you of the dangers of contaminated shellfish.

Path Since you can drive directly onto the shore, you can guess how firm and level the track from the end of the road is.

Beach This is one of the few beaches along this coast not suitable for picnicking. Although it is level and capacious, the upper shore is made up largely of fist-sized rocks backed by a heavy fringe of tall grass and other salt-tolerant vegetation. Farther down, larger boulders are interspersed with a few clusters of huge rocks. Enterprising and determined folk have cleared a strip a considerable distance toward the low-water line so that small boats can be launched here. Should you arrive with kayaks, eager to dip your paddles, you will probably want to check your trusty tide tables. The lowest tides expose about 150 m of shore, negotiable but not exactly convenient.

Suitability for children If you come to this spot in pursuit of adult interests—there are some—you can set your resilient and curious child loose without worrying overmuch about injury or even boredom. Still, if you come to this beach, it will be for your sake, not your child's.

Suitability for groups Three types of group might come here—kayakers, birdwatchers and artists. Such groups will find easy parking and will not feel intrusive, as they might at the similar spot on nearby Argyle Road.

View The lovely and varied view is one of the chief attractions of this spot, probably best enjoyed at high tide. This section of shore is the southernmost area—until you approach Parksville—where your sea view can include many mountains. In addition, the shore of Comox to the north leading to Cape Lazo and, to the south, Sandy Island (or, in local parlance, Tree Island) and the spit at the north of Denman provide lots of picturesque detail to any sketch or photograph.

Winds, sun and shade You are likely to find yourself a little sheltered from the strongest blasts of a northwest wind, but not so for a southeast wind. Since no tall trees grow along the shore, and since the shore is nearly flat, you will find no shade.

Beachcombing Walking is easy for a considerable distance in either direction, though it can be a little rough underfoot at several spots. You will probably find walking north more interesting than walking south. To the south, around 2 km distant, you will bump up against a "booming ground," where logs are grouped into giant rafts, or booms, to be towed to mills. To the north, you will find that the beach becomes increasingly wide at low tide until you round a corner and suddenly find the shore changing character dramatically.

Seclusion Given that this access brings you to the middle of a well-settled residential area, you will be surprised that you have considerable seclusion at this particular bit of shore. One hundred metres or so to the north, you will see several highly visible shorefront houses, but not to the south, where a screen of low trees provides an impenetrable barrier—at least to the upper shore.

57
DOROTHY ROAD

A gentle slope through an area of grass to a pebbly upper shore and a cleared strip to the water's edge, suitable for launching kayaks

Location, signs and parking Approximately 4 km north of Union Bay, in a lightly treed area, look for the signs saying Dorothy Road and No Exit. After about 75 m along Dorothy Road, you will cross David Road. Drive another 50 m along the grass-and-gravel roadbed with a clear view of the shore. You will find parking for several cars near the end of the road. No signs are posted to warn you or prohibit you, but you can guess what you should and shouldn't do in the middle of a residential area.

Path You will understandably feel a little odd, since no fence or hedge separates the road area from the neighbours' lawn on the left. A clear and easily traversable grassy area leads you down a gentle slope to a nearly overgrown path through high beach grass to the shore, some 20 or 30 m away.

Beach If you are bent on devouring a novel or a portable banquet, you are best off turning to the right, where the upper beach of pebbles and shell fragments is largest. Since only a very few logs come to rest on this beach, you will have to make do without back support. The lower beach has obviously been what anthropologists describe as "culturally modified." Enterprising souls—with strong backs and lots of determination—have pushed aside hundreds of large round boulders, leaving a broad strip of golf-ball-sized gravel more or less to the water's edge. Poles implanted on either side of this strip have no doubt been useful in guiding boats back to the strip when the tide is in. Since the tide doesn't drop very far, kayakers could use this cleared strip if they are headed toward Tree Island.

Suitability for children Both the approach to the shore and the shore itself make reaching it, and getting about on it, child's play—so to speak. Even so, this is not the kind of place where you can come for a pleasant visit without worrying about your child's comfort or amusement. Beach play is possible, but its pleasures a little too subtle for most children.

Suitability for groups It would have to be a very discreet group indeed that would not be intrusive in coming to the middle of this dense residential area.

View Collectors and painters of unusual views will want to put this spot on their list of places to visit. Most striking in the foreground is an intriguing cluster of pilings a short distance offshore. Most scenic is the northern tip of Denman Island, known as Longbeck Point, and, to the north, the island and its islets connected at low tide to Denman. Officially called Sandy Island Marine Provincial Park, the island has long been called Tree Island by locals. The islets to the north are, appropriately, called the Seal Islets.

Winds, sun and shade Whether refreshing on a hot day, or chilling on a cool day, both a northwest wind and southeast wind can be felt here, albeit neither head-on. On a cool but sunny day, you don't need to worry about avoiding shade, since there is none!

Beachcombing If you want to do a little beach exploring, you are probably best off turning over low-tide rocks in quest of sea snails, shore crabs and the like rather than striding along the shore. You can walk a considerable distance along the shore to the north, but you will be doing so along a fairly lumpy beach and in front of a virtually unbroken strip of shorefront houses. To the south, in less than 1 km you will come across booming grounds and, beyond, a large estuary.

Seclusion For many, the chief drawback of this spot is its exposure to shorefront houses, resulting from the lack of screening bushes or trees. On the other hand, it is unlikely that, if you do settle down with your watercolour set or munchable novel, you will have to make small talk with other visitors to this little-known and little-used spot.

58
UNION BAY BOAT LAUNCH
A historically interesting roadside spot with picnic table and launching area

Location, signs and parking There is no map for this spot, since it is right on the highway. Smack dab in the middle of "downtown" Union Bay and immediately opposite the historic building that houses the post office, the Union Bay Boat Launch is clearly signposted. On a summer's day you are likely to find lots of vehicles and trailers in the large gravel parking area, as hopeful fishermen head for the open sea. Of the various signs here, some relating to the use of the concrete launching ramp, most interesting to visitors are the ones providing information about the history of Union Bay and the giant wharf that used to ship coal around the world.

Path You don't need to worry about a path to the beach since, of course, you can drive your vehicle to the launching spot. Note that there is a rough and ready washroom in the parking area.

Beach This area is divided into three sections, one to the north of the breakwater, the breakwater itself and one to the south of the breakwater. Head to the area north of the breakwater if your primary purpose is to get your eager little kayak into the water. Many boaters use the compact gravel slope and little bay beside the breakwater, rather than the concrete ramp, to launch their trailered boats, but the spot is obviously good for kayaks as well. The second section, the breakwater, provides a level viewing spot and picnic table alongside a giant propeller displayed as a historical curiosity. To the south of the breakwater, it is possible to make your way to the shore as well, though the gravel beach is not particularly attractive.

Suitability for children This is a good place to bring children for a short visit, but it is hardly the place to spend a summer's afternoon if you are looking for prime beaching activities. If you want a good spot to break up a long driving trip, stopping will give your hyperactive children a good opportunity not just to use the washroom but also to clamber around the breakwater, marvel at the giant propeller and throw a few rocks at the beach to the south of the breakwater.

Suitability for groups Only a kayaking group or group wanting to stretch their legs midway through a long car trip by wandering around the historical bits and pieces would choose to come here. The picnic table could well be built into your plans for leavening such a car trip.

View By far the most interesting sights here are not of expansive vistas, but of close-up curiosities. To the list of those already described, add the black slag promontory across the tiny bay and the historic buildings of Union Bay itself.

Winds, sun and shade The little harbour by the launching strip is well protected from all winds, while the top of the breakwater is exposed to all. The little beach north of the breakwater is largely sheltered from northwest winds by the breakwater, a fact to keep in mind if parts of your breakwater-top picnic become airborne. On the other hand, on a cool day, you don't need to worry about being immersed in chilly shade, since you won't find any.

Beachcombing The most obvious feature beckoning shore explorers is the black promontory of coal slag across the little bay. Since, however, visitors are not permitted to trespass on this area, you will have to content yourself with a little lightweight strolling along the shore in front of Union Bay itself.

Seclusion Seclusion is the last quality you should be expecting if you come to Union Bay. You will find none. Decide in advance that you will enjoy watching the comings to and fro of little boats, however, and you won't miss the lack of seclusion.

59

BAYNES SOUND REST AREA

Not just lots of facilities for breaking up a drive, but also a pleasant access to shore-front views and activities

Location, signs and parking There is no map for this spot, since it is along the edge of the highway. Midway between Union Bay and Buckley Bay and about 3.5 km from either, Baynes Sound Rest Area is clearly visible as a long paved parking strip running parallel to the highway immediately above the shore. This area is bristling with signs, some of them prohibiting various kinds of behaviour, some of them informative. Many of these are ones you might expect, forbidding fires, demanding that dogs be kept on leash and so on. The one to note that is most likely to affect your planning is that forbidding the collecting of oysters because the shore here is a commercial oyster lease. The most interesting sign is the one that displays photographs and information about Union Bay, the "friendly port" a few kilometres north.

Path Alongside the parking area but somewhat screened from it by the drop in the bank is a series of picnic tables eagerly awaiting picnickers. The large and well-maintained washrooms are probably the chief attraction for most visitors casually driving by.

You can get onto the shore at a few spots, none of them demanding more than a few metres' stroll down a slight incline through gravel. Kayakers could easily launch their craft here but should come at high tide to avoid walking through the commercial oyster lease.

Beach The beach is reasonably well screened from the highway and the parking area by small firs and shorefront bushes. Because the shoreline is protected from large waves, the upper beach is largely covered with beach grass and other salt-tolerant plants. In a few places, though, cleared areas of small gravel and crushed seashells would make pleasant areas to while away a snack's worth of beaching time. Except for these spots, however, the gradually sloping shore is largely made up of rounded boulders, some of them huge.

Suitability for children This spot is a good one to keep in mind if your car-bound children have far more energy than they know what to do with. Here you can easily pull over en route to dinner at your in-laws and set your children free to jump off boulders, hurl a few rocks and do their best to obey your instructions to keep their feet dry. The clean and easily accessible toilets make an obviously child-friendly feature. Still, this is not the kind of spot you would seek out for an afternoon's outing with your children.

Suitability for groups As with kids, so with groups—at least up to a point. For most cavalcades of friends or family, this is the kind of place to pull over for a little sea air and a few shorefront calisthenics to break up a long trip. Some groups, however, could well plan to come to this spot. For birders, photographers and watercolourists, this is a good choice. The combination of parking and park facilities along with some truly lovely views along the shoreline make this an easy and attractive destination for such specialized outings.

View While most features of the view are distant and therefore not hugely dramatic, put together they invite lots of photos or, at least, gentle oohs and ahhs. The largely treed and curving shoreline, particularly to the south, extends for several kilometres. Far to the north, the steep shores of Cape Lazo, the intriguing profile of Sandy Island and the low-tide spit connecting it to Denman Island are especially appealing. Many visitors will be intrigued by the herring skiffs and other commercial fishing boats often moored along this stretch of coast.

Winds, sun and shade You won't find much protection from wind or shade here. The winds, however, run more or less parallel to the shore.

Beachcombing Given the presence of commercial oyster leases along the shore, any tromping should be done near the high-water line. In any case, the rounded boulders can make strolling a little more of an adventure than you might intend. This is a good spot to stretch your legs after and before too much time in a car; it is not a great spot to plan a shorefront expedition.

Seclusion Thank heavens for the screening properties of the ubiquitous Douglas fir. Although the highway is only a few metres away from the shore, a dense band of shorefront vegetation can give you enormous visual relief from the procession of cars. You may be surprised, too, how few people make their way down to the shore rather than just use the facilities and push onwards. Still, you would be more than a little sanguine to seek this spot out for a secluded hour or two of contemplation or conversation.

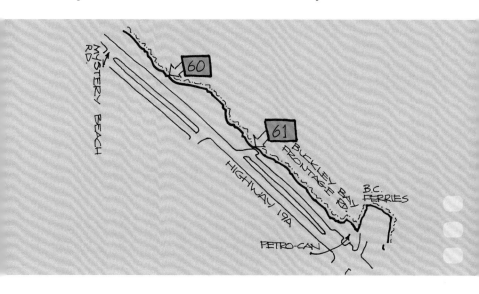

60
JOE WALKER COMMUNITY PARK
A narrow strip of beautiful forest and rocky beach with trails and park facilities

Location, signs and parking Although this park is right beside the highway, you will have to have your wits and eyes finely tuned to find it. Located about 1.5 km north of the ferry to Denman Island in Buckley Bay, the park has no sign clearly visible from the road. Your best bet in finding it is to watch for Mystery Beach Road if you are approaching from the north and McKay Road if you are approaching from the south. About 500 m from both roads, the entrance to the park is identifiable by a widened patch on the shoulder of the highway and by a bit of metal handrailing visible above the surrounding bushes. These subtle clues are, strangely, all you have to go on! The instant you pull over onto the correct spot, however, you will see many additional confirmations that this is the spot you have been looking for. The first sign visible, unique to this park, is a cartoon-illustrated plea not to cut or "prune" trees! A large, hand-carved, wooden sign bearing the name of the park and the additional words Regional District of Comox-Strathcona is visible only once you have walked to the centre of the park near the shore. In addition, you will see nailed to a tree a detailed notice of various dangers associated with collecting shellfish. Oddly, this is not one of the ubiquitous Department of Fisheries notices, but one produced by the Centre for Disease Control. A final, touching sign, thanks one Joe Millard for his work in maintaining the park and, interestingly, identifies this to be Mystery Beach. Mystery Beach is also, by the way, the name of the small subdivision directly across the highway but almost completely screened from it by trees.

Path While paths lead through the forest of cedars and firs, beachgoers will be interested primarily in the four concrete steps, with a handrail, leading down from the shoulder of the road to a gently sloping dirt track a dozen or so metres before another short set of concrete steps and the picnic area. Here you will find several picnic tables, a picnic bench and a large concrete barbecue protected from West Coast drizzle by a solid wooden shelter. A sign points to toilets in the woods. A metal fire ring has been placed on the gravelly beach area, but it doesn't seem to be much used.

Beach Pleasant though it be, the beach itself would not be much of a reason to seek this spot out were it not for the park facilities on offer. An area of shore grass has been cleared, so some people may enjoy sitting on this patch of gravel, but most picnickers will no doubt prefer to open their Tupperware on the picnic tables. The lowest tides drop less than 100 m, so the water is usually not very far away. Rounded boulders and rocks cover most of the lower beach.

Suitability for children The park facilities more than the shore itself make this a good place to bundle your children. After all, it counts for a lot that you have available not just picnic tables and toilets but a large barbecue and—as long as there is no fire closure—a good spot for making incendiary devices out of marshmallows. As for beach activities, you will, of course, have to count out sandcastles and barefoot scampering. Don't overlook the rollicking good fun that can be had with constructing rock castles (strange, but true), hunting for the largest or most strikingly coloured crab, or skipping the world's best skipping stone.

Suitability for groups The same features that make this a good spot for children also make it a good spot for a group. The same features of the beach that make it an imperfect spot for certain kinds of children also make it an imperfect spot for certain kinds of groups. In addition, build into your reckoning that the only parking is along the shoulder of a busy road (albeit an accommodatingly wide shoulder at this point).

View This is not the kind of view that pulls your seeking eyes toward distant horizons or distant peaks. It is, however, like all views on the east coast of the island, an interesting combination of island shapes and foreshore. Because you are in the centre of a very gently curving shore and because Denman Island is directly across Baynes Sound from you, your view is made up almost entirely of low treed banks and rocky shores.

Winds, sun and shade Both a northwest wind and a southeast wind cruise by the shore at something of an angle, but both can feel more than a little fresh. The amount of shade you will find varies with time of day and position on the beach. The good news is that you can be as finicky as you like with your demands. Though the morning is the sunniest and the afternoon the shadiest, you can arrive at virtually any time of day and find both.

Beachcombing If you want to walk off that carbonized marshmallow carefully prepared for you by your youngest and dearest, you may find the forest paths the most comfortable. You can walk for considerable distance in either direction along the shore, though the upper shore is smoothest. In addition, be aware that the highway is never more than a few metres away, though often screened by trees.

Seclusion If your ears are tuned into road noise, then the swoosh of cars through the trees could dispatch any impressions you have of solitude. If you can ignore the sounds, though, you can enjoy a total sense of solitude on a long stretch of forested shore where you are likely to be the only visitor. Take advantage of that in all the ways your little heart desires.

61 BUCKLEY BAY FRONTAGE ROAD

A good spot for launching kayaks or even small boats from trailers on a compacted gravel shore

Location, signs and parking While some maps identify this road as Frontage Road, expect to see "Buckley Bay Frtg Rd" on the road sign. Getting onto the road is best done not from the highway itself but from the north end of the Petro-Can station by the Buckley Bay Ferry. The spot you are looking for is almost 1 km north of the Petro-Can station, where Frontage Road takes a sharp turn away from the water. The only sign you will see here is one bearing a no-parking symbol. Since the words "here to corner" have been covered with tape, it is not very clear where exactly it is that you are not to park.

Path You will find no path to speak of, but a well-used dirt track slopes from the paved road for a few metres directly onto the compacted gravel shore. This easy access to the shore, in combination with the characteristics of the beach, makes launching a kayak a breeze.

Beach Evergreens extend to a band of salt-tolerant beach vegetation on the upper shore. Because of this vegetation, you won't find a good area for picnicking or sitting on the shore. You won't even find a good, solid beach log on which to plant your rump. Much of the lower beach is covered with rocks, mostly fist-sized but in some cases full-on boulders. Enterprising (or desperate) souls have cleared a car-width track to the shore. The comparative smoothness of this strip, in combination with a tide that doesn't go out very far, means that kayakers will find this an easy spot to get their panting little boats into the protected waters of Buckley Bay.

Suitability for children You wouldn't seek out this spot to reward your deserving child with a spot of beach frolic. If you are here anyway and happen to have a bouncing child in need of a good romp, you will find that the shore can offer up several amusements. The boulders harbour weird and wonderful critters; the smaller rocks make perfect water-bound missiles; the water itself, never distant, is just as wet here as at even the sandiest beach. And that, for many children, is more than enough.

Suitability for groups Apart from the oddly ambiguous parking situation, this would be a good choice for a clutch of kayakers eager to make up a flotilla. Most other sorts of groups would prefer a spot where the picnicking and beachcombing are more inviting.

View The view is made up primarily of two bookending elements. One is the shoreline of Denman Island directly opposite, just under 2 km distant. The other is the gentle curve of treed shore embraced by points of land both to the north and to the south.

Winds, sun and shade Neither a northwest wind nor a southeast wind is as unchecked here as it is at many more exposed parts of the coast. Because the shore faces northeast and is slightly indented, it is partially sheltered from wind. The upper beach does get a little shade in the late afternoon, but since it isn't a very desirable spot for sitting anyway, the presence or absence of shade is more or less irrelevant.

Beachcombing A walk along the upper shore, above the boulders and occasional oyster lease, is easy in both directions, but not especially enticing. To the south, you will be walking more or less in the front yards of houses and after a few hundred metres will run up against the ferry to Denman Island. To the north, after a short stretch of houses, you will be walking close to the shore-hugging highway.

Seclusion Given the proximity to houses, the access spot is amazingly secluded. You are subject neither to being seen nor seeing. Now, if only you could find a pleasant little patch on which to while away a sunny hour or two.

From the Tozer Road access (62), you will see the little ferry between Buckley Bay and Denman Island constantly plying the waters of Baynes Sound. Like the ferry from Campbell River to Quadra Island, this ferry is your key to a whole world of hidden beaches. Denman Island has some beautiful and intriguing beaches, and Hornby Island has even more. Some are small sandstone coves with pebble shores, and some are gorgeous stretches of sand, among the most beautiful you will find on planet Earth. Not just hidden beaches down forested tracks but also large parks abound: Fillongley and Boyle Point parks on Denman, Helliwell and Tribune Bay parks on Hornby. Some beaches, like that at Whaling Station Bay, are easily spotted but best visited from well-hidden side routes. Full information about the beaches of both of these islands appears in volume four in this series of books, *Secret Beaches of the Salish Sea.*

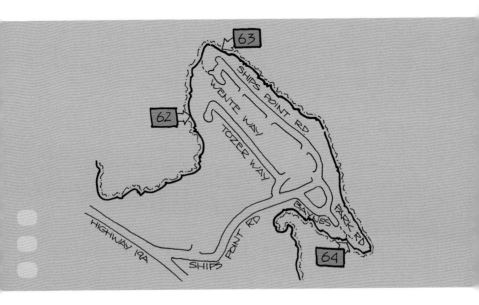

62

TOZER ROAD

An unusual, well-hidden access with striking views of the Cowie Creek (formerly Cougar Creek) estuary and Beaufort Range

Location, signs and parking Using the Fanny Bay Hall as a landmark, turn onto Ships Point Road. After approximately 1.5 km, turn left onto Tozer Road. After another 1.5 km, Tozer Road takes a sharp left and comes to a halt in a large turnaround. You will find room around the shoulder for more cars than will ever find their way here. At the trailhead you will see a sign with the icon of a pair of binoculars, your clue to the central interest here, the Fanny Bay Conservation Unit.

Path The level path of crushed gravel leads about 50 m between a meadow on the left and, on the right, a screen of trees between you and the house behind it. As you approach the shore you will see a trail running along the top of what locals call "the dike."

Beach Select this spot for the two qualities for which it is outstanding— wildlife viewing and soaking up the views of mountains and sunsets. Selecting this spot just for its beach would be a little odd, though the upper beach of shell fragments could well be used for a minor picnic and rest stop, particularly if you don't mind the small concrete retaining wall of the house on your right. Low tide exposes an estuary of several hundred metres of gravel and muddy sand.

Suitability for children Though they no doubt exist, children would be hard to find who would want to come to a spot that is best suited to holding still and just looking.

Suitability for groups Bring a group by all means, but let it be a small group of naturalists, photographers, artists or walkers. The noisy gabble of eager picnickers would be at odds with the tranquility of the scenery.

View It is what you see that makes your journey here so worthwhile. For studying the birdlife, come at high tide and bring binoculars to focus on the throngs of waterfowl (surf scoters are the most common). From September to May you will hear lots of "ork-ork-ing" and see the dark forms of California sea lions across the bay. Springtime, when the mountains are still gleaming with snow that catches sunrises and sunsets, is another choice time to visit. To the north you can see not just the Beaufort Range tapering into the distance but also the sea meadows and forests along the shores of Fanny Bay toward Union Bay. On the other side of Baynes Sound, Denman Island extends several kilometres toward its northern tip.

Winds, sun and shade Look to your easel if a northwest wind is howling, since it howls straight down Baynes Sound. If the wind is from the southeast, however, the rest of the world might be blown to bits and you will be witnessing the stillness of a millpond. Throughout the day, as long as the sun is unobscured by clouds, full sunlight is on the shore.

Beachcombing You can walk along the upper shore to the north if you are careful to keep well above the oyster tenure. The best walking, however, is along the trails through the sea meadows and along the dike.

Seclusion The access trail brings you to the edge of a residential subdivision. Thus, while you have houses on one side, on the other you have a soul-stirring sense of natural spaces and blessed quiet—except perhaps for the barking of sea lions!

While you're here, you might want to pull over on Fanny Bay Road where you see the sign for the Fanny Bay Conservation Boundary. Here you can get some unique perspectives on the roadside sea meadows.

63
WENTE WAY
Shoreside parking in woods by a gently sloping upper beach of crushed shell, with good views of the Beaufort Range and sunsets

Location, signs and parking Turn onto Ships Point Road by the Fanny Bay Hall and stay on it for just over 3 km. At the virtual end of the winding road you will see the Wente Way road sign and the road itself curving left. At the bend in Wente Way you can turn right, though you may have the uncomfortable feeling you are in private property. In fact, the whole wooded area between houses is access land, though you will see scant places to park. The road leading directly onto the shore is used by vehicles managing the oyster tenure that occupies the entire shoreline of Ships Point. While being careful not to block this road by parking here, you might nevertheless wish to drive far enough forward that you can enjoy an apple fritter or two as the first course of a foul-weather car picnic. The only signs are an official-looking one telling you not to camp or park overnight and an unofficial-looking one, painted onto a large circular saw blade and bearing the words OYSTER LEASE TO HIGH WATER, KEEP OFF.

Path Both routes to the shore could hardly be easier. You can choose either to walk down the dirt roadway or to take the wide, even path for a more gradually sloping route.

Beach The uppermost beach is a dry, loose mix of coarse sand, pebbles and shell fragments, though with none or few of the beach logs typical of nearby beaches. This is the part of the beach that you can use for picnicking or spending a sun-soaked afternoon with a fat novel. The rest of the beach, mostly firmly packed pebbles and small gravel and about 75 m wide at the lowest tide, is off limits, since it is part of the oyster tenure.

Suitability for children Given the magnetic pull that water exerts over even the most restrained children, you are best off coming here without children. Since they, like you, will have to stay on the uppermost fringe of beach, they are unlikely to be happy for long, or at least, any longer than it takes to devour an oatmeal cookie or two.

Suitability for groups Although this beach is backed by a large chunk of access land, the restriction on using the beach below the high-tide line means that the only group likely to be happy here is one that is content to stay put with their sketch pads, camera tripods and binoculars.

View It is really the extraordinary view that will bring you here. This is one of very few spots on the coast where you can look back onto the northern part of the Beaufort Range tapering toward Cumberland. Along the shore you will also see the curve of Fanny Bay beyond Cowie Creek estuary and the wooded shores toward Buckley Bay. On a clear day you can even see the sand Willemar Bluffs in Comox, framed by the southern shore of Denman Island. Between, expect to see the little ferry plying back and forth between Denman Island and Vancouver Island. During the winter months you are likely not only to hear the din of barking California sea lions on the logs in Fanny Bay but also to see them cruising by the shore. Come in the evening for perhaps the best sunset-viewing spot between Campbell River and Deep Bay.

Winds, sun and shade Since northwest winds funnel down Baynes Sound, you will feel them, whether refreshingly or chillingly. If almost all beaches along the strait are shivering with the blasts of a strong southeast wind, however, you can come here and bake on a windless beach. Though you can find patches of shade on the shore during the first part of the day, by the afternoon the beach is in full sun, so you will have to move up under the trees if you need protection.

Beachcombing It is both easy and pleasant to walk a full circle route along the regular surface of the uppermost beach. If you turn right along the shore, you will come to Ship's Point Regional Park about 2. 5 km distant and, if you like, return along Baynes Drive and Ships Point Road. The trick, as you will have figured out by now, is keeping to the uppermost fringe of beach created by winter waves and above regular high tides.

Seclusion On one side is a private residence, on the other a bed and breakfast house. In fact, since the trees crowd forward, from most spots on the edge of the beach you will neither see nor be seen.

64
SHIP'S POINT PARK
A quiet, peninsula-tip park, with unusually mixed shore surfaces and views in nearly all directions

Location, signs and parking A first step in sorting out where you're going is recognizing the diversity in the naming of your destination. You will be looking for a sign saying Ship's Point Park by going down a road called Ships Point Road, on a chunk of geography called Ship Peninsula. Ships Point Road leaves the highway between Mud Bay and Fanny Bay opposite a prominent landmark, the Fanny Bay Community Hall. Drive about 1.5 km before turning right onto Baynes Drive. About 200 m down this loop road you will see Park Road, and, within a few metres, a large, carved wooden sign with the name of the park. You should park here, though a dirt track, used by oyster farmers, leads directly through the park and onto the shore itself. In fact, one prominent sign tells you that "the taking or destroying of shellfish," unsurprisingly, should not be on your agenda of activities here. Other signs tell you (graphically) that your funmobile will be towed if you park between a very liberally minded 11 p.m. and 5 a.m. As for dog owners, you, too, are asked to be responsible, by cleaning up after Aloysius Cuddlecake III.

Path You can choose one of several routes to the shore, depending on whether you want to face east, west, or somewhere between. All routes are level, smooth and short. Those with walking difficulties will be happy here, and all the more because a park bench is positioned virtually on the shore. One of the paths, on the west side of the small promontory, leads to a washroom—though it is best described as "rustic."

Beach While the ingredients for the beach are predictable, the effect is not. In fact, you won't find any other shore quite like this one anywhere. At low tide, nearly 400 m of gently shelving shale and compacted gravel dotted with patches of huge boulders extends from the tip of the promontory. The shore tapers to just over 100 m on the northeast side of the promontory, but the west side is likewise vast. The upper beach, especially at the tip of the promontory, is oddly attractive. Composed of decorative patches of salt-tolerant vegetation and large areas of near-white sand and crushed shell, it invites some heavy-duty lounging.

Suitability for children This isn't really a swimming beach except at the highest tides, when the water does become wonderfully warm. For any child, though, with the smallest trace of curiosity and energy, the flat surfaces of the broad shore encourage lots of running, climbing and shell collecting.

Suitability for groups If you have a group of friends who are beach connoisseurs and would enjoy a striking and unusual spot, you will win bouquets of kudos by bringing them here. The park can't accommodate more than a few cars full of visitors, however, and doesn't offer the most conventional kinds of beach experience.

View You won't find many spots along this coast that offer quite such a range of views. From the view up Baynes Sound between Ship Peninsula and Denman Island, past Chrome Island lighthouse and the southern strait, around to the tapering skyline of the Beaufort Range, the view is richly varied. Only at Deep Bay and the approach to Cape Lazo will you get a similar perspective onto the main landforms of the

Vancouver Island area. It would be criminal to forget your camera on this outing.

Winds, sun and shade Given the sweep of the shoreline around the promontory, you can get just about as much wind and shade as you like, depending on the time of day and the direction of the wind. If a south-east wind is chillier than you can handle, however, you might have to tuck well up into the trees on the west side of the peninsula.

Beachcombing Along with savouring an unusual view, beach walking is the main attraction of this unusual spot. Come at low tide, though, or you won't be able to fully appreciate the size and diversity of the point extending from the south of park. As you should already know by now, you have to be mindful that this is an oyster tenure. Tread lightly and take nothing.

Seclusion Although you are within 100 m of phalanxes of houses, you will feel more or less in the embrace of Mamma Nature. The thickets of firs behind you and the spaces in front of you will all convince you that you are deeply and truly alone. If you chose this spot to pop a question, you might not be the first to do so.

65
ARBUTUS BAY ROAD
Level access to a trail through a meadow of low estuary vegetation to broad gravel tidal flats

Location, signs and parking There is no map provided for this spot because it leads directly from the highway. Since Arbutus Bay Road does not appear on most maps (including Google Maps), you will have to keep a particularly sharp lookout for the road sign. About 2 km north of the railway crossing in Mud Bay, look for a NO THRU ROAD sign and, tucked beneath, the road sign for Arbutus Bay Road. Since the road is only a few dozen metres long, and because you can see the open coast at the end of it, you will immediately realize you are on the right track. You will find probably more parking than you need in the wide, level gravel area at the end of it. One sign tells you that you mustn't park overnight or camp. The other, a somewhat battered paper sign inside a plastic sleeve, is directed toward fishermen who should be reminded of the correct protocol when they are hunting down the wary coastal cutthroat trout.

Path It is really the path that is the chief interest of this intriguing spot. In fact, the transition from non-shore to shore is so subtle and gradual that you will find yourself unsure whether you are on a sea meadow path or beach path. The well-beaten trail, initially running alongside a private fence and used by fishermen (remember the sign for the cutthroat trout?), leads through thickets of calf-high shore vegetation past depressions of pebbles and pools.

Beach This is not the kind of beach to choose for most beach-going activities. You will find no area good for sitting, let alone picnicking or sunning. What you will find, though, is a beautiful area where walking through the meadow-like expanses of salt-tolerant vegetation and out to the gravel shore beyond provides you with striking views and an unusual experience. Because the lowest tides expose more than 300 m of shore, you will probably find the area most attractive at a mid tide.

Suitability for children Bring children only if you have the kind of child who enjoys accompanying a parent on an exploratory stroll or photography expedition. This is not the place to bring children who want to play on a beach.

Suitability for groups Parking is easy, and you won't feel that a small group intrudes on a neighbourhood. If you have friends or family who enjoy birdwatching, sketching or photographing, they are likely to find this spot well worth seeking out. Most others will not.

View Lovers of wide open spaces and dramatic ocean views will be disappointed with this spot. Those with an eye for patterns of shoreline and expanses of nearly untouched beach vegetation will find strangely beautiful the gentle sweeps of shore from Ships Point (in some contexts called Ship Peninsula or Ship's Point), across Denman Island and toward Deep

Bay in the south, with only the tiniest glimpse of the open strait beyond. Some will be intrigued by the lines of floats to the south belonging to a mariculture business. Others—not so much.

Winds, sun and shade Most winds, and particularly those from the northwest, are a little muted here. Since you will find no shore for sitting, the absence of shade is hardly an issue.

Beachcombing While walking toward the shore is both the chief activity and attraction at this spot, walking along the upper shore in either direction is neither attractive nor easy. Surprisingly, though, the low-tide shore is considerably less muddy or squelchy than you might expect.

Seclusion You must begin your walk to the shore virtually in someone's front yard. Likewise, once out on the intertidal meadows you will see that several houses dot the curving bay behind you. Still, your overall feeling will be of visiting a quiet and rarely seen shoreline, midway between land and sea.

While you're here, consider pulling onto the shoulder of the highway about 200 m north of Arbutus Bay Road where, within a few metres, you will see the sign for Coal Creek Conservation Area and a picturesque view of sea meadows and ruined pilings.

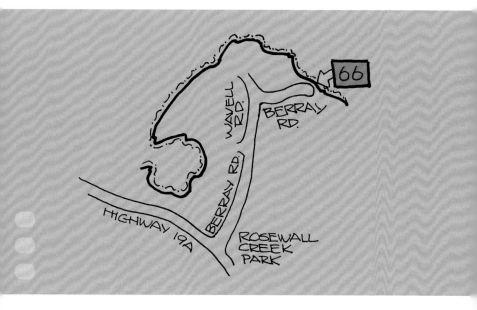

66
BERRAY ROAD
Remarkable views over
a huge area of estuary
vegetation and tidal flats

Location, signs and parking A few minutes south of Mud Bay, in a heavily wooded section of highway, look for the prominent signs for Rosewall Creek Provincial Park and prepare to turn onto Berray Road. Although your destination is simply the end of Berray, driving on local roads is not always as simple as you might think. In fact, after a kilometre or so, Berray Road suddenly changes name to Wavell Road. Persevere. After about a half kilometre, you will come to a T-junction—and discover Berray Road on your right! Allow yourself to feel amused. Carry on to the end of Berray Road, where you will find easy parking for several cars along the shoulder. The only sign you will see here is one that, in macabre fashion, warns you against the perils of collecting clams and oysters.

Path It is difficult to find many access spots where you can park as close to the shore as you can here. You might have to climb over the odd beach log, but otherwise will find little between your vehicle and the upper shore. This is a perfect spot for a car picnic, but don't come to this protected spot during a storm expecting to watch lashing waves and frothing derring-do.

Beach Only the first few metres of shore are anything like a conventional beach. In fact, this area of loose shell fragments and pebbles can be a very pleasant spot to set up an easel or tripod or solve the riddle of the universe or your partner's psychology. Below this area, though, the shore is far, far from looking anything like a beach in the traditional sense. What you will see is a huge area, almost 400 m wide at low tide, comprised of patterns of low estuary vegetation, tidal flats and pools.

Suitability for children Children who accompany their parents to this spot could play a little around the upper beach or submit to being fed oatmeal and raisin cookies and a smoothie. This is far, far from being anything like a good place to bring children if your primary goal is to treat them to a little beach fun.

Suitability for groups A small group would not have to worry about finding places to park or intruding on a closed neighbourhood. All that ordinary groups would have to worry about is finding a positive reason to come here. Yet extraordinary groups will want to make a special note of checking out this access. In fact, watercolourists, photographers and birders will find this a splendid spot and will want to revisit it during different seasons and different times of day.

View You won't find many more confined views on the entire coast— or, in certain light conditions, many more striking ones. A series of low, overlapping contours extends, in the north, from Mud Bay and Ship Peninsula/Ships Point, across Denman Island and, to the south, Deep Bay. Early morning light from the south of Denman gives a particularly haunting effect to a view that shows only the most subtle signs of human intervention.

Winds, sun and shade You will find that the same winds that can create enormous furor elsewhere along the coast are here often as muted and subtle as the scenery. In fact, on a hot day, this spot can be very hot, not just because breezes can be so little felt, but also because every burning ray of the sun can be felt so fully. Put simply, you will find no shade.

Beachcombing This is a shore for contemplation, appreciation or viewing. It is not great for walking. If you do want to make your way out across the littoral, especially if you want a closer look at a mysterious shorebird, you will probably be most comfortable if you wear boots.

Seclusion You would be hard pressed to find many spots nearby that offer as much seclusion as this one does. Come at any time of day in any season and expect to see few or no other people here. Expect, as well, to feel that you can sit in this quiet spot for hours without human interruption.

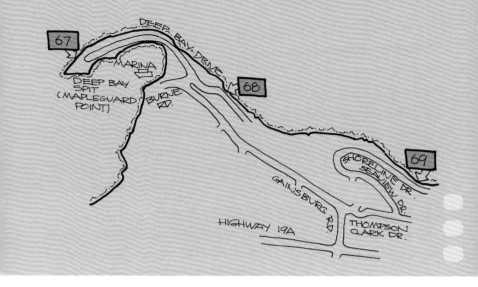

67

DEEP BAY SPIT

A striking geographical formation with a steeply sloping shore of sand and gravel and remarkable views of the Beaufort Range

Location, signs and parking Although you will find no clear landmark for your turn along this treed section of highway about 3 km north of Bowser, you will see a widened section of highway with a left-turn lane and the sign for Gainsburg Road clearly visible. Carry on for about 2 km until a T-junction with Burne Road. Turn right, and after less than 100 m, take the first left onto Deep Bay Drive. Follow Deep Bay Drive as it takes you through a residential area on Deep Bay Spit—also known as Mapleguard Point—and comes to an end in a paved turnaround area. You may do a bit of a double-take when you see the symbol for no parking, until you notice that that restriction applies only between 11 p.m. and 6 a.m., when residents have exclusive right to park there. You will also see four signs on a single post, all forbidding some of the beaching activities you might have been planning, including lighting fires and collecting shellfish. Another sign reiterates that you may not park overnight, while yet another tells you that "motorized vehicles" are not allowed down the narrow path ahead. Who would have thought?

Path The tip of the spit is a level, bushy area shaped roughly like a triangle, each side about 75 m long. The main path leads straight ahead through sky-high grass and then curves toward the southern side of the spit. The path is level, even and generally kept clear by constant use. It can, however, feel a little crowded with vegetation. As the path approaches the beach, you will see two weathered but serviceable picnic tables.

Beach The most popular and most conventionally appealing beach area faces the bay created by the spit. The steeply sloping beach is composed primarily of loose coarse sand and, near the low-tide line, egg-sized gravel. If you carry on around the beach, you will find that it becomes less steep but also rockier. Most beachgoers will probably find the beach most attractive at high tide, but, since the tide never withdraws very far, tides aren't a huge issue.

Suitability for children Generally, this is a good place to bring your water-loving children. While they won't find the tidal flats and tidal pools of some beaches, they will find lots of loose, clean sand in which to lose toy trucks and bury feet. Parents will be happy, too, that the familymobile is just a short walk away and that at any tide, children can get up to watery mischief without going very far from their sun-stupefied supervisors. One caution, though: the bottom drops off quickly. Unless your children are confident swimmers or have reliable PFDs, you should probably hover around them. If you head away from the tip of the spit, you will find the bottom doesn't drop off quite as quickly, but you should still be wary.

Suitability for groups This is a great place to impress and please a few houseguests from the Interior, but not much more than that. Although the beach area itself could accommodate lots of visitors, the lack of facilities and the built-up residential area immediately beside the beach are not conducive to bringing large groups.

View You can come at any time of year and enjoy about 270 degrees of view if you walk around the whole shore. Come in the spring when Mount Arrowsmith and the Beaufort Range are still thick with snow, however, and you could drive away with some stunning photographs. Indeed, this is one of a very few spots along this coast where you are far enough away from the main chunk of Vancouver Island that you can look back onto it with full appreciation.

Winds, sun and shade This may well be the warmest beach on Vancouver Island. One of the advantages of having 270 degrees of view is that you also have 270 degrees of exposure to or protection from winds. This means that while beachgoers elsewhere are fighting off bad cases of goosebumps, you will be deliciously warm. It also can mean—be warned—that you might be sizzling hot when everyone else is exactly the right temperature. Not a trace of shade is to be had from dawn until dusk, a fact that should figure prominently in your planning and the contents of your beach bag.

Beachcombing While the tide doesn't go out very far on the north side of the spit, if you walk clockwise you will find the opposite to be true. Carry on past the first few houses and you will come to gigantic tidal flats, mostly of gravel. At the lowest tides, the gravel bar extends a full half kilometre out to sea. In fact, you can have the extraordinary experience of walking literally halfway across Baynes Sound to Denman Island!

Seclusion Although this beach is never crowded, it is well used in summer weather. You won't be without company if you stay on the sandy side of the point. If you want to be alone with your thoughts or some reasonable facsimiles thereof, however, you need only walk along the shore and, at low tide, out along the gravel flats. Voila!

While you're here, consider pulling over onto the shoulder of Deep Bay Drive about 600 m before the end of the road. Picturesque views across the marina on the inside of the road or across Baynes Sound on the outside of the road can make for great photographs.

68

DEEP BAY DRIVE

Shorefront parking with views
of Chrome Island lighthouse
and access to a mixed beach
with low-tide sand

Location, signs and parking Although you won't see any landmarks on
this wooded section of highway, you will see a major turnoff with a designated left-turn lane and the Gainsburg Road sign. Follow Gainsburg
Road for under 3 km, take Burne Road on your right for a few dozen
metres, and Deep Bay Drive on your right. After about 200 m, the road
turns suddenly toward the shore. A widened section of shoulder just
outside the entrance to an RV park serves as parking space. This is an
excellent spot for a winter car picnic. Dig out your Thermos and your hot
chocolate. If you planned to bring your aged VW van here for an overnight stay, forget it. Overnight parking is verboten. If you've planned to
dig up your dinner, you'll have to check with Fisheries first. The shellfish
can be contaminated and you really, really don't want to suffer paralytic
poisoning.

Path Considerable energy and goodwill have gone into making a few
steps out of large boulders. The result is that most for whom walking is
a challenge can be on the shore within seconds.

Beach This is one of those "sandwich" beaches where the top and bottom
are, indeed, sand, and the middle is an expanse of barnacle-bristling rocks
and boulders. The large area of high-tide sand and logs is perfect for picnicking and sunning. The low-tide sand is great for wading and concocting
sandcastles. The area between would not be quite as appealing were it not
for a huge tidal pool just to the south of the stairs to the shore.

Suitability for children This is a great place to bring children for whom
the nearby Deep Bay Spit isn't quite perfect. Unlike that spot, this one
has only the most gradual drop into deep water and, to boot, has lots of
low-tide sand for miniature construction projects.

Suitability for groups Most groups would be much better off at the nearby Deep Bay Spit/Mapleguard Point access. Still, a few cars full of novelty seekers could park here and refresh their senses in a lovely picnic spot.

View The view is unusually varied. Looking to the north, you will be aware that this is the southern exit from Baynes Sound. Across the narrow channel, you will see the wooded banks of Denman Island and, behind it, Mount Geoffrey on Hornby Island. Looking to the south, however, you will find yourself with an interesting perspective not only on Chrome Island lighthouse but also on the expanses of the southern part of the Strait of Georgia stretching away to the horizon.

Winds, sun and shade If you have been baking at nearby Deep Bay Spit and need some relief, you may want to move to this spot where, in the afternoon, you can find both some shade on the upper beach and a little more sea breeze, particularly if the breeze is from the southeast.

Beachcombing Lovers of walking on varied shoreline will be in paradise if they come at low tide. They can start to the north with the vast gravel bar extending into the middle of Baynes Sound before rounding the steep-shored sweep of Deep Bay Spit. At that point they can cut back along the road to begin a southern exploration of the largely secluded gravel shore and, after a 15 minutes' walk, the beginning of an intertidal zone with huge, irregular tidal pools.

Seclusion This beach is not even the tiniest bit secluded. In the middle of a nest of houses and beside an RV park, it could hardly be otherwise. Still, the access isn't used very much, and if you walk south you will soon be surprisingly alone.

While you're here, you might want to visit Deep Bay Marina on Burne Road, particularly if you wish to use a ramp to launch your kayak.

69

SHORELINE DRIVE (BOWSER)

A wooded roadside viewpoint with a picnic bench and easy access to a mixed shore with large areas of soft sand and rock

Location, signs and parking Using a GPS or Google Maps? Be careful! Another Shoreline Drive just south of Campbell River has been especially created just to mislead you. Turn off the highway onto Gainsburg Road as if you were headed to Deep Bay, but, after 200 m, turn right onto Thompson Clark Drive for another 200 m and left onto Seaview Drive for about 500 m until it changes name to Shoreline Drive and curves down toward the eponymous shoreline. (Be warned, another section of Thompson Clark Drive, completely separate from this one, runs off Jamieson Road south of here.) Once you have driven a short distance parallel to the shore, you will find a broad gravel shoulder with a waste bin, park bench and two signs. One tells you that you may not park overnight; the other gruesomely alerts you to the dangers of paralytic poisoning from contaminated shellfish. This can be a good spot for car picnicking, but in summer you might be looking through a screen of irrepressible bushes.

Path If your energy level can rise to a hop, skip and jump, then that's all you need to get down the short slope onto the beach. The former path has been eroded and taped closed, but, we can all hope, will soon be revivified.

Beach This isn't a great beach to choose for sitting on the upper shore—though you do have the option of sitting on the park bench. Because this part of the shore is overhung with maples and alders, for most of the day it will seem a little shady and enclosed. The lower part of the beach, however, is extensive and varied. Two large gravel bars, almost 150 m wide, nearly enclose a shallow area and large sandy patch. The sand is peculiarly soft, almost a little muddy, but is perfectly usable for sand play.

Suitability for children You will want to time your visit for low tide if you come with your children, and you will want to bring an arsenal of buckets and spades. Wading through the extensive shallows and pursuing sea creatures will engage many children but can take place only if you remember water shoes. The easy route from the car is an obvious advantage if your children are needy or reluctant to climb steep paths.

Suitability for groups Constrained parking and the lack of a good picnic area on the beach itself mean that most groups might wonder why you navigated them here.

View This is one of the closest viewing spots you will get for tiny, bare Chrome Island and its distinctive lighthouse. Bring your binoculars to see it properly, however. To the north you will see Denman Island and the southern part of Baynes Sound, with Hornby Island's Mount Geoffrey looming behind. To the south, Texada and Lasqueti islands dominate your view of landforms across the strait.

Winds, sun and shade You will find neither lots of protection from nor lots of exposure to winds. You will, however, find lots of shade, especially in the afternoon and especially on the upper shore.

Beachcombing If you are intrigued by the watery depressions and undulations of the shore here, you will find lots more along the shore in either direction. If you want to visit the more interesting landforms, head north toward Deep Bay Spit. If you want maximum isolation, head south. In either case, be prepared for walking carefully over several sections of rounded and irregular rocks.

Seclusion Although this is a roadside spot, the only other people you are likely to encounter are the residents of the half dozen houses at the end of the road a short distance south. In fact, you are most likely to be completely alone and unobserved.

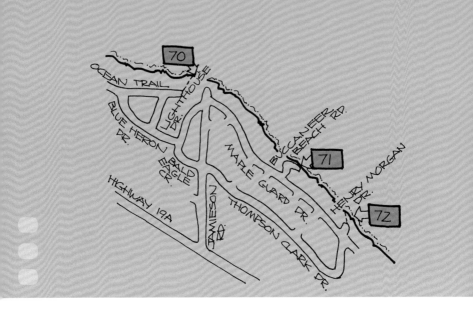

70

MOSS PARK

A long winding path down a
beautifully forested ravine to
a mixed shore with huge tidal
pools, wet sand and boulders

Location, signs and parking If you know the myth of the labyrinth, you will identify with the heroic Theseus as you wind your convoluted way to this spot. A few kilometres north of Bowser, look for Jamieson Road and follow it for about half a kilometre to Bald Eagle Crescent, where you should turn left. An additional left onto Blue Heron Drive, first right onto Lighthouse Drive, and right again onto Ocean Trail will bring you within metres of your goal. You will see room for several cars on the wide, paved end of Ocean Trail and a lovingly handcrafted sign made from a burl slab that reads MOSS PARK. Currently, no other signs are posted to tell you anything about the park, but clearly it is a local park used by the residents in the immediate area—and particularly important to them, because it is one of the few ways down to the shore from the top of the high wooded bank that stretches along several kilometres of coast.

Path The path to the shore is one of the main reasons for seeking out this spot. Although it is little more than a dirt trail, it winds about 100 m down the picturesque side of a heavily forested ravine.

Beach The shore is little short of peculiar. While you can find huge tidal pools and gravel bars at a few spots farther south along the coast, nowhere will you find a spot where the shore is so heavily indented and carved with such a variety of elements. Peculiarly, too, the large sandy areas exposed by low tide are fairly squelchy as well as being dotted with huge boulders. Presumably, the sand is slightly muddy because the shore here is largely protected from wave action. The small stream that tumbles down the ravine and cuts across the shore a short distance to the south may likewise contribute to the soft shore.

Suitability for children Small or unadventurous children are not the kind most likely to have fun here. First, of course, they have to be got or get themselves not just down but also back up a daunting path. Second, they need to have the energy and curiosity to enjoy romping over rough rocks and squishing through giant tidal pools.

Suitability for groups This is not the place to bring your sedate and conservative picnicking colleagues. It is, though, the perfect place to bring a group of friends or family members who love to find new places, hidden shorelines and unusual beaches. As long as they don't clog up the end of the road with cars, a group of watercolourists or shore wanderers can easily be accommodated on the largely empty expanses of shore they will find. With a group, though, you almost certainly will want to come at low tide, since the upper shore is comparatively confined at a high tide.

View You are partly tucked behind Denman Island and, visible above it, Mount Geoffrey on Hornby Island. Lighthouse lovers will want to bring a telephoto lens and get some good close-ups of Chrome Island lighthouse off the south end of Denman Island. This is also one of the only beach spots where you can get a great view, to the north, of the peaks and permanent snowfields of Strathcona Park.

Winds, sun and shade Unlike most spots farther south, almost all of which are exposed to every chilling buffet of wind and burning ray of sun, this access provides considerable protection from the elements. You will feel both a northwest and southeast breeze, but not fully. You will also find plenty of sizzling sun, but not on the upper shore and not in the afternoon. In fact, if you want a sun-baked picnic, it may well have to be a brunch.

Beachcombing This is the perfect section of shore to choose if you are game to wander far out onto rocky bars and crests of boulders and wade through large tidal pools. It is also a good choice for those who like a shifting view as they round promontories. If you head north for a few hundred metres, you can walk into a bay where even at mid tide you can find an attractively sandy beach not otherwise easily accessible.

Seclusion When your inclination to find a place all to yourself ramps up to full-scale yearning, this is the perfect spot for you. Because of the high wooded bank, you will have the sense that there is no one even close by. Because of the labyrinth of roads required to find this hidden park, you will almost certainly find yourself the only one on the shore. Take full advantage of the situation!

Moss Park

71
BUCCANEER BEACH
A secluded spot below a high, treed bank, with a broad band of coarse sand on the upper beach and a rocky lower shore

Location, signs and parking The simplest, though not quite the shortest, route to Buccaneer Beach is to turn off the highway in the northern outskirts of Bowser onto Jamieson Road. Follow it nearly to its end and turn right onto Maple Guard Drive. After a few hundred metres search out tiny Buccaneer Beach Road (replete with NO EXIT sign) zigzagging down the treed bank. Parking at the end is difficult for more than three or four cars, especially because you have to take care not to block a private driveway.

Path Since the road is parallel to the shore, and virtually on it, you don't need to do much more than to manage a few steps to get you through a small strip of grass onto the shore. While beachgoers don't need much physical strength to get onto the shore, they will have to be prepared to make their way through a broad area of soft, sliding sand. Note the park bench and rubbish bin, both potentially germane to your beaching plans.

Beach Most visitors will probably be charmed chiefly by the large area of dry sand, beach vegetation and logs, all well above summer high tides. This large area, close to the car and relatively private, calls out for the most decadent picnic imaginable, from crab-and-brie panini to triple chocolate torte. At high-tide, the beach is most attractive. At low tide, though chiefly rocks and barnacles, the beach has a few large tidal pools well worth exploring. Although the tide drops about 75 m at all but the lowest tides, kayakers would find it easy to execute an uneventful and low-energy launch.

Suitability for children The large upper beach of coarse sand invites lots of barefoot romping and log jumping between fits of snacking on chocolate chip cookies and apple slices. Water shoes are a must, though, especially if your intrepid child is intrigued by the sculpins and starfish in the large tidal pools created by the retreating tide.

Suitability for groups The major limitation for a group, apart from the lack of facilities, is the limited parking. If you can squeeze your prairie in-laws into two or three cars, though, you can bring them to this spot with the expectation of finding lots of space to picnic, throw Frisbees and wander without intruding.

View To the north your view is largely foreground. You will find your eye passing from the curving shore to the graceful undulations of Denman and Hornby islands. To the south, however, your view is mostly of the distant islands and open horizon of the southern strait.

Winds, sun and shade For good or ill, this is one of the few spots along this stretch of coast that is subject to invading bands of afternoon shade— at least on the upper beach. Since there are so many spots to the south where you can't find shade even when you want to, keep this spot in mind when the sun is hotter than you want and you crave delicious shade.

Beachcombing Tighten the laces of your sturdiest shoes, take a deep breath and head out for as long a beach walk as your inclination takes you. Choose north if you want a shore at the base of a high forested bank, huge tidal pools and few people to disturb your thoughts. Choose south if you want to combine your walk with a visit to the village, about 8 km distant, and a snack. In either case, you will find yourself having to opt

Buccaneer Beach

for the comparatively smooth upper beach of loose pebbles or the much more solid but rougher lower beach.

Seclusion The beach is delectably secluded most of the time. The small parking area and the wooded banks ensure that. Here is your big chance to pop that big question, whether to your honey or to the Almighty.

72

HENRY MORGAN DRIVE

A broad, crushed-gravel trail descending from a high, wooded bank to a secluded shore of high-tide pebbles and low-tide rock

Location, signs and parking A few minutes north of Bowser, turn onto Jamieson Road. Take the second turn right onto Thompson Clark Drive and follow it through its many curves until it crosses—or seems to cross—Maple Guard Drive. In fact, the few metres of road immediately across Maple Guard constitute the Henry Morgan Drive that you're looking for. You will see no instructional or invitational signs, but from the only parking area, on the shoulder of the road at its end, you will see the beginning of a broad, crushed gravel path.

Path The path, about 70 or 80 m long, drops more than a dozen metres as it takes you through a fine stand of cedars, grand firs and maples.

Beach Probably the most immediately appealing part of the beach is the large area of loose pebbles and beach succulents well above most high tides. Curiously, few logs have accumulated in this spacious pebbly area. The lowest tides expose about 100 m of barnacle-covered boulders and some skookum tidal pools. A broad pathway slightly to the left of the access to the water's edge has been cleared through the boulders.

Suitability for children Pre-toddlers could be easily hefted down the trail and provided a comfortable nest among the pebbles. Getting older children both down to the beach and back up again might prove to be more than some parents are up to. In addition, the enticements of the beach are not huge for most children, given the density of barnacle-covered boulders. Still, at high tide, when only the large area of pebbles is exposed, the beach is a pleasant place for a picnic and a splash.

Suitability for groups Parking isn't plentiful, but a few cars could crowd onto the shoulder of the road. The spot would be suitable for the kind of group that wants a quiet and secluded picnic area or enjoys exploring a large chunk of shore accessible to only a few.

View This is one of the few spots in the area where you will want to pause en route to the shore for a slice of hilltop view over the southern end of Baynes Channel and, beyond, Denman and Hornby islands. These same two islands dominate your view from the beach, but if you turn south, you will see the curve of shore extending south of Bowser and, if you strain your eyes just a tad, the distant bumps of Mount Arrowsmith.

Winds, sun and shade In principle, both a northwest wind and a southeast wind blow more or less parallel to the shore rather than directly onto it. On the upper beach you should feel a somewhat reduced version of the blusters and breezes of both winds. On a hot day, you will find some areas of shade in which to huddle, but don't expect the entire shore to be swathed in shade, since the broad cleared area and gradual slope of the bank allow summer sun onto your picnic and paddling.

Beachcombing A certain class of beachcomber will want to seek out this spot, come hell or high water. This is the kind of beachcomber who prizes above all the opportunity to walk for many kilometres, seen by few and seeing few, savouring both the woods on the high banks and the unusually large strips of tidal pool and gravel bar running along the shore. Those wanting to punctuate their wandering with a snack should head south. Within a couple of kilometres, they can climb Bowser Road and find themselves in the village.

Seclusion Most of the high bank above the shore is lined with houses, but its height and trees create an impression of delicious seclusion on the shore. Because the spot is well off the highway and well away from the centre of Bowser, accessible only to those with the patience to wind through a complex network of roads, it receives few visitors.

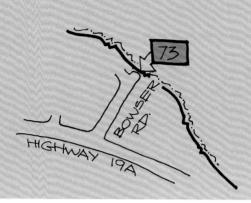

73

BOWSER ROAD
Near the centre of Bowser,
good for launching kayaks and
getting easy access to an upper
beach of pebbles and sand

Location, signs and parking Finding Bowser Road could hardly be simpler. In the centre of Bowser, you will see Bowser Building Supply and, right beside it, Bowser Road. Descend the two blocks toward the coast, and you will find yourself in an area of hard-packed gravel and enough parking space for several cars. On a hot day, take advantage of the shade provided by the firs on the right side of the area. Even though this spot is very much in the middle of the village, the only prohibitions spelled out by the PUBLIC BEACH ACCESS sign clearly posted here are against unleashed pooches and, bizarrely, motorbikes. Obviously, however, given the location, you will want to think twice, or possibly thrice, before having a beach fire or parking overnight.

Path Although this isn't the best car-picnicking spot in the world, you can park close enough to the shore that you might well enjoy bringing the snack you've picked up at a village eatery to enjoy while you watch the wheeling gulls. In warm weather, however, you will appreciate that only a few steps will bring you to either a picnic bench or the shore immediately below it.

Beach The shore seems to attract very few picnic-friendly logs, but otherwise it is reasonably well suited as a site for making short shrift of your chicken salad. Even at high tide, several metres of sand and gravel remain high and dry. Unfortunately, the sandiest and therefore most comfortable part of the shore is dotted with rounded boulders. The pebbly strip slightly down the beach is probably best for spreading out your picnic blanket. The broken concrete chunks of a former project gone horribly awry do little to beautify the otherwise pristine beach. High tide is by far the best time to launch a kayak. Though the tide doesn't drop a huge distance, the lower shore is covered with an obstacle course of boulders. You can also take advantage of the venerable launching strip a short distance down the shore to your right.

Suitability for children High tide, when the barnacles and boulders are well submerged, is best for children who want to bone up on their dog-paddling skills or skip rocks until their arms ache. At low tide, only children interested in investigating the lonely lives of rock crabs and blennies will be delighted with the boulder-covered shore.

Suitability for groups You will find plenty of parking for several cars but, in this close neighbourhood, more than a few people here will be intrusive.

View The east end of Denman Island is visible to the north, partially obscuring Hornby. Texada Island, with the scars of the open-pit mine more visible than you want, dominates the central part of your view. The shore angles southward in such a way that, on a clear day, you can make out the telltale lumps of Mount Arrowsmith.

Winds, sun and shade Because of the curve of the shoreline, you will be partially sheltered from a northwest wind, especially on the upper beach. If a sou'easter is a-howling, though, you will have to batten down your hatches. Don't forget your sunscreen and broad-brimmed hat on a sunny day: while your car might be shaded, you won't be.

Beachcombing You can walk comfortably for several hundred metres in either direction, until, in both directions, you stumble upon some huge tidal pools. One of the advantages of the boulder-covered lower shore is that, more than the gravelly shore that dominates the coast many kilometres to the south, this one provides habitat for all kinds of interesting low-tide creatures.

Seclusion In the immediate vicinity of the access strip, and also to the south, you will have a hard time finding anything remotely like solitude. Be prepared, however, for a pleasant surprise if you are looking for a little Quality Time with just you and the waves. Turn north, and after a 100 m you will find yourself at the base of a high, wooded bank and blessed with solitude.

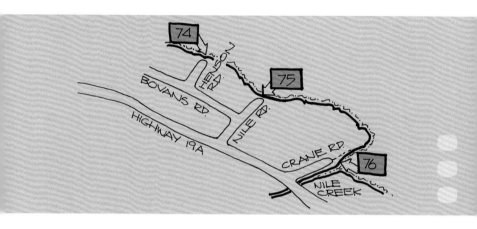

74

HENSON ROAD
Lots of shorefront parking, best visited at high tide for kayak launching or car picnicking in foul weather

Location, signs and parking Midway between Qualicum Bay and Bowser, look for a broad swath of cleared land and power lines crossing the highway. Turn onto Nile Road, almost immediately left onto Bovans Road, and, after almost 300 m, right onto Henson Road. Henson Road grinds to a halt about 75 m later in a road-width area. Though this is a good spot for car picnicking, be careful not to pull too far forward, as your tires can easily sink into the sand in dry weather. One sign tells you that you should make no plans to spend overnight. Another warns of the dangers of contaminated shellfish.

Path As those practised in the art of measurement will confirm, the beach is spitting distance from the parking area. From an exposed, treeless area, a few steps bring you past some shore-stabilizing boulders down a metre or so to the beach.

Beach Although at first glance the beach might seem to be an undistinguished expanse of rough gravel and barnacles, a few features should quickly stand out for beachgoers with an expert eye. Most obvious is the line of broken pilings, the intriguing wreckage of someone's having underestimated the power of the elements. Second is the area of coarse sand and pebbles on the log-free upper beach, an invitation to roost in warm weather. Third—for kayakers—is the comparatively short distance over easily trod gravel to the waterline.

Suitability for children Because the beach is so nearly level, the only threat it poses for children comes in the form of the foot-lacerating barnacle. On the other hand, most children will be happy here if, at low tide, they enjoy lifting rocks in pursuit of sea critters or, at high tide, like getting thoroughly drenched. Otherwise, this is not the perfect beach for the younger set.

Suitability for groups Kayaking groups or walkers could do far worse than begin their adventure here, where access to the shore is easy and parking is fairly ample. Picnickers and baskers, however, will be happier where sand and facilities are more plentiful.

View From this northeast-facing shore, the view is dominated by Denman and Hornby islands to the north, and, to the south, the rolling skyline of Texada Island and the open horizon of the southern strait.

Winds, sun and shade You won't feel the full head-on whammy of a northwest wind, since it blows roughly along the beach rather than onto it. The southeast winds associated with low-pressure systems, however, are about as strong here as they are anywhere. In this exposed, treeless spot you won't find even an iota of shade.

Beachcombing Although you will have to be prepared to tread a little carefully over the slightly irregular surface, you will find nothing significant to impede your walking a considerable distance in either direction. Several hundred metres to the south, Nile Creek cuts across the shore. To the north, you will come to an area where the gravel beach is varied with some large tidal pools.

Seclusion Although you are unlikely to find many fellow visitors to this beach, you are likely to feel as if you stand out like a very sore thumb on the edge of this residential area. Don't expect even the slightest visual barrier between you and the phalanxes of shorefront houses on either side of the access road.

75
NILE ROAD
A small parklike area with a park bench, gravelly shore and good view of Denman and Hornby islands

Location, signs and parking Partway between Bowser and Qualicum Bay (not to be confused with Qualicum Beach), Nile Road has lots of easily spotted landmarks, even though the south-facing road sign is not easily spotted. At the point where a huge swath of cleared land cuts across the highway, replete with power pylons festooned with cables, turn onto the wide, paved road. Nile Road takes you perhaps 200 m to a loop-shaped turnaround area lined with a few large boulders. Here you will find easy parking for at least a dozen cars. The only sign is a bedraggled paper notice, inadequately covered with plastic, with lots of fine print alerting you to the dangers of collecting shellfish.

Path If the international unit of measurement known as the "stone's throw" means much to you, then you will realize how quickly you can find yourself settled on the park bench with your thoughts, drinking in the view and the contents of your Thermos. Although you can catch glimpses of a monstrous hydro facility a few metres to the south, the park-like setting of firs and grass should distract you.

Beach While both the path and the shore itself are nearly level, low tide exposes a considerable expanse of gravel and barnacles. Kayakers will find this a good spot to get their craft afloat, but will be happiest avoiding very low tides. Picnickers and sun worshippers will enjoy the large area of dry loose sand near the park bench, but may want to bring a blanket or beach chairs, since the usual all-purpose beach logs do not seem to make themselves available here.

Suitability for children This is one of those beaches common to this stretch of coast that most water-loving children can enjoy best at high tide—but only if their feet are well protected. At low tide, children who enjoy molesting hermit crabs and starfish will be happiest.

Suitability for groups A clutch of picnickers will find that spacious parking for several cars and the distance from irritable locals are the chief draws of this spot. The only facilities are the park bench and a rubbish bin.

View The shore here is angled in such a way that your view is almost due north. That means that your vista starts with the distant shore of Bowser and leads across Denman and Hornby islands. From this far north, Texada Island, by far the largest island in the Strait of Georgia, no longer dominates the entire view across the strait, but is still a mighty presence. On a clear day you can see a small area of the mainland peaks that provide such a dramatic skyline to the views north of Comox.

Winds, sun and shade Because the shore faces almost due north, you will feel a northwest wind more or less directly. A southeast wind, however, which is generally chillier, tends to shear past you a little. If you are trying to cater both to those who want sun and to those who want shade with their sandwiches, this is a good picnic spot. From noon onward, patches of both creep across the soft sandy area.

Beachcombing If you're after a stroll or a stride, you will have plenty of nearly level shore at your disposal. Two details to remember, however, are, first, to head north if you aren't up to wading across Nile Creek a short distance south. Second, make sure you have something considerably more substantial than flip-flops to protect you from the irregular surface.

Seclusion The gigantic hydro installation to your south and the thick patch of firs to your north almost ensure that, if you and your sweetie are the only ones who have found your way to this relatively obscure spot, you will have the freedom to murmur or even serenade without the benefit of an audience.

While you're here, you might want to drive a little farther north along Henson Road until you see the Gladys Road sign and an open, clear track to a similar section of this beach that is probably quieter, but not quite so good for car picnicking.

76

CRANE ROAD

An unusual access to the south shore of Nile Creek where it empties into the sea across a huge area of low-tide gravel

Location, signs and parking Roughly midway between Bowser and Qualicum Bay, look for the Nile Creek bridge and, a dozen or so metres north, Crane Road. Crane Road runs parallel to Nile Creek toward the coast for a very short distance. Park in the wide gravel turnaround area posted with two signs, one that prohibits camping and overnight parking, another that prohibits the taking of lethally contaminated shellfish. You don't need to be a rocket scientist to realize which two particular plans you should strike from your list when hunting down this beach.

Path If you like to hop, skip and jump your way to the shore, rest assured you can use exactly that method of getting the very few gravelly and nearly level metres from your car onto the first part of the shore. Those with walking difficulties could hardly find a more convenient place to get onto the shore—though, be warned, not onto the open coast.

Beach All of your hopping, skipping and jumping brings you onto the shore, yes, but actually onto the south shore of a little gravelly inlet created by the outflowing Nile Creek. At high tide, this is a pleasant and protected place to visit. At low tide, it might seem a little landlocked, since the beach can look more like a creek bank than an ocean shore. When the tide is low, the water's edge retreats well over 100 m down the estuary. Be prepared for a bit of a trek if you want to settle down with your picnic fodder and a full view of the briny offerings of the strait.

Suitability for children Any negotiable shore with water at its edge—which is to say any shore between Qualicum and Campbell River—can provide energy-releasing fun for a wound-up child. Still, this shore is not tailor-made for maximizing most children's beach-going pleasure. If you come at low tide, you will probably find that your child is most interested in romping in the small creek as it makes its way toward the open ocean across the tidal flats. Come at high tide if your child is most interested in getting as thoroughly wet as possible as quickly as possible. The water in the most protected part of the shore drops off fairly quickly at high tide and is most likely to be warm.

Suitability for groups You and your beach-bound buddies will find lots of parking for several cars and lots of place to spread out, especially at low tide. Be sure, though, that the fairly limited activities at this shore fit with the druthers of your group. And remember that you will find no facilities—other than a waste bin for your picnic leftovers.

View From the creek bank, your view is limited but very pretty in a wild sort of way. You will be looking primarily across the creek bed or, at high tide, across a small inlet at mid-sized firs and, tucked among them, a few houses. At low tide, of course, your view at the distant water's edge can be of the full sweep of the strait.

Winds, sun and shade This is a great spot to keep in mind if an obstreperous northwest wind is creating frothing waves and goosebumps on exposed flesh. Stay close to the parking area, tucked around the corner from the open ocean, and you will feel only the most tempered bit of breeze. An equally obstreperous southeast wind, on the other hand, is not the least bit tempered here. Bring all the sun protection you need, because you will find none from overhanging trees.

Beachcombing Like most estuaries, Nile Creek is likely to be a good spotting ground for ducks and, during the autumn, spawning salmon. Those who like a long walk along a gravelly shore will find nothing to stop them for several kilometres if they turn north. To the south, of course, they will first have to get themselves across Nile Creek, a feat most easily achieved near the low-tide line during a dry season.

Seclusion Many houses line the shore both across Nile Creek and along the open coast, but nearly all of them are tucked well into the many trees. Because the beach is not likely to attract the Average Beachgoer, you, in your individualistic beach-going mode, are likely to be alone, or nearly alone.

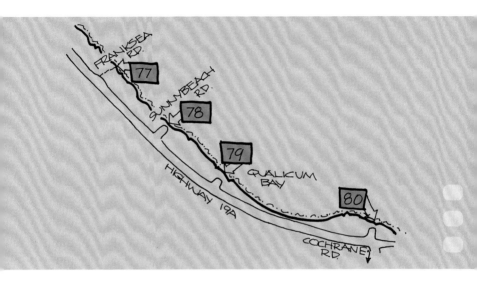

77
FRANKSEA ROAD
A rolling path through a beautiful patch of forest to a fine beach of pebbles and low-tide sand

Location, signs and parking Although this is called Franksea Road Beach Access—at least according to a venerable and barely legible sign posted there—you cannot find it by looking for Franksea Road as you drive along this section of highway. Neither on most maps nor in reality is there such a road. Instead, along the straight section of highway several minutes north of Qualicum Bay, look for a house number 6209 on a post by a brown picket fence. Voila! If you are driving south, spotting a 60 km sign should further help locate this elusive but immensely worthwhile spot.

You should see a dirt pull-off area along the side of the road under a large cedar and, if you peer into the woods, the small, fading sign announcing this to be Franksea Road Beach Access. This sign provides the additional information that the trail was built by "Adventurers Anonymous, A District 69 Youth Group." Looking for a spot for a beach fire? Don't come here: the sign tells you that fires are not welcome. It also, gently, tells you to keep your dog "under control" without specifically requiring that it be on a leash. Given the difficulty of finding this spot and the fact that you may well be the only one here, you and your controlled pooch are unlikely to create offence.

Path The path is a delight. Through a pretty patch of cedars and firs, this wide but little-used trail takes you about 30 m directly to the shore.

Beach Those familiar with the popular Sunnybeach Road access, a short distance south, will instantly recognize this much quieter beach to be otherwise nearly identical. The upper shore, with areas both of pebbles and dry sand, slopes fairly quickly to a wide low-tide swath of fine sand that extends a considerable distance in either direction. Although gener-ally backed with only a few beach logs, and dotted with patches of shore

Franksea

vegetation, the upper beach is inviting to anyone with languorous or gastronomic inclinations. Come at high tide for a delicious swim over a sandy bottom. Come at low tide for hundreds of metres of sandy waterfront at your barefoot disposal.

Suitability for children Sunnybeach Road, the nearby sister to this spot, has the advantage of providing proximity to your parked car as well as facilities. On the other hand, this beach has the same wonderful beach but with very few fellow visitors. Flip-flops or other beach shoes will help to get you onto the sandy area, but even the pebbly area of the upper shore should provide little impediment to little feet. It is the large swath of low-tide sand that is the real draw for children, of course. Parents will also appreciate that the tide does not usually drop very far, so supervising the antics of the next generation at the water's edge can be easily done from the vantage point of the dry upper shore.

Suitability for groups The lack of parking space, other than along the shoulder of a fairly busy road, is the main restriction on this area for your wine-tasting club's annual picnic. If they don't need park facilities, though, they should be thrilled to the tips of their wine-tasting toes—or tongues—at this beautiful, and beautifully hidden, beach.

View Because this strip of shore essentially faces east, the view is dominated by the low undulations of islands, the horizon of the southern strait and the gentle, broad sweep of Vancouver Island's shore.

Winds, sun and shade With considerable protection here from a northwest breeze, you might find this area can become baking hot on the warmest days. Come in the latter part of the afternoon, however, and you will find patches of shade spreading across the upper shore.

Beachcombing This access is located near the northern end of a long spread of low-tide sand. Barefoot beachcombers will want to head south. Shod beachcombers can choose either direction, but should be prepared either to get wet feet or go unshod. To the north in particular, the oxymoronically named Nile Creek cuts across the shore, though in the driest part of the year, it is not much of an obstacle.

Seclusion Seclusion, or something close to it, is one of the glories of this beach for those who want a quiet place to unburden their heart. While houses line the low shore for considerable distance on both sides, the patch of woods surrounding the access path is large enough to provide a wonderful sense of privacy. The fact that the spot is so tricky to find likewise increases the chances that you will have to share the shore with no one.

78

SUNNYBEACH ROAD

A splendid beach for children, complete with lots of sand, warm water, picnic tables and washrooms

Location, signs and parking A few minutes' drive north of Qualicum Bay, look for a standard road sign indicating Sunnybeach Road, and, immediately below it, a sign forbidding overnight parking and camping. The groomed gravel road takes you a few dozen metres to several parking spots alongside a high wooden fence. Be mindful that this wide area is also used by locals pulling in to collect their mail from the mailboxes perching on the right side. In blustery weather, if no one else is here, you can drive virtually onto the beach and have a front-row seat for gazing on the wheeling gulls and busy waves. You will see surprisingly few signs, given the well-developed nature of this spot. You are simply told not to dump refuse and not to pursue lethal shellfish. That's it. You are, however, offered two picnic tables, washrooms (of sorts) and a picnic bench, all in a compact but attractively treed area.

Path Getting to the beach could hardly be easier. Those unsteady on their legs or lugging beach hardware will be well served.

Beach Like most of the large sandy beaches on this stretch of coast, this one starts off with a strip of pebbles and gravel. It is possible to picnic or ponder on this upper shore, though you will see some locals bringing beach chairs and setting them up on the sandy section below this strip. Of course, it is this area of fine, firm sand extending a considerable distance on either side of the access that makes this spot popular with locals. Although the tide does not go out a long way (kayakers take note), at low tide there is plenty of sand for accidentally throwing Frisbees into deep water, struggling with a skimboard or doing your level best to get a kite airborne.

Suitability for children This is the best beach for children for a considerable distance in either direction. While crocs or flip-flops are crucial for negotiating the strip of gravel, once onto the sand your firstborn can go berserk with soggy and gritty pleasure. The proximity of car, picnic tables and washroom make this close to a perfect choice for children.

Suitability for groups The ample parking, the great beach and the facilities would, at first blush, suggest this is a good spot for a minor multitude eager for sandwiches and sand. Before you invite an entire pack of cubs or galaxy of astrophysicists, you should be aware that this spot is well used by locals. Keep your group small or come at an unlikely time of day or during unlikely weather. Franksea Road, a short distance north, is a little-used access to the same beach, though it has no facilities.

View The shoreline here is almost east-facing and, in addition, part of a large, gently curving bay. The result is that your view starts, in the north, with the northern end of Hornby Island and extends to the open horizon of the southern strait.

Winds, sun and shade This stretch of shore should be a little more protected from a northwest wind than it often seems to be, but of course on a hot day, a sea breeze is deliciously welcome. If a southeast wind is blowing, this shore gets every morsel. While most of the shore is in sun most of the day, if you're trying to avoid a scorcher, in the latter part of the afternoon you can find some shade on the upper beach and on the park bench. Almost as welcome might be the fact that your trusty car can huddle in the shade during any part of the day.

Beachcombing You won't find much variation underfoot as you comb the shore for treasures. However, you will be happy to forego the nobbles and bumps, inlets and bars of some shores when you stride easily for long stretches along this nearly straight shoreline.

Seclusion This is a popular spot. You will have to come at an unsavoury time of day or murky time of year to have it to yourself and your significant other. You can't stroll your way to privacy, either; the low, level shore is, understandably, thoroughly lined with houses positioned to drink in every fragment of view the beach has to offer.

79

QUALICUM BAY—NORTH

Access to the tidal flats of
Qualicum Bay, close to cafés
and restaurants

Location, signs and parking Immediately beside Lighthouse Motel, more or less in the centre of Qualicum Bay, you will see a short gravel road leading directly to the shore between the motel on your right and an RV park on your left. On a post to your left as you make your way down this road you will see two signs, one encouragingly telling you that this is a public beach access, one discouragingly warning you against the perils of collecting the apparently edible creatures of the shore. Dog owners take note: if you come to this beach to give your dachshund a salty saunter, bring a leash. Motorcyclists also take note: if, unfathomably, you should want to take your motorcycle onto the rocky shore, you can't. Car drivers take note: you will find plenty of parking for almost a dozen vehicles.

Path Although not quite as much a piece of cake as the paths at some other spots nearby, this one nevertheless is easy for all but the most tee-tering beachgoers. A sort of ramp of rough gravel descends a few metres from a park bench to the shore. Note the well-placed rubbish bin for your picnic scraps.

Beach While not exactly a front-runner in the most beautiful beach contest, the shore is certainly varied and interesting. The upper shore is a curious mix of shiny, smooth boulders and fine gravel, almost, but not quite, appealing for sitting and sunning. The usual—and puzzling—absence of beach logs, and the looming concrete retaining wall of the motel's patio to your right, don't add to the appeal of the upper beach for those most in search of a sunning spot. A swath of large, rounded boulders likewise lies between you and the extensive tidal flats beyond. Still, the beach is intriguing for those who are eager to search out star-fish, crabs and shells among the low-tide rocks and in the low-tide pools.

A short distance to the south, in the centre of Qualicum Bay, you will see a walloping tidal pool, some slightly squelchy patches of sand and a raised gravel bar.

Suitability for children Some children will be forgiven for finding this spot's proximity to the ice cream store a short walk away to be its most appealing feature. In fact, wily parents might well keep this fact in mind as they negotiate plans for a walk out along the curious, but sometimes challenging, shore and circling back into the centre of the village.

Suitability for groups As with children, so with whole groups. This might be a great spot to bring a group who would like to embellish a café or pub visit with a wander and prod in the world of crustaceans and mollusks.

View Notwithstanding that this is downtown "lighthouse country," this is primarily a viewing spot for islands, not for lighthouses. In fact, there are few other spots on this section of coast where you see the undulating forms of islands almost to the exclusion of the mountains and stretches of open horizon that typify many other spots. From your left, check off Denman, tiny Chrome and hulking Hornby islands, all close by. Across

the strait massive Texada, overshadowing much smaller Lasqueti, makes up the rest of your view. If you have truly powerful binoculars, you might actually be able to see the two lighthouses after which this area has been named, one on Chrome Island, the other, Sisters Lighthouse, off the northern tip of Texada Island.

Winds, sun and shade Don't expect protection from either wind or sun. If the wind is a little friskier than you find ideal, though, you may get a little shelter if you move back onto the park bench to ponder the great ponderables and mull over the life of the lowly oyster.

Beachcombing Low-tide exploring of the broad, varied shore provides the chief interest of this beach (along with the aforementioned nearby food treats!). Do bring sturdy shoes and be prepared to wade, though. Even at the lowest tide, many sections of the extensive shore are under water.

Seclusion The desire to get away from It All, or even some of the All, should not lead you to seek out this spot. Although you won't find the beach crowded, you will find the shore in both directions not only spotted with various breeds of shore-goer but also lined with houses and resorts.

View of Chrome Island Lighthouse

80

QUALICUM BAY—SOUTH
The best access to the
south end of Qualicum Bay
tidal flats

Location, signs and parking A minute or two south of the main cluster of shops and eateries in Qualicum Bay, look for a set of mailboxes on the ocean side of the highway immediately opposite a sign for Cochrane Road. Confusingly, you will see two short dirt tracks leading toward the shore. The southernmost one, with the warning against the dire consequences of eating clams or oysters, is the one for you, your beachware and your beachwear. Parking is probably best on the shoulder of the highway, since a concrete barrier has been placed a short distance down the smoother of the two dirt tracks.

Path Twenty metres of easy, level strolling take you down the dirt track, over the concrete barrier and onto the shore.

Beach Most beachgoers will be forgiven for finding the beach directly in front of this access a little uninspiring. In the absence of signs forbidding fires or late-night parking, some have evidently found the spot good for a beach fire and wiener roast. Until it is carried away by winter storms, a log is positioned to act as a seat near the remains of a firepit. It is also possible to find a reasonably comfortable roosting spot in a small area of loose pebbles and gravel. Low down, the beach is largely covered with an unbroken expanse of fist-sized rocks, though a gravel bar enclosing a large tidal pool adds visual variety. Since the tide doesn't go out a huge distance, as it does immediately to the north, and since the shore is mostly level, this is a feasible spot for launching a kayak.

Suitability for children The best bet for enticing a child to this beach is the promise of concocting a s'more or setting a marshmallow alight. Still, sure-footed and energetic children will have fun exploring the large tidal pool or, with their parents, walking the short distance north to the tidal flats of the main part of Qualicum Bay—and its ice cream shops.

Suitability for groups The limited parking and upper beach area make this suitable for no more than a car or two's worth of beachgoers.

View This is a good spot to get the sense of how Denman and Hornby islands link, punctuated by tiny Chrome Island with its signature lighthouse. Don't forget that this section of coast is marketed as "lighthouse country," though Chrome Island lighthouse is the only lighthouse that you can see clearly during the day. Directly across, huge Texada Island dominates the skyline while its smaller cousin, Lasqueti Island, nestles up against its southern flank. The Sisters Lighthouse, the other lighthouse in question, is just off the north of Texada.

Winds, sun and shade Because this shore faces largely northeast, neither a northwest nor southeast wind smacks you straight in the face—or not quite. We all know about sea breezes and how they tend to feel straight on, even when they're not. Those looking for a spot to enjoy polishing off *War and Peace* while not being burnt to a crisp should note that this is one of the few shores that treats you to lots of afternoon shade.

Beachcombing Those whose primary aim is to enjoy the extensive tidal flats and gigantic tidal pool in the middle part of Qualicum Bay will find that they are probably happiest parking here and walking along the shore, rather than parking along the cramped shoulder in the middle of the bay and then having to scramble down the steep rubble of broken rock. To the south, your walking will take you to a large public camping and RV resort on the shores of Big Qualicum River.

Seclusion This is a quiet area of shore, but not a particularly secluded one. The beach immediately below the access is well buffered by foliage from adjoining houses, but to the north the area is well peopled.

While you're here, you may wish to check out two similar spots, both a little farther south from Qualicum Bay, but both with slightly better shorefront parking and, in one case, with a park bench. Look for tracks to the shore leaving the highway by houses numbered 5361 and 5524.

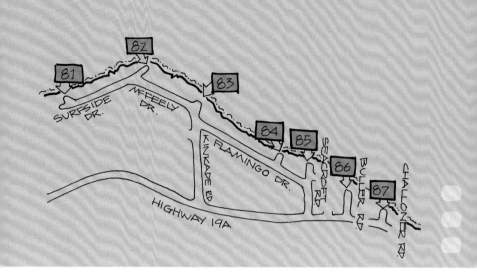

81
SURFSIDE DRIVE—WEST
Easy access to a huge low-tide area of sandbars and gravel bars

Location, signs and parking Reaching this spot from the highway might seem like a bit of a trek, though the sequence of roads that brings you here could hardly be simpler. Opposite the Riverside Resort, turn off the highway onto Kinkade Road and follow it until it merges to the left into McFeely Drive and, soon after, bumps into Surfside Drive. Follow Surfside to the left until nearly its end. You will see opening up on your right a short, wide bit of road leading to the shore. You will find plentiful parking for several cars near the end of the gravel area and a few signs to curb your inclination to let your mastiff run off leash, to light fires, to camp, and, oddly, to ride motorbikes on the beach. Those in quest of the cunning clam or oyster will have to go elsewhere: they're contaminated here. For your information, too, in case it is relevant to something devious you have in mind, you are told this is part of the Parksville Qualicum Beach Wildlife Management Area. Those in quest of the perfect car picnicking spot might be misled by looking at a map and thinking that they will have an unimpeded view of their seagull friends. In fact, residential lots on either side of the entrance jut forward, creating something like tunnel vision for the intrepid car picnicker.

Path You will see no path. You will, however, see an easy patch of gravel and coarse sand that allows you and all of the beaching goods you want to get to the shore with almost no effort. Those with walking difficulties are particularly well served because few logs usually block the way as they do at many similar spots along this stretch. In fact, those with walking difficulties need go no farther than a park bench positioned with a splendid view of the shore.

Beach The remarkable size and variety of the beach seems to be the result of the outflow from the Little Qualicum River that cuts at an angle across the shore to the north. The result is an amazing series of sand and gravel bars. At a half tide, indeed, you can stand in shallow water and see stretching out to sea a series of bars and patches, some of them similarly ankle deep or even above the water level. Sunbathers and picnickers might wish that the upper beach were a titch sandier and, perhaps, graced with a few more all-purpose logs. Still, they should have no difficulty finding a pleasant spot to plonk themselves down among the loose pebbles and coarse sand.

Suitability for children This beach isn't quite perfect for children—the patches of barnacle-covered gravel see to that. Children looking to skimboard or run unhampered in bare feet will not be thrilled. Otherwise, though, this beach has a lot to offer. Flying kites, building sandcastles and battlegrounds, hunting out crabs and similar critters and so on are all enticing options. Parents should keep two considerations in mind, though. First, don't forget the all-powerful barnacle: water shoes or crocs are a must. Second, be mindful that there is some danger on an incoming tide that a tiny non-swimmer will be cheerfully wandering along a sand or gravel bar only to discover that a beeline toward shore means dropping into scarily deep water.

Suitability for groups Two characteristics of this beach make it great for even a multi-car picnic extravaganza. A huge parking area and a huge, low-tide beach area can accommodate the reunion of even the most enthusiastically fertile family. Still, this is a residential subdivision, not a park.

Since most groups are happiest where they can find tables and washrooms, they will probably want to go elsewhere.

View One of the most interesting aspects of the view is not across the strait but toward Mount Arrowsmith, across the meadows that line one side of Surfside Road. Another is that this is one of the few spots along this coast where you can look up from your salt-stained library book and see the Beaufort Range and the mountains extending north along Vancouver Island.

Winds, sun and shade While a northwest wind can pack a wallop just around the corner from this spot, at the upper beach you will find some protection, especially if you are sitting on the park bench. Don't expect any such protection from a southeast wind, however. On a cool but sunny day, you don't have to worry about being further cooled by shade. There is almost none. If you really want a shady spot, you can find a little in late afternoon cast by a small fir to the left of the parking area.

Beachcombing For certain kinds of beachcombers, this shore is paradise. If you would love to wander far, far away from shore through tidal pools and across a mixed shore while hunting for colourful seashells, you could hardly do better. Be aware, though, that you will be happiest with crocs or flip-flops that you can easily remove and refit. Also be aware that, while the most extensive shore lies to the north, the Little Qualicum River does provide a barrier.

Seclusion You certainly won't find any seclusion from the many houses that line the low, treeless shore. You may, or may not, find seclusion from other beachgoers. While hardly a hot spot, this access route to the shore is occasionally used by others.

While you're here, you can find an even quieter, though less spacious, approach to much the same beach by driving down a narrow track beside a house numbered 1013. Also note that Surfside Drive borders on the signposted Marshall-Stevenson Wildlife Sanctuary.

82

SURFSIDE DRIVE—EAST

A large, sun-baked expanse
of beach logs and gravel
leading to a lower beach
with a distinctive gravel bar

Location, signs and parking Kinkade Road leaves the highway just south of the Riverside Resort and morphs into McFeely Drive as it approaches the shore. When you reach Surfside Drive, turn right. A very short distance brings you to a large, paved turnaround and a small forest of signs. The most informative signs indicate, through icons, that you must not light beach fires, camp, ride motorcycles (strange, but true) or let your dog off leash. Two larger signs reinforce two of the prohibitions, namely against campfires and against camping or overnight parking. One of the ghoulish Fisheries notices, complete with skull and crossbones, warns you of the dangers of eating contaminated shellfish. A small, functional sign identifies the spot as being part of the Parksville Qualicum Beach Wildlife Management Area but doesn't go further in saying how this might affect your behaviour.

Path A largely level, open area takes you past a short section of bank-stabilizing boulders onto an extensive stretch of beach plants, loose sand and pebbles, and beach logs. Be prepared for a little unstable footing, but don't worry overmuch about having to manoeuvre unwieldy family members over the beach logs, since at this spot they are well spaced.

Beach It's hard to know where the beach itself starts and the upper shore stops. Certainly the most distinctive trait of this spot is the huge, almost dunelike area of exposed logs and pebbles. Otherwise, the beach is most interesting for the gravel bar that scoops toward the north and, at mid tide, creates an interesting waterline. Most visitors will probably want to spread out their array of lotions and reading material on the upper beach. High tide is the time to come if you want to combine sunning with swimming. Even then, be prepared with beach shoes, since you will be swimming over gravel bristling with some devilish little barnacles.

Opportunistic kayakers might note that the tide doesn't go out nearly as far here as at most other nearby spots.

Suitability for children It would be an unusual child who would beg to be brought to this beach. Even so, at high tide in particular, most children will find lots of entertainment in the form of logs to leap over, pebbles to skip and, of course, water molecules to send flying.

Suitability for groups The spot is suitable to a bevy of picnickers who would like a large area that they are almost guaranteed to have all to themselves. The ample parking for a small group and the large section of beach suitable for lounging against logs, even at high tide, are its most apparent attractions.

View To the north, your view of distant Denman and Hornby islands is unrestricted. The middle of the strait is dominated by the graceful bumps of Texada and, a little south, Lasqueti islands. Tiny Sangster Island seems to bob, alone in the middle of the strait, off the edge of Lasqueti Island. Most distinctive about this spot, though, is that it is one of the very few beaches from which you can see Mount Arrowsmith—at least if you look behind the beach across the estuary.

Winds, sun and shade On a hot day, come with sunglasses and sunscreen, since you will find no shade. On a blustery day, come with windbreakers or sweaters, since you will find no protection from the wind.

Beachcombing Any stroll along the shore will almost certainly begin with the interesting sandbar. After that, the beach is your oyster—so to speak. Turn left if, after a short distance, you would like to find yourself on a huge stretch of low-tide estuary created by the Little Qualicum River. Do, however, come psyched up for the fact that though the beach is largely level, if you try hard you could twist an ankle on the irregular surface of small rocks.

Seclusion There are few beaches with less privacy—houses press forward along the entire stretch of low shore on either side of the access strip. Nary a twig stands between you and the gleaming picture windows. On the beach itself, however, you may well be the only ones drinking in this particular segment of sea air.

83

KINKADE ROAD

A peculiar but level approach to
a wide sun-baked upper shore
of beach logs and gravel, and
a lower shore of unusually
long sand and gravel bars

Location, signs and parking A few minutes north of Qualicum, look for the Riverside Resort and, a short distance south, Kinkade Road crossing the highway. Follow Kinkade Road to where it bends to the left. (Beware Google Maps, which indicates another Kincade Road, with a different spelling, a hundred metres past the bend.) In the bend, pull over onto the shoulder by a set of concrete barriers and a large sign immediately in front of a green utility structure, reading SURFSIDE WATER CONSERVATION LEVEL. You will find room for several cars along the shoulder, though no clearly defined parking area. From this spot you will see no signs indicating that this is a public beach access, but once you walk toward the shore, you'll see a dizzying number of signs, several repeating each other. Planning a beach party? You will see signs telling you—twice—that you can-not light fires and telling you—twice—that you may not camp or park overnight, though without specifying when you must leave, as such signs often do. Shellfish gatherers, take note that your chowder ingredients must come from elsewhere, since they are contaminated here. Weirdly, motorcycles are explicitly forbidden on a beach where they couldn't pos-sibly drive. Lastly, dog owners looking for a place to set Fifi the bulldog free among the waves should be aware that Fifi must here be on leash. Interestingly, though, another sign tells you that this is part of the Parksville Qualicum Beach Wildlife Management Area, but does so on a sign markedly different from those employed south of this spot. This one says nothing explicit about keeping your dog off the beach during the March and April brant migration period, so you might be a little guarded about what animals you bring to this beach and exactly when.

Path You will probably see no path at first, but once you walk past the concrete barriers you will spot a clear, level and well-beaten path snaking alongside a barrier of boulders apparently marking the weirdly shaped edge of the private property on the right. About 30 easy metres will bring you to the shore. Those unsteady on their feet should have no difficulty going the distance but will have to be prepared to clamber over some logs that can block the beach itself.

Beach The most immediately striking feature of the beach is the wide expanse of sun-bleached logs. While a first glance suggests this area of logs would be a good place to settle down with a fat bestseller, you would need padding from the golf-ball-sized rocks that make up the top part of the shore. For more comfortable sitting, head farther along the upper beach to a strip of finer pebbles and coarse sand. Although the tide descends quite far over the largely gravel-and-barnacle shore, at mid tide the shoreline is interestingly varied. You will have a hard time resisting the temptation to explore a long gravel bar projecting from your left in front of the access point. Even at low tide, an irregular, shallow "inlet" provides warm paddling water not far from the upper beach.

Suitability for children This is one of those beaches, dominated by gravel and barnacles, where so much of a child's fun depends on the height of tide and the child's personality. At low tide, the child who loves poking around for starfish, limpets, chitons and shore crabs could be delighted. The child who likes only the sensation of bare feet on sand will not. At high tide, when the water laps up to the area of coarse sand and pebbles, the options for leaping from log to log and chaotically splashing are enough to keep most children somewhere on the scale between vaguely contented and exhilarated.

Suitability for groups Most small groups would find enough parking and a large enough upper beach area to be able to lounge, stroll and munch comfortably and unintrusively. Even so, the beach is not likely to be a huge draw for most groups.

View At most tide levels, the large gravel bar will attract the first notice of most visitors. Otherwise, the most striking features are the sweep of foreshore to the south, and, across the strait, the charmless, open-pit mines of Texada Island.

Winds, sun and shade Don't expect much protection from sun or wind at this exposed spot, though a northwest wind doesn't strike the shore as directly as does a southeast wind.

Beachcombing Most visitors will no doubt want to begin a shore wander with an exploration of the intriguing gravel bar. You can walk a considerable distance in either direction without much to hinder your steps or your thoughts. For the most dramatic change in view, though, you might prefer to turn north. As you round the curving shoreline, you will find not only that your view of islands to the north suddenly opens up, but also that you will be gazing across the huge, low-tide estuary created by the Little Qualicum River.

Seclusion On one side of the access path, a few trees provide a little screening from the local residents. On the other side, while no such screen exists, the houses are set far away across a stretch of short grass.

84
FLAMINGO DRIVE—WEST
An easy, level approach to a broad upper beach of coarse sand and pebbles amid beach logs and beach grass

Location, signs and parking From the highway, turn down Seacroft Road, a few minutes north of Qualicum. Turn left onto Flamingo and continue along it about 100 m until you see an obvious open stretch of gravel leading to the shore. Park on the grassy area at the end of the road. You will find lots of space here for several cars, though you most likely won't encounter any. Apart from a venerable and nearly indecipherable concrete access sign largely hidden in the vegetation, you will see no sign anticipating that you—or any other beach-lover—is expected here and needs welcoming, warning or prohibiting.

Path The distance to the shore from your car full of beach lovers and beaching devices will largely depend on how far forward you wish to park in the unmaintained grassy area at the end of the road. You won't find a groomed path, but should have no difficulty manoeuvring yourself and even stubby little others onto the nearly level shore.

Beach Although the lower beach is largely small gravel—and, it follows, barnacles—the entire shore is attractively sculpted with gravel bars projecting from the shore in either direction, each of them forming a gigantic tidal pool at low tide. The majority of visitors, however, will probably find the beach most inviting at high tide, when the broad area of coarse sand, pebbles, beach logs and beach grass makes a welcoming swath for picnicking and soaking up far more sun than is healthy for you before taking a cooling dip. Water shoes, crocs or flip-flops are essential, unless you have a very high pain threshold.

Suitability for children As with adults, so with children. Come near high tide on a warm day and your well-shod children will enjoy a gleeful hour's splashing while you loll among the logs. Rest assured that the shore slants gradually enough that your wee ones won't disappear into the depths, but not so gradually that they need to wade out toward the horizon to get past their waists. Low tide, however, can make for less gleeful wandering around the stretches of gravel in quest of distant low-tide sand.

Suitability for groups A group of two or three cars hunting down a private picnic spot could do far worse than choose this spot to spread out their Tupperware containers. The spot is probably better for a picnic dinner than a picnic lunch, however, since it is during the evening that tides tend to be in and the beach is at its most attractive and most swimmable. Don't forget that there are no park facilities.

View The view is expansive, spreading from horizon to horizon via Lasqueti and Texada islands. Even so, this spot is located in the centre of a small, shallow bay. The result is a pleasantly framed view, but one that excludes both Denman and Hornby islands, key ingredients of most viewpoints along this coast.

Winds, sun and shade Because of the slight tilt of the bay toward the south, you will find a little protection from a northwest wind if it happens to be raising goosebumps on goosebump-prone flesh. From a southeast wind, usually accompanied by cooler weather anyway, you can expect no such muffling. As for shade, this spot provides none. You can, however, probably find a shaded spot to park your car.

Beachcombing You will have to be prepared for a little loose footing along the upper beach and uneven footing on the lower beach. Even so, you will find nothing much standing in the way of your wandering a considerable distance along the shore in either direction. To the north, however, you will find not just a huge expanse of shore, but lots of channels and huge tidal pools. To the south, less than 3 km away, via more spits and pools, lie the sands of Qualicum Beach.

Seclusion It is the relative isolation of this spot, along with the difficulty of finding it, that is most likely to provide you with seclusion—at least from other beachgoers. From the neighbouring houses you will get little seclusion, though the houses on either side of the access spot are set back a little, especially on the left.

85

FLAMINGO DRIVE—EAST
A quiet access best suited to those looking for a good kayak-launching shore, car-picnic vantage point or shade-protected resting area

Location, signs and parking From the Island Highway a few minutes north of Qualicum Beach, look for the Seacroft Road sign just north of Deez Bar and Grill. Simply follow it for 200 m to its end. The pavement goes right to the edge of the boulder-reinforced shore, so you can arrive with binoculars and Thermos on even the most inhospitable day and have a ringside seat on whatever the Strait of Georgia has on offer. One sign tells you that this is—as if you need reminding—a public access. Dog owners, however, do need to be reminded to keep their chihuahuas well away during March and April, and to clean up after their dogs at other times of the year. Think: plastic bags. This is, you are told, a wildlife management area, but you are "welcome" nevertheless. Overnight parking, or even late night beach partying, is, predictably, not allowed.

Path Although you can virtually drive to the beach, in fact you are 2 m above it at the top of a steep bank of boulders. The dirt track to the shore is short but could be difficult to manage for the very young or the very old.

Beach The beach itself is not likely to be the main draw for those choosing this spot. It is safe and pleasant for swimming at high tide and, at low tide, is chiefly interesting for the huge tidal pools and channels separated by gravel bars extending more than 200 m to the low-tide line. Picnicking, too, is possible, and even appealing, since this is one of the few beaches in the area where you can picnic in the shade. Many would understandably choose to picnic at the park bench at the top of the bank, since the beach itself has only a narrow area of loose pebbles and usually collects few logs. This is a reasonably good place to launch kayaks, the steep little path notwithstanding. The tide does not generally go out nearly as far here as at most spots in the area, and the shore is largely smooth underfoot.

Suitability for children Don't select this spot from among others in the area if your aim is to provide your eager children with a summer afternoon's worth of sand and sea. The shore is level and poses no threats other than the dreaded barnacle, but is not a great play beach.

Suitability for groups Only a group that wants to take advantage of the unusual features of the spot—the shaded beach or the decent kayak launching, for example—would want to choose this spot, in spite of the capacious and shaded parking.

View The view, like so much else about this beach, is without striking features, though the sense of the wide open Strait of Georgia extending to the horizon in either direction is nowhere stronger than here. The shore is slightly concave to the north, however, and does provide a small treed point to frame your view.

Winds, sun and shade A northwest wind hits the shore at an angle but can nevertheless seem a little fresher than you sometimes want. A southeast wind, though usually not as strong in this area as in others, hits the shore directly. This exposure to winds, in combination with the afternoon shade, can make the upper beach comparatively cool.

Beachcombing Choose an extremely low tide for the most interesting beach exploring. To the north, the tide withdraws more than 300 m and exposes a convoluted series of gravel formations and sandbars, channels and huge tidal pools. To the south, after about 2.5 km you will come upon the sands of Qualicum Beach via an interestingly varied shore.

Seclusion One of the features of this spot that makes it such a prime choice for car picnicking is that you won't feel as if you are jammed in between houses full of curious neighbours. High fences as well as plenty of space can make you feel you have an exclusive front-seat view of a winter blow. Make sure you have a large Thermos and a restful CD.

86
BULLER ROAD
A few steps from the end of the road to a varied shore comprising a sandy upper beach, a huge tidal pool and steep gravel bar

Location, signs and parking Buller Road leaves the Island Highway on the northern outskirts of Qualicum. Unlike Challoner Road, immediately south, which entices the visitor with two PUBLIC ACCESS signs, Buller Road faces the potential visitor with two No Thru Road signs. In fact, however, even as you turn onto Buller Road, you can see the open coast beckoning a short distance ahead. If you still feel any doubt that this is a public access, you will be reassured by three signs, all three more or less concerned with the spot as a brant goose feeding area during the spring migration. While the first two signs tell you to keep your puppy well away during March and April and to clean up after her during the rest of the year, the third, hearteningly, welcomes you to the Parksville Qualicum Beach Wildlife Management Area. You will also see a robust garbage stand bearing the fascinatingly heraldic coat of arms of Qualicum—replete, anthropologists take note, with a teepee! Considerably less charming is the steel manhole cover bearing the words RDN

Sanitary Sewer. Take heart: unlike some similar spots, this one has no murky little stream running down the beach.

Path Some will want to enjoy their visit here from the viewpoint of the park bench poised immediately above a patch of bank-stabilizing boulders. Even visitors with walking issues, however, will have little difficulty taking the few steps down the sloping path to the shore.

Beach Those beachgoers interested in garnering sunbeams will be most interested in the upper beach of coarse sand and pebbles. More active beach-goers will want to come at low tide and explore the huge tidal pool and steep-sided gravel bar extending to the south. Another unusual feature of the shore is the two sets of ragged boulders and trapped beach logs on either side of the upper shore. The shore immediately to the south of the access path is susceptible to collecting mounds of dead seaweed, though seaweed accumulations vary enormously from week to week throughout the year.

Suitability for children Most children would probably be happiest here at high tide, either munching thoughtfully on a peanut-butter-and-honey sandwich or getting as quickly and thoroughly wet as they can. More curious children, their feet armoured with sturdy water shoes, could also be happy at low tide exploring the unusual gravel bar. If you arrive at an intermediate tide, however, be aware that small children might start wading over the gravel bar from north to south, only to discover as they turn toward shore that the depth suddenly increases by almost a metre. The possibilities for panic, and worse, hardly need spelling out.

Suitability for groups A few cars stuffed with family members from Back East, hungry for pasta salad and a beach exploration, could be charmed by this spot for an hour or two, especially if you want a spot all to your-selves. In general, though, even small groups would be happiest at more conventional, sandy beaches.

View The angle of the shore is such that your view is primarily toward the southern horizon and the distant bumps of Lasqueti and Texada islands. Both Denman and Hornby islands, signature components of most views along this coast, are completely obscured by the northern shoreline.

Winds, sun and shade Winds from the northwest tend to angle past the shore slightly here, but only slightly. Southeast winds, in contrast, come ashore more or less head-on. If you are cooler than you like, you can get some shelter from winds by snuggling down beside either of the two piles of rocks and logs extending down the shore. If you need shade on a blistering day, this is not the place to come unless you can provide your own. On the other hand, you need not worry, as you will at many points farther south, that trees will cast cooling afternoon shade on your swim.

Beachcombing Like most other access spots along this stretch of coast, this is good for those who like to chalk up several seaside kilometres— and don't mind making their way along an irregular surface. Sturdy footwear will make for a more comfortable walk.

Seclusion Plenty of houses line the shoreline here, so don't expect to go unobserved in your shorefront antics. Equally, though, don't expect to meet many other beachgoers. Almost everyone in this area heads for the sandy stretches to the south.

87

CHALLONER ROAD

A well-signposted but slightly constricted approach to a distinctive shore of dunes, gravel bars, tidal pools and sandy patches

Location, signs and parking Both the boldly affirmative Public Access sign and the Challoner Road sign should make your quest for this spot easy sailing. Less easy sailing, however, might be your approach to the shore itself if, as sometimes happens, Challoner Road is lined with cars (apparently belonging to guests of the adjoining resort). If you feel up to squeezing past these cars, you will find limited parking at the end of the short, paved road. At the welcoming end of the scale you will find two park benches and another Public Access sign identical to the first. On the finger-wagging end of the scale, you will find signs telling you to keep your dog well away during brant migration season, March and April, and to clean up after this same dog during the rest of the year. A more colourful and informative sign tells you about the wildlife management area you are entering. As for overnight parking (and we know what that means), don't even think about it.

Path A level path of loose sand winds for about 30 m through a dunelike area of venerable beach logs and dune plants. While this arrangement should make for an easy approach to the shore for most beachgoers in most conditions, be aware that those with walking difficulties might find the loose sand a bit of a struggle.

Beach The beach is unusual, though its components are not. Most striking is the high gravel bar cutting across the access spot from the left, a huge tidal pool behind it, depending on the tide, and to the right, a large area of low-tide sand. The sandiest upper shore is directly in front of a resort to the south of the public access. The upper beach in front of the access path is composed largely of pebbles and coarse sand. Those looking for a spacious picnic or sun-soaking shore will be well rewarded.

Suitability for children While the smallest of the breed will have to be toted through the long stretch of loose sand and logs, most children should find this a great beach for sand and water play. Experienced parents will make sure that a beach bag contains the usual protection against the elements, including, in this case, barnacles. While kites and castles are well within the play possibilities here, skimboards and Frisbees are a little less suited because of the comparatively small areas of sand.

Suitability for groups The main drawbacks to this spot for a group's gleeful frolicking are, first, the lack of much parking space and, of course, the lack of facilities. Otherwise, the large picnicking area, well away from dwellings on either side, and the enticingly diverse beach make this a great spot for an outing.

View Hornby Island is almost tucked out of sight to the north, and the southern shore of Qualicum Beach Bay sweeps out to the horizon to the south. In between, you will find about as open and expansive a view as you will find anywhere on the east coast of the Island.

Winds, sun and shade If a northwest wind is a little on the fresh side, you will find some protection on this somewhat south-facing shore. The logs of the upper beach can also provide a smidgeon of buffering. A southeast wind, however, will be as frisky here as it is farther out in the strait.

On a sunny day, with little wind, this can be a hot spot. Don't expect a trace of shade, so come prepared with all the SPF you can muster.

Beachcombing This is a great place to undertake a bracing or inspiring stroll by the sea. Nothing will stand in your way of getting as many kilometres under your belt as you want. Come at a fairly low tide, however, to vary your terrain between the smooth but slanted mid-shore and the more level but often irregular lower shore.

Seclusion Largely because of the trees and the long expanse of logs and grass, the spot is surprisingly secluded from neighbouring dwellings and resorts. On the other hand, this stretch of shore is used by many beachgoers, especially those who arrive at the nearby resort, eager to find their first sand dollar and pat their first turret into position.

88

QUALICUM BEACH—NORTH
A well-signposted and level access to a broad gravel shore at the north end of the bay at Qualicum Beach

Location, signs and parking No map is provided for this spot, since it is immediately beside the highway. This is one of the few signposted public access spots between Qualicum Beach and Campbell River. To confirm your location, look for the house numbered 3263 and the short, wide strip of road leading directly to the shore. You will find space for several cars in the gravel area at the end of the road, but you are better off keeping to the left of the space so as not to block the drive of the house on that side. Because the shore here is within the feeding and recovery grounds for the spring migration of brant geese, you will see signs telling you to keep your beach-loving hound far distant during March and April. Other signs tell you that even during the rest of the year, you are responsible for cleaning up after your beloved pooch, that shellfish are contaminated and that parking between 11 p.m. and 6 a.m. is forbidden.

Path A slightly grim-looking metal structure covers the end of a drain-pipe emptying onto the beach in the middle of the access spot; thickets of beach grass block your way onto the shore on either side of this structure. A park bench to the left, however, is perched immediately above the most inviting section of the upper beach. In fact, if you're after a spot that allows you a full beach view from the comfort of a bench, this is one of the few spots along this section of coast allowing that combination.

Beach You are far enough north of the central beach that you are a long way from its appealing expanses of sand. If you can overlook the some-what slimy area of beach created by the trickle from the drainpipe, you will find that, at a very low tide, the configuration of gravel bars to the north creates an intriguing shoreline. If you are primarily after a sandy spot in the full sun to spread out your picnic wares, you will find exactly that on the upper shore immediately below the bench.

Suitability for children Getting the younger set to and from the car is a piece of cake. Older children could enjoy a low-tide—but well-shod—romp along the interesting gravel bars to the north. Very small children will be happy enough nestled into the loose sandy parts of the upper shore. Most children, however, will be happiest at high tide, when they can make watery mayhem—though, again, only if they have a skookum pair of water shoes.

Suitability for groups This is a spot most suited to a family or two, but not to even a very small throng. Take your entourage south to the main beach.

View The view from this spot has many advantages over that from the more obviously accessible spots immediately south. Whether from your car during cold weather or from the shore during warm weather, you will find that you can see far south across the sweep of bay toward Qualicum Beach and the distant horizon of the southern strait. To the north, Hornby Island is almost, but not quite, tucked out of sight.

Winds, sun and shade Because this stretch of shore tilts slightly south-ward, a northwest wind slides past without too much fuss. A southeast wind, however, has no compunctions about making itself felt. The com-plete absence of shade on a day with little wind can make for a broiling afternoon. Come prepared.

Beachcombing The beach is level and broad in both directions, though you may prefer to head north if you want to keep away from fellow explorers. Come at low tide if you want to put the most distance under your hoofs. You don't need to worry about clambering over boulders or rough shore, but you will nevertheless need to be buffered against barnacles.

Seclusion The shore immediately in front of the access and for a considerable distance in either direction is jam-packed with eager little houses pressing forward for every bit of sea view they can get. Don't expect anything approaching seclusion—but don't expect, either, to see many others sharing the shore.

89
QUALICUM BEACH— BRANT VIEWING AREA
Huge gravel parking area and easy access to a mixed shore of sand, gravel and massive boulders at the north end of Qualicum Beach

Location, signs and parking No map is provided for this spot, since it is immediately beside the highway. This could well be the least "secret" spot in this book—but, also, of all prominently placed spots, the least noticed. A short distance north of the main sweep of Qualicum Beach, look for a low-trimmed hedge separating the highway from a long gravel strip immediately back of the shore. In this area you will find parking for a few dozen cars and some signs, three of them directed toward dog owners. Like the access immediately north, this one forbids you and your eager beagle from stepping onto the beach from March 1 to April 30, the period when migrating brant geese are trying to recoup their energies. Unlike the neighbouring access, however, this one doesn't require you to wield your leash during the summer months. Leashed or unleashed, however, your pooch needs you to clean up after it. Another sign, oddly perched on a beach stump, warns you against the dangers of gathering chowder supplies here.

Path Although some spots in the large parking area are farther away from the easiest access routes to the shore than others, at others you can park virtually on the upper shore. Keep that in mind when the winter storms are inspiring you to bring a freshly baked blueberry muffin and cuppa for a little soul-stirring seaside picnic. On the south end of this area, note a parklike strip of lawn with shade trees and several picnic tables.

Beach The ample parking notwithstanding, this spot will compete with the main part of the beach as an alternative only for visitors with special interests. With the long stretches of perfect sand and ample parking so nearby, most beachgoers will see little point in coming to a spot where they have to walk across expanses of gravel and boulders to get to their sandy pleasures. For those who do not belong to this large majority, however, this spot is one they will want to remember and seek out for its attractive advantages. First is an area of sand backed by thickets of graceful beach grass, perfect for laying down a picnic blanket and more comfortable than the gravel covering the upper shore of the main beach. Second is a diversity of shore life and textures. Here shore-goers will find low-tide sand, yes, but also mounds of boulders with the limpets, chitons, sea snails, hermit crabs, blennies, clingfish and so on that are not to be found on the sandy beach. Third is the viewing platform extending out and over the shore, perfect for setting up a tripod during brant viewing season in early spring.

Suitability for children Most children will want to head straight for the main sandy beach a few hundred metres away, of course. But come here in any sunny weather and you are likely to find adventurous children climbing over and around the mounds of giant boulders, wading through the tidal pools and generally ignoring the sand.

Suitability for groups For a group that would like a spot virtually all to themselves, this spot has huge advantages over the main beach. The extensive parking, the picnic tables and the pleasant upper beach for resting mean that you can bring a dozen or two beach-lovers here and have a beautiful seaside spot almost entirely to yourselves.

View Since you are on the western end of the gently curving bay of Qualicum Beach, your view will tend toward the gentle curve of the bay and the southern part of the strait. Mountain enthusiasts will take note of the permanent snowfields of Mount Tantalus on the mainland, probably the most spectacular peak visible between Qualicum and Lantzville.

Winds, sun and shade The main part of Qualicum's beach tends to feel a northwest wind less than the coast immediately north and south. This spot feels even less of that wind. Southeast winds, though rarely strong here, do blow more or less directly onto the shore. Rarely, but violently, the Qualicum offshore wind creates dramatic "cat's paws" on the riffled water. You will find no shade on the beach itself but, on a hot day, can move up to the grassy area, where a few leafy shade trees march along the lawn.

Beachcombing This is a shore almost purpose-made for beach exploring, even though the mounds and ridges of boulders testify to a lot of "cultural modification." The breadth of the beach at low tide, along with its sheer variety of surfaces and shore life, will no doubt attract most visitors to shift into investigation mode. Warm up your macro lens.

Seclusion You will find nothing even remotely secluded about this spot—but will be surprised that so few visitors use it.

Qualicum Beach—Brant Viewing Area

BEST BETS

All beachgoers will find favourite spots, and for the most personal of reasons. Perhaps one beach will become a favourite because of the configuration of tidal pools. Another one might have a particularly cozy little nest among beach logs. Yet another might have much-needed public toilets. As a starting point, however, many will find the following recommendations handy.

1. Varied shore

1	Seagull Road
2	Shell Road
4	Heard Road
9	Laval Road
12	Driftwood Road—North
13	Driftwood Road—Middle
15	Elma Bay Place
17	Williams Beach
22	Coleman Road
23	Coral Road
24	Perrey's Beach
25	Seal Bay
39	Longview Road—West
40	Longview Road—East
46	Goose Spit
47	Hilton Road
48A	Marine Drive—West
53	Amber Way
58	Union Bay Boat Launch
64	Ship's Point Park
67	Deep Bay Spit
69	Shoreline Drive (Bowser)
70	Moss Park
71	Buccaneer Beach
81	Surfside Drive—West
86	Buller Road
87	Challoner Road
88	Qualicum Beach—North
89	Qualicum Beach—Brant Viewing Area

2. Car picnicking

2	Shell Road
3	Shoreline Drive (Campbell River)
4	Heard Road
7	Langton Road
16	Seaview Road
17	Williams Beach
19	Pantuso Road
22	Coleman Road
23	Coral Road
27	Wilkinson Road
31	Little River Road
36	Kin Beach—South
40	Longview Road—East
41	Point Holmes
42	Lazo Road
45	Curtis Road—West
46	Goose Spit
47	Hilton Road
48A	Marine Drive—West
52	Gartley Road
53	Amber Way
56	Argyle Road
66	Berray Road
68	Deep Bay Drive
69	Shoreline Drive (Bowser)
71	Buccaneer Beach
74	Henson Road
76	Crane Road
79	Qualicum Bay—North
81	Surfside Drive—West
85	Seacroft Road

3. Launching kayaks

5	Sailor Road (mid to high tide)
9	Laval Road, Pacific Playgrounds Marina
16	Seaview Road
19	Pantuso Road (mid to high tide)
20	Kitty Coleman Provincial Park
22	Coleman Road (high tide)
23	Coral Road (high tide)
27	Wilkinson Road (high tide)
29	Singing Sands Road

30	Mayfair Road
31	Little River Road
33	Booth Road
34	Astra Road
36	Kin Beach—South (high tide)
41	Point Holmes (launching ramp)
45	Curtis Road—West (mid to high tide)
46	Goose Spit
47	Hilton Road (mid to high tide)
48A	Marine Drive—West (mid to high tide)
51	Bartel Road (mid to high tide)
52	Gartley Road
56	Argyle Road (mid to high tide)
57	Dorothy Road
58	Union Bay Boat Launch
59	Baynes Sound Rest Area
61	Buckley Bay Frontage Road
63	Wente Way (high tide)
67	Deep Bay Spit (or nearby marina)
68	Deep Bay Drive (high tide)
71	Buccaneer Beach
73	Bowser Road
74	Henson Road
75	Nile Road
78	Sunnybeach Road
82	Surfside Drive—East (mid tide)
85	Seacroft Road (mid tide)
86	Buller Road (high tide)

4. Viewing sunsets

28	Florence Road
29	Singing Sands Road
39	Longview Road—West
49	Carey Place
62	Tozer Road
63	Wente Way
67	Deep Bay Spit
81	Surfside Drive—West

5. Taking small children

6	Oyster Bay Rest Area
9	Laval Road
10	Saratoga Beach
11	Seaman Road
12	Driftwood Road—North
15	Elma Bay Place
17	Williams Beach
23	Coral Road

24	Perrey's Beach
35	Kin Beach—North
37	Windslow Road—North
38	Elks and Royal Purple Park
39	Longview Road—West
42	Lazo Road
44	Curtis Road—East
45	Curtis Road—West
46	Goose Spit
52	Gartley Road
71	Buccaneer Beach (high tide)
77	Franksea Road (low tide)
78	Sunnybeach Road (low tide)
81	Surfside Drive—West (low tide)
87	Challoner Road (low tide)
88	Qualicum Beach—North

6. Taking adventurous children

1	Seagull Road
3	Shoreline Drive (Campbell River)
4	Heard Road
8	Oyster River Nature Trails
13	Driftwood Road—Middle
18	Eagles Drive Park
20	Kitty Coleman Provincial Park
21	Davey Janes Road
25	Seal Bay
36	Kin Beach—South
39	Longview Road—West
43	Andrew Avenue
47	Hilton Road
49	Carey Place
58	Union Bay Boat Launch
64	Ship's Point Park
67	Deep Bay Spit
70	Moss Park
83	Kinkade Road
85	Seacroft Road
86	Buller Road
89	Qualicum Beach— Brant Viewing Area

7. Long beach walks

1	Seagull Road
3	Shoreline Drive (Campbell River)
4	Heard Road
6	Oyster Bay Rest Area
8	Oyster River Nature Trails
9	Laval Road
10	Saratoga Beach

16	Seaview Road	45	Curtis Road—West
18	Eagles Drive Park	46	Goose Spit
19	Pantuso Road	49	Carey Place
21	Davey Janes Road	50	Gartley Point Road
22	Coleman Road	57	Dorothy Road
25	Seal Bay	58	Union Bay Boat Launch
26	Cloudcroft Road	59	Baynes Sound Rest Area
27	Wilkinson Road	62	Tozer Road
28	Florence Road	63	Wente Way
31	Little River Road	67	Deep Bay Spit
32	Harvard Road	73	Bowser Road
36	Kin Beach—South	74	Henson Road
39	Longview Road—West	81	Surfside Drive—West
40	Longview Road—East	83	Kinkade Road
47	Hilton Road	84	Flamingo Drive—West
49	Carey Place	89	Qualicum Beach—
50	Gartley Point Road		Brant Viewing Area

12. Medium or large groups

60	Joe Walker Community Park
63	Wente Way
64	Ship's Point Park

6	Oyster Bay Rest Area
17	Williams Beach (no facilities)
20	Kitty Coleman Provincial Park
69	Shoreline Drive (Bowser)
70	Moss Park
71	Buccaneer Beach
72	Henry Morgan Drive
75	Nile Road
76	Crane Road
77	Franksea Road

35	Kin Beach—North
38	Elks and Royal Purple Park
41	Point Holmes (limited facilities)
46	Goose Spit (limited facilities)
48A	Marine Drive—West
	(picnic facilities)
59	Baynes Sound Rest Area
	(picnic facilities)
60	Joe Walker Community Park
	(medium group)
67	Deep Bay Spit
	(medium or small group)
89	Qualicum Beach—
	Brant Viewing Area
	(lots of parking, no facilities)

11. Afternoon sun

6	Oyster Bay Rest Area
9	Laval Road
10	Saratoga Beach
11	Seaman Road
17	Williams Beach
19	Pantuso Road
22	Coleman Road
23	Coral Road
27	Wilkinson Road
28	Florence Road
29	Singing Sands Road
30	Mayfair Road
31	Little River Road
35	Kin Beach—North
36	Kin Beach—South
37	Windslow Road—North
38	Elks and Royal Purple Park
41	Point Holmes
42	Lazo Road
43	Andrew Avenue
44	Curtis Road—East

13. Throwing Frisbees or flying kites

4	Heard Road
6	Oyster Bay Rest Area
10	Saratoga Beach
11	Seaman Road
12	Driftwood Road—North
13	Driftwood Road—Middle
15	Elma Bay Place
17	Williams Beach
24	Perrey's Beach
35	Kin Beach—North
37	Windslow Road—North

38	Elks and Royal Purple Park
39	Longview Road—West
41	Point Holmes
45	Curtis Road—West
46	Goose Spit
52	Gartley Road
68	Deep Bay Drive
77	Franksea Road
78	Sunnybeach Road
81	Surfside Drive—West
83	Kinkade Road
86	Buller Road
87	Challoner Road

14. Bird viewing

6	Oyster Bay Rest Area (north end)
14	Driftwood Road—South (Black Creek)
24	Perrey's Beach (great blue herons)
46	Goose Spit
48A	Marine Drive—West
49	Carey Place
50	Gartley Point Road
59	Baynes Sound Rest Area
62	Tozer Road
63	Wente Way
64	Ship's Point Park
66	Berray Road
67	Deep Bay Spit
68	Deep Bay Drive
76	Crane Road
81	Surfside Drive—West (wildlife sanctuary)
82	Surfside Drive—East (wildlife sanctuary)
88	Qualicum Beach—North (especially brant season)
89	Qualicum Beach— Brant Viewing Area (especially brant season)

15. Protection from a southeast wind

6	Oyster Bay Rest Area (north end)
47	Hilton Road
50	Gartley Point Road
58	Union Bay Boat Launch
62	Tozer Road
63	Wente Way
67	Deep Bay Spit

| 76 | Crane Road |
| 81 | Surfside Drive—West |

16. Protection from a northwest wind

10	Saratoga Beach
11	Seaman Road
41	Point Holmes
42	Lazo Road
43	Andrew Avenue
44	Curtis Road—East
45	Curtis Road—West
46	Goose Spit
58	Union Bay Boat Launch
64	Ship's Point Park
66	Berray Road
73	Bowser Road
76	Crane Road
77	Franksea Road
78	Sunnybeach Road
83	Kinkade Road

INDEX TO ENTRIES

THEO DOMBROWSKI is a retired teacher who was involved for many years in international education, primarily at Lester B. Pearson College of the Pacific outside Victoria, BC. A writer, photographer and artist, he has a Ph.D. in English and spent many years teaching literature and writing. He studied drawing and painting at the Banff School of Fine Arts and the University of Victoria Fine Arts Department and has worked as a professional artist. He lives in Nanoose Bay, BC. Theo is donating his proceeds from sales of this book to the local environmental group Georgia Strait Alliance and to the international humanitarian support group Médecins Sans Frontières/Doctors Without Borders (MSF). Originals and copies of the illustrations in this book can be purchased by contacting the author at booksandart@shaw.ca. Proceeds will go to MSF.

Acknowledgements Thanks to David Pinel, Joan Cavers, Bruce Whittington, and Eileen Dombrowski

OTHER BOOKS IN THE SECRET BEACHES SERIES

**SECRET BEACHES
OF SOUTHERN VANCOUVER ISLAND**
Qualicum to the Malahat
ISBN 978-1-894974-97-4

SECRET BEACHES OF GREATER VICTORIA
View Royal to Sidney
ISBN 978-1-894974-98-1

Coming in spring 2012
SECRET BEACHES OF THE SALISH SEA
The Gulf Islands